THE REPUBLIC

THE REPUBLIC

PLATO

SIRIUS

SIRIUS
This edition published in 2025 by Sirius Publishing,
a division of Arcturus Publishing Limited,
26/27 Bickels Yard, 151–153 Bermondsey Street,
London SE1 3HA

ISBN: 978-1-3988-5145-0
AD005624UK

Printed in China

Contents

Introduction

Plato, best known as the father of Western philosophy, was born in approximately 428BC in Athens. Little is known about his early life, but it is likely that he belonged to an aristocratic family. Like most noble Greek boys of the time, he was taught grammar, music and gymnastics.

One teacher who had a greater effect on him than any other was the celebrated philosopher Socrates and Plato became one of his many devoted followers. During his time as a student, Plato put his ideas into words. Each of his works followed the format of a Socratic dialogue – that is, he presented his ideas through a fictional conversation held between Socrates and various Athenian citizens. Plato's writing was prolific but he is best known today for *The Republic*.

In his later life, Plato travelled across the Mediterranean to Italy, Egypt and Cyrene. On his return to Athens, he founded the Academy, an institute of higher learning that included a shrine to the Goddess of wisdom, Athena.

The Republic was written around 380BC. It primarily focuses on the meaning of justice – of the character of the just city, and what it meant to be a just man. After examining the various options for forms of government, Plato concludes that just government is only possible under the rule of a philosopher king. *The Republic* features the famous 'Allegory of the Cave'. Plato examined the belief system of a group of people who had spent their entire lives facing a blank wall inside a cave. When a fire is lit behind them, they see the dancing shadows on the wall in front of them and give them names, believing them to be real. In Plato's argument, the philosopher is the freed prisoner, seeing reality for the first time and no longer fooled by the deceptive shadows.

Plato's work influenced generations of writers, philosophers and historians. In Ancient Rome, Cicero and Tacitus regarded him as the paramount Greek thinker. In another age, St Augustine built on Plato's ideas of a model republic to create an imagined 'City of God', while during the Enlightenment philosophers such as John Locke and Jean-Jacques Rousseau drew inspiration from the theories of the state that Plato expressed in *The Republic*. Without Plato, the history of philosophy would be very different.

Translator's Introduction

The *Republic* of Plato is the longest of his works with the exception of the *Laws*, and is certainly the greatest of them. There are nearer approaches to modern metaphysics in the *Philebus* and in the *Sophist*; the *Politicus*, or *Statesman*, is more ideal; the form and institutions of the State are more clearly drawn out in the *Laws*; as works of art, the *Symposium* and the *Protagoras* are of higher excellence. But no other Dialogue of Plato has the same largeness of view and the same perfection of style; no other shows an equal knowledge of the world, or contains more of those thoughts which are new as well as old, and not of one age only but of all. Nowhere in Plato is there a deeper irony or a greater wealth of humour or imagery, or more dramatic power. Nor in any other of his writings is the attempt made to interweave life and speculation, or to connect politics with philosophy. The *Republic* is the centre around which the other Dialogues may be grouped; here philosophy reaches the highest point to which ancient thinkers ever attained. Plato among the Greeks, like Bacon among the moderns, was the first who conceived a method of knowledge, although neither of them always distinguished the bare outline or form from the substance of truth; and both of them had to be content with an abstraction of science which was not yet realised. He was the greatest metaphysical genius whom the world has seen; and in him, more than in any other ancient thinker, the germs of future knowledge are contained. The sciences of logic and psychology, which have supplied so many instruments of thought to after-ages, are based upon the analyses of Socrates and Plato. The principles of definition, the law of contradiction, the fallacy of arguing in a circle, the distinction between the essence and accidents of a thing or notion, between means and ends, between causes and conditions; also the division of the mind into the rational, concupiscent, and irascible elements, or of pleasures and desires into necessary and unnecessary – these and other great forms of thought are all of them to be found in the *Republic*, and were probably first invented by Plato. The greatest of all logical truths, and the one of which writers on philosophy are most apt to lose sight, the difference between words and things, has been most strenuously insisted on by him, although he has not always avoided the confusion of them in his own writings. But he does not bind up truth in logical formulae, – logic is still veiled in metaphysics; and the science which he imagines to 'contemplate all truth and all existence' is very unlike the doctrine of the syllogism which Aristotle claims to have discovered.

Neither must we forget that the *Republic* is but the third part of a still larger design which was to have included an ideal history of Athens, as well as a political and physical philosophy. The fragment of the *Critias* has given birth to a world-famous fiction, second only in importance to the tale of Troy and the legend of Arthur; and is said as a fact to have inspired some of the early navigators of the sixteenth century. This mythical tale, of which the subject was a history of the wars of the Athenians against the Island of Atlantis, is supposed to be founded upon an unfinished poem of Solon, to which it would have stood in the same relation as the writings of the logographers to the poems of Homer. It would have told of a struggle for Liberty, intended to represent the conflict of Persia and Hellas. We may judge from the noble commencement of the *Timaeus*, from the fragment of the *Critias* itself, and from the third book of the *Laws*, in what manner Plato would have treated this high argument. We can only guess why the great design was abandoned; perhaps because Plato became sensible of some incongruity in a fictitious history, or because he had lost his interest in it, or because advancing years forbade the completion of it; and we may please ourselves with the fancy that had this imaginary narrative ever been finished, we should have found Plato himself sympathising with the struggle for Hellenic independence, singing a hymn of triumph over Marathon and Salamis, perhaps making the reflection of Herodotus where he contemplates the growth of the Athenian empire – 'How brave a thing is freedom of speech, which has made the Athenians so far exceed every other state of Hellas in greatness!' or, more probably, attributing the victory to the ancient good order of Athens and to the favor of Apollo and Athene.

Again, Plato may be regarded as the 'captain' (ἀρχηγὸς) or leader of a goodly band of followers; for in the *Republic* is to be found the original of Cicero's *De Republica*, of St. Augustine's *City of God*, of the *Utopia* of Sir Thomas More, and of the numerous other imaginary States which are framed upon the same model. The extent to which Aristotle or the Aristotelian school were indebted to him in the *Politics* has been little recognised, and the recognition is the more necessary because it is not made by Aristotle himself. The two philosophers had more in common than they were conscious of; and probably some elements of Plato remain still undetected in Aristotle. In English philosophy too, many affinities may be traced, not only in the works of the Cambridge Platonists, but in great original writers like Berkeley or Coleridge, to Plato and his ideas. That there is a truth higher than experience, of which the mind bears witness to herself, is a conviction which in our own generation has been enthusiastically asserted, and is perhaps gaining ground. Of the Greek authors who at the Renaissance brought a new life into the world Plato has had the greatest influence. The *Republic* of Plato is also the first treatise upon education, of which the writings of Milton and Locke, Rousseau, Jean Paul, and Goethe are the legitimate descendants. Like Dante or Bunyan, he has a revelation of another life; like Bacon, he is profoundly impressed with the unity of knowledge; in the early Church he exercised a real influence on theology, and at the Revival of Literature on politics. Even the fragments of his words when 'repeated at second-hand' have in all ages ravished the hearts of men, who have seen reflected in them their own higher nature. He is the father of idealism in philosophy, in politics, in literature. And many of the latest conceptions of modern thinkers and statesmen, such as the unity of knowledge, the reign of law, and the equality of the sexes, have been anticipated in a dream by him.

Argument

The argument of the *Republic* is the search after Justice, the nature of which is first hinted at by Cephalus, the just and blameless old man – then discussed on the basis of proverbial morality by Socrates and Polemarchus – then caricatured by Thrasymachus and partially explained by Socrates – reduced to an abstraction by Glaucon and Adeimantus, and having become invisible in the individual reappears at length in the ideal State which is constructed by Socrates. The first care of the rulers is to be education, of which an outline is drawn after the old Hellenic model, providing only for an improved religion and morality, and more simplicity in music and gymnastics, a manlier strain of poetry, and greater harmony of the individual and the State. We are thus led on to the conception of a higher State, in which 'no man calls anything his own', and in which there is neither 'marrying nor giving in marriage', and 'kings are philosophers' and 'philosophers are kings'; and there is another and higher education, intellectual as well as moral and religious, of science as well as of art, and not of youth only but of the whole of life. Such a State is hardly to be realised in this world and would quickly degenerate. To the perfect ideal succeeds the government of the soldier and the lover of honour, this again declining into democracy, and democracy into tyranny, in an imaginary but regular order having not much resemblance to the actual facts. When 'the wheel has come full circle' we do not begin again with a new period of human life; but we have passed from the best to the worst, and there we end. The subject is then changed and the old quarrel of poetry and philosophy which had been more lightly treated in the earlier books of the *Republic* is now resumed and fought out to a conclusion. Poetry is discovered to be an imitation thrice removed from the truth, and Homer, as well as the dramatic poets, having been condemned as an imitator, is sent into banishment along with them. And the idea of the State is supplemented by the revelation of a future life.

The division into books, like all similar divisions, is probably later than the age of Plato. The natural divisions are five in number; – (1) Book I and the first half of Book II down to the paragraph beginning, 'I had always admired the genius of Glaucon and Adeimantus', which is introductory; the first book containing a refutation of the popular and sophistical notions of justice, and concluding, like some of the earlier Dialogues, without arriving at any definite result. To this is appended a restatement of the nature of justice according to common opinion, and an answer is demanded to the question – What is justice, stripped of appearances? The second division (2) includes the remainder of the second and the whole of the third and fourth books, which are mainly occupied with the construction of the first State and the first education. The third division (3) consists of the fifth, sixth, and seventh books, in which philosophy rather than justice is the subject of inquiry, and the second State is constructed on principles of communism and ruled by philosophers, and the contemplation of the idea of good takes the place of the social and political virtues. In the eighth and ninth books (4) the perversions of States and of the individuals who correspond to them are reviewed in succession; and the nature of pleasure and the principle of tyranny are further analysed in the individual man. The tenth book (5) is the conclusion of the whole, in which the relations of philosophy to poetry are finally determined, and the happiness of the citizens in this life, which has now been assured, is crowned by the vision of another.

Or a more general division into two parts may be adopted; the first (Books I–IV) containing the description of a State framed generally in accordance with Hellenic notions of religion and morality, while in the second (Books V–X) the Hellenic State is transformed into an ideal kingdom of philosophy, of which all other governments are the perversions. These two points of view are really opposed, and the opposition is only veiled by the genius of Plato. The *Republic*, like the *Phaedrus*, is an imperfect whole; the higher light of philosophy breaks through the regularity of the Hellenic temple, which at last fades away into the heavens. Whether this imperfection of structure arises from an enlargement of the plan; or from the imperfect reconcilement in the writer's own mind of the struggling elements of thought which are now first brought together by him; or, perhaps, from the composition of the work at different times – are questions, like the similar question about the *Iliad* and the *Odyssey*, which are worth asking, but which cannot have a distinct answer. In the age of Plato there was no regular mode of publication, and an author would have the less scruple in altering or adding to a work which was known only to a few of his friends. There is no absurdity in supposing that he may have laid his labours aside for a time, or turned from one work to another; and such interruptions would be more likely to occur in the case of a long than of a short writing. In all attempts to determine the chronological order of the Platonic writings on internal evidence, this uncertainty about any single Dialogue being composed at one time is a disturbing element, which must be admitted to affect longer works, such as the *Republic* and the *Laws*, more than shorter ones. But, on the other hand, the seeming discrepancies of the *Republic* may only arise out of the discordant elements which the philosopher has attempted to unite in a single whole, perhaps without being himself able to recognise the inconsistency which is obvious to us. For there is a judgment of after-ages which few great writers have ever been able to anticipate for themselves. They do not perceive the want of connection in their own writings, or the gaps in their systems which are visible enough to those who come after them. In the beginnings of literature and philosophy, amid the first efforts of thought and language, more inconsistencies occur than now, when the paths of speculation are well worn and the meaning of words precisely defined. For consistency, too, is the growth of time; and some of the greatest creations of the human mind have been wanting in unity. Tried by this test, several of the Platonic Dialogues, according to our modern ideas, appear to be defective, but the deficiency is no proof that they were composed at different times or by different hands. And the supposition that the *Republic* was written uninterruptedly and by a continuous effort is in some degree confirmed by the numerous references from one part of the work to another.

The second title, *Concerning Justice*, is not the one by which the *Republic* is quoted, either by Aristotle or generally in antiquity, and, like the other second titles of the Platonic Dialogues, may therefore be assumed to be of later date. Morgenstern and others have asked whether the definition of justice, which is the professed aim, or the construction of the State is the principal argument of the work. The answer is, that the two blend in one, and are two faces of the same truth; for justice is the order of the State, and the State is the visible embodiment of justice under the conditions of human society. The one is the soul and the other is the body, and the Greek ideal of the State, as of the individual, is a fair mind in a fair body. In Hegelian phraseology the State is the reality of which justice is the ideal. Or, described in Christian language, the kingdom of God is within, and yet develops into a Church or external kingdom; 'the house not made with hands, eternal in the heavens' is reduced to the proportions of an earthly building. Or, to use a Platonic image, justice and the State are the warp and the woof which run through the whole texture. And when the constitution of the State is completed, the conception of justice is not dismissed, but reappears under the same or different names throughout the work, both as the inner law of the individual soul, and finally as the principle of rewards and punishments in another life. The virtues are based on justice, of which common honesty in buying and selling is the shadow, and justice is based on the idea of good, which is the harmony of the world, and is reflected both in the institutions of States and in motions of the heavenly bodies. The *Timaeus*, which takes up the political rather than the ethical side of the *Republic*, and is chiefly occupied with hypotheses concerning the outward world, yet contains many indications that the same law is supposed to reign over the State, over nature, and over man.

Too much, however, has been made of this question both in ancient and in modern times. There is a stage of criticism in which all works, whether of nature or of art, are referred to design. Now in ancient writings, and indeed in literature generally, there remains often a large element which was not comprehended in the original design. For the plan grows under the author's hand; new thoughts occur to him in the act of writing; he has not worked out the argument to the end before he begins. The reader who seeks to find some one idea under which the whole may be conceived, must necessarily seize on the vaguest and most general. Thus Stallbaum, who is dissatisfied with the ordinary explanations of the argument of the *Republic*, imagines himself to have found the true argument 'in the representation of human life in a State perfected by justice and governed according to the idea of good'. There may be some use in such general descriptions, but they can hardly be said to express the design of the writer. The truth is, that we may as well speak of many designs as of one; nor need anything be excluded from the plan of a great work to which the mind is naturally led by the association of ideas, and which does not interfere with the general purpose. What kind or degree of unity is to be sought after in a building, in the plastic arts, in poetry, in prose, is a problem which has to be determined relatively to the subject-matter. To Plato himself, the inquiry 'what was the intention of the writer' or 'what was the principal argument of the *Republic*' would have been hardly intelligible, and therefore had better be at once dismissed.

Is not the *Republic* the vehicle of three or four great truths which, to Plato's own mind, are most naturally represented in the form of the State? Just as in the Jewish prophets the reign of Messiah, or 'the day of the Lord', or the suffering Servant or people of God, or the 'Sun of righteousness with healing in his wings' only convey, to us at least, their great spiritual ideals, so through the Greek State Plato reveals to us his own thoughts about divine perfection, which is the idea of good – like the sun in the visible world; – about human perfection, which is justice – about education beginning in youth and continuing in later years – about poets and sophists and tyrants who are the false teachers and evil rulers of mankind – about 'the world' which is the embodiment of them – about a kingdom which exists nowhere upon earth but is laid up in heaven to be the pattern and rule of human life. No such inspired creation is at unity with itself, any more than the clouds of heaven when the sun pierces through them. Every shade of light and dark, of truth, and of fiction which is the veil of truth, is allowable in a work of philosophical imagination. It is not all on the same plane; it easily passes from ideas to myths and fancies, from facts to figures of speech. It is not prose but poetry, at least a great part of it, and ought not to be judged by the rules of logic or the probabilities of history. The writer is not fashioning his ideas into an artistic whole; they take possession of him and are too much for him. We have no need therefore to discuss whether a State such as Plato has conceived is practicable or not, or whether the outward form or the inward life came first into the mind of the writer. For the practicability of his ideas has nothing to do with their truth; and the highest thoughts to which he attains may be truly said to bear the greatest 'marks of design' – justice more than the external frame-work of the State, the idea of good more than justice. The great science of dialectic or the organisation of ideas has no real content; but is only a type of the method or spirit in which the higher knowledge is to be pursued by the spectator of all time and all existence. It is in the fifth, sixth, and seventh books that Plato reaches the 'summit of speculation', and these, although they fail to satisfy the requirements of a modern thinker, may therefore be regarded as the most important, as they are also the most original, portions of the work.

It is not necessary to discuss at length a minor question which has been raised by Boeckh, respecting the imaginary date at which the conversation was held (the year 411 BC which is proposed by him will do as well as any other); for a writer of fiction, and especially a writer who, like Plato, is notoriously careless of chronology, only aims at general probability. Whether all the persons mentioned in the *Republic* could ever have met at any one time is not a difficulty which would have occurred to an Athenian reading the work forty years later, or to Plato himself at the time of writing (any more than to Shakespeare respecting one of his own dramas); and need not greatly trouble us now. Yet this may be a question having no answer 'which is still worth asking', because the investigation shows that we can not argue historically from the dates in Plato; it would be useless therefore to waste time in inventing far-fetched reconcilements of them in order avoid chronological difficulties, such, for example, as the conjecture of C. F. Hermann, that Glaucon and Adeimantus are not the brothers but the uncles of Plato, or the fancy of Stallbaum that Plato intentionally left anachronisms indicating the dates at which some of his Dialogues were written.

Characters

The principal characters in the *Republic* are Cephalus, Polemarchus, Thrasymachus, Socrates, Glaucon, and Adeimantus. Cephalus appears in the introduction only, Polemarchus drops at the end of the first argument, and Thrasymachus is reduced to silence at the close of the first book. The main discussion is carried on by Socrates, Glaucon, and Adeimantus. Among the company are Lysias (the orator) and Euthydemus, the sons of Cephalus and brothers of Polemarchus, an unknown Charmantides – these are mute auditors; also there is Cleitophon, who once interrupts, where, as in the Dialogue which bears his name, he appears as the friend and ally of Thrasymachus.

Cephalus, the patriarch of house, has been appropriately engaged in offering a sacrifice. He is the pattern of an old man who has almost done with life, and is at peace with himself and with all mankind. He feels that he is drawing nearer to the world below, and seems to linger around the memory of the past. He is eager that Socrates should come to visit him, fond of the poetry of the last generation, happy in the consciousness of a well-spent life, glad at having escaped from the tyranny of youthful lusts. His love of conversation, his affection, his indifference to riches, even his garrulity, are interesting traits of character. He is not one of those who have nothing to say, because their whole mind has been absorbed in making money. Yet he acknowledges that riches have the advantage of placing men above the temptation to dishonesty or falsehood. The respectful attention shown to him by Socrates, whose love of conversation, no less than the mission imposed upon him by the Oracle, leads him to ask questions of all men, young and old alike, should also be noted. Who better suited to raise the question of justice than Cephalus, whose life might seem to be the expression of it? The moderation with which old age is pictured by Cephalus as a very tolerable portion of existence is characteristic, not only of him, but of Greek feeling generally, and contrasts with the exaggeration of Cicero in the *De Senectute*. The evening of life is described by Plato in the most expressive manner, yet with the fewest possible touches. As Cicero remarks (*Ep. ad Attic*. iv. 16), the aged Cephalus would have been out of place in the discussion which follows, and which he could neither have understood nor taken part in without a violation of dramatic propriety.

His 'son and heir' Polemarchus has the frankness and impetuousness of youth; he is for detaining Socrates by force in the opening scene, and will not 'let him off' on the subject of women and children. Like Cephalus, he is limited in his point of view, and represents the proverbial stage of morality which has rules of life rather than principles; and he quotes Simonides as his father had quoted Pindar. But after this he has no more to say; the answers which he makes are only elicited from him by the dialectic of Socrates. He has not yet experienced the influence of the Sophists like Glaucon and Adeimantus, nor is he sensible of the necessity of refuting them; he belongs to the pre-Socratic or pre-dialectical age. He is incapable of arguing, and is bewildered by Socrates to such a degree that he does not know what he is saying. He is made to admit that justice is a thief, and that the virtues follow the analogy of the arts. From his brother Lysias we learn that he fell a victim to the Thirty Tyrants, but no allusion is here made to his fate, nor to the circumstance that Cephalus and his family were of Syracusan origin, and had migrated from Thurii to Athens.

The 'Chalcedonian giant', Thrasymachus, of whom we have already heard in the *Phaedrus*, is the personification of the Sophists, according to Plato's conception of them, in some of their worst characteristics. He is vain and blustering, refusing to discourse unless he is paid, fond of making an oration, and hoping thereby to escape the inevitable Socrates; but a mere child in argument, and unable to foresee that the next 'move' (to use a Platonic expression) will 'shut him up'. He has reached the stage of framing general notions, and in this respect is in advance of Cephalus and Polemarchus. But he is incapable of defending them in a discussion, and vainly tries to cover his confusion in banter and insolence. Whether such doctrines as are attributed to him by Plato were really held either by him or by any other Sophist is uncertain; in the infancy of philosophy serious errors about morality might easily grow up – they are certainly put into the mouths of speakers in Thucydides; but we are concerned at present with Plato's description of him, and not with the historical reality. The inequality of the contest adds greatly to the humour of the scene. The pompous and empty Sophist is utterly helpless in the hands of the great master of dialectic, who knows how to touch all the springs of vanity and weakness in him. He is greatly irritated by the irony of Socrates, but his noisy and imbecile rage only lays him more and more open to the thrusts of his assailant. His determination to cram down their throats, or put 'bodily into their souls' his own words, elicits a cry of horror from Socrates. The state of his temper is quite as worthy of remark as the process of the argument. Nothing is more amusing than his complete submission when he has been once thoroughly beaten. At first he seems to continue the discussion with reluctance, but soon with apparent good-will, and he even testifies his interest at a later stage by one or two occasional remarks. When attacked by Glaucon he is humorously protected by Socrates 'as one who has never been his enemy and is now his friend'. From Cicero and Quintilian and from Aristotle's *Rhetoric* we learn that the Sophist whom Plato has made so ridiculous was a man of note whose writings were preserved in later ages. The play on his name which was made by his contemporary Herodicus, 'thou wast ever bold in battle', seems to show that the description of him is not devoid of verisimilitude.

When Thrasymachus has been silenced, the two principal respondents, Glaucon and Adeimantus, appear on the scene: here, as in Greek tragedy, three actors are introduced. At first sight the two sons of Ariston may seem to wear a family likeness, like the two friends Simmias and Cebes in the *Phaedo*. But on a nearer examination of them the similarity vanishes, and they are seen to be distinct characters. Glaucon is the impetuous youth who can 'just never have enough of fechting' (cf. the character of him in Xen. *Mem*. iii. 6); the man of pleasure who is acquainted with the mysteries of love; the 'juvenis qui gaudet canibus', and who improves the breed of animals; the lover of art and music who has all the experiences of youthful life. He is full of quickness and penetration, piercing easily below the clumsy platitudes of Thrasymachus to the real difficulty; he turns out to the light the seamy side of human life, and yet does not lose faith in the just and true. It is Glaucon who seizes what may be termed the ludicrous relation of the philosopher to the world, to whom a state of simplicity is 'a city of pigs', who is always prepared with a jest when the argument offers him an opportunity, and who is ever ready to second the humour of Socrates and to appreciate the ridiculous, whether in the connoisseurs of music, or in the lovers of theatricals, or in the fantastic behaviour of the citizens of democracy. His weaknesses are several times alluded to by Socrates, who, however, will not allow him to be attacked by his brother Adeimantus. He is a soldier, and, like Adeimantus, has been distinguished at the battle of Megara.

The character of Adeimantus is deeper and graver, and the profounder objections are commonly put into his mouth. Glaucon is more demonstrative, and generally opens the game. Adeimantus pursues the argument further. Glaucon has more of the liveliness and quick sympathy of youth; Adeimantus has the maturer judgment of a grown-up man of the world. In the second book, when Glaucon insists that justice and injustice shall be considered without regard to their consequences, Adeimantus remarks that they are regarded by mankind in general only for the sake of their consequences; and in a similar vein of reflection he urges at the beginning of the fourth book that Socrates falls in making his citizens happy, and is answered that happiness is not the first but the second thing, not the direct aim but the indirect consequence of the good government of a State. In the discussion about religion and mythology, Adeimantus is the respondent, but Glaucon breaks in with a slight jest, and carries on the conversation in a lighter tone about music and gymnastics to the end of the book. It is Adeimantus again who volunteers the criticism of common sense on the Socratic method of argument, and who refuses to let Socrates pass lightly over the question of women and children. It is Adeimantus who is the respondent in the more argumentative, as Glaucon in the lighter and more imaginative portions of the Dialogue. For example, throughout the greater part of the sixth book, the causes of the corruption of philosophy and the conception of the idea of good are discussed with Adeimantus. Then Glaucon resumes his place of principal respondent; but he has a difficulty in apprehending the higher education of Socrates, and makes some false hits in the course of the discussion. Once more Adeimantus returns with the allusion to his brother Glaucon whom he compares to the contentious State; in the next book he is again superseded, and Glaucon continues to the end.

Thus in a succession of characters Plato represents the successive stages of morality, beginning with the Athenian gentleman of the olden time, who is followed by the practical man of that day regulating his life by proverbs and saws; to him succeeds the wild generalisation of the Sophists, and lastly come the young disciples of the great teacher, who know the sophistical arguments but will not be convinced by them, and desire to go deeper into the nature of things. These too, like Cephalus, Polemarchus, Thrasymachus, are clearly distinguished from one another. Neither in the *Republic*, nor in any other Dialogue of Plato, is a single character repeated.

The delineation of Socrates in the *Republic* is not wholly consistent. In the first book we have more of the real Socrates, such as he is depicted in the *Memorabilia* of Xenophon, in the earliest Dialogues of Plato, and in the *Apology*. He is ironical, provoking, questioning, the old enemy of the Sophists, ready to put on the mask of Silenus as well as to argue seriously. But in the sixth book his enmity towards the Sophists abates; he acknowledges that they are the representatives rather than the corrupters of the world. He also becomes more dogmatic and constructive, passing beyond the range either of the political or the speculative ideas of the real Socrates. In one passage Plato himself seems to intimate that the time had now come for Socrates, who had passed his whole life in philosophy, to give his own opinion and not to be always repeating the notions of other men. There is no evidence that either the idea of good or the conception of a perfect State were comprehended in the Socratic teaching, though he certainly dwelt on the nature of the universal and of final causes (cp. Xen. *Mem.* i. 4; *Phaedo* 97); and a deep thinker like him in his thirty or forty years of public teaching, could hardly have falled to touch on the nature of family relations, for which there is also some positive evidence in the *Memorabilia* (*Mem.* i. 2, 51 foll.) The Socratic method is nominally retained; and every inference is either put into the mouth of the respondent or represented as the common discovery of him and Socrates. But anyone can see that this is a mere form, of which the affectation grows wearisome as the work advances. The method of inquiry has passed into a method of teaching in which by the help of interlocutors the same thesis is looked at from various points of view.

The nature of the process is truly characterized by Glaucon, when he describes himself as a companion who is not good for much in an investigation, but can see what he is shown, and may, perhaps, give the answer to a question more fluently than another.

Neither can we be absolutely certain that, Socrates himself taught the immortality of the soul, which is unknown to his disciple Glaucon in the *Republic*; nor is there any reason to suppose that he used myths or revelations of another world as a vehicle of instruction, or that he would have banished poetry or have denounced the Greek mythology. His favorite oath is retained, and a slight mention is made of the daemonium, or internal sign, which is alluded to by Socrates as a phenomenon peculiar to himself. A real element of Socratic teaching, which is more prominent in the *Republic* than in any of the other Dialogues of Plato, is the use of example and illustration (τὰ φορτικὰ αὐτῷ προσφέροντες): 'Let us apply the test of common instances.' 'You', says Adeimantus, ironically, in the sixth book, 'are so unaccustomed to speak in images.' And this use of examples or images, though truly Socratic in origin, is enlarged by the genius of Plato into the form of an allegory or parable, which embodies in the concrete what has been already described, or is about to be described, in the abstract. Thus the figure of the cave in Book VII is a recapitulation of the divisions of knowledge in Book VI. The composite animal in Book IX is an allegory of the parts of the soul. The noble captain and the ship and the true pilot in Book VI are a figure of the relation of the people to the philosophers in the State which has been described. Other figures, such as the dog in the second, third, and fourth books, or the marriage of the portionless maiden in the sixth book, or the drones and wasps in the eighth and ninth books, also form links of connection in long passages, or are used to recall previous discussions.

Plato is most true to the character of his master when he describes him as 'not of this world'. And with this representation of him the ideal State and the other paradoxes of the *Republic* are quite in accordance, though they can not be shown to have been speculations of Socrates. To him, as to other great teachers both philosophical and religious, when they looked upward, the world seemed to be the embodiment of error and evil. The common sense of mankind has revolted against this view, or has only partially admitted it. And even in Socrates himself the sterner judgment of the multitude at times passes into a sort of ironical pity or love. Men in general are incapable of philosophy, and are therefore at enmity with the philosopher; but their misunderstanding of him is unavoidable: for they have never seen him as he truly is in his own image; they are only acquainted with artificial systems possessing no native force of truth – words which admit of many applications. Their leaders have nothing to measure with, and are therefore ignorant of their own stature. But they are to be pitied or laughed at, not to be quarrelled with; they mean well with their nostrums, if they could only learn that they are cutting off a Hydra's head. This moderation towards those who are in error is one of the most characteristic features of Socrates in the *Republic*. In all the different representations of Socrates, whether of Xenophon or Plato, and the differences of the earlier or later Dialogues, he always retains the character of the unwearied and disinterested seeker after truth, without which he would have ceased to be Socrates.

Benjamin Jowett

Book I

I went down yesterday to the Piraeus with Glaucon the son of Ariston, that I might offer up my prayers to the goddess; and also because I wanted to see in what manner they would celebrate the festival, which was a new thing. I was delighted with the procession of the inhabitants; but that of the Thracians was equally, if not more, beautiful. When we had finished our prayers and viewed the spectacle, we turned in the direction of the city; and at that instant Polemarchus the son of Cephalus chanced to catch sight of us from a distance as we were starting on our way home, and told his servant to run and bid us wait for him. The servant took hold of me by the cloak behind, and said: 'Polemarchus desires you to wait.'

I turned round, and asked him where his master was.

'There he is,' said the youth, 'coming after you, if you will only wait.'

'Certainly we will,' said Glaucon; and in a few minutes Polemarchus appeared, and with him Adeimantus, Glaucon's brother, Niceratus the son of Nicias, and several others who had been at the procession.

Polemarchus said to me: 'I perceive, Socrates, that you and our companion are already on your way to the city.'

'You are not far wrong,' I said.

'But do you see', he rejoined, 'how many we are?'

'Of course.'

'And are you stronger than all these? For if not, you will have to remain where you are.'

'May there not be the alternative,' I said, 'that we may persuade you to let us go?'

'But can you persuade us, if we refuse to listen to you?' he said.

'Certainly not,' replied Glaucon.

'Then we are not going to listen; of that you may be assured.'

Adeimantus added: 'Has no one told you of the torch-race on horseback in honour of the goddess which will take place in the evening?'

'With horses!' I replied. 'That is a novelty. Will horsemen carry torches and pass them one to another during the race?'

'Yes,' said Polemarchus, 'and not only so, but a festival will he celebrated at night, which you certainly ought to see. Let us rise soon after supper and see this festival; there will be a gathering of young men, and we will have a good talk. Stay then, and do not be perverse.'

Glaucon said: 'I suppose, since you insist, that we must.'

'Very good,' I replied.

Accordingly we went with Polemarchus to his house; and there we found his brothers Lysias and Euthydemus, and with them Thrasymachus the Chalcedonian, Charmantides the Paeanian, and Cleitophon the son of Aristonymus. There too was Cephalus the father of Polemarchus, whom I had not seen for a long time, and I thought him very much aged. He was seated on a cushioned chair, and had a garland on his head, for he had been sacrificing in the court; and there were some other chairs in the room arranged in a semi-circle, upon which we sat down by him. He saluted me eagerly, and then he said:–

'You don't come to see me', Socrates, 'as often as you ought. If I were still able to go and see you I would not ask you to come to me. But at my age I can hardly get to the city, and therefore you should come oftener to the Piraeus. For let me tell you, that the more the pleasures of the body fade away, the greater to me is the pleasure and charm of conversation. Do not then deny my request, but make our house your resort and keep company with these young men; we are old friends, and you will be quite at home with us.'

I replied: 'There is nothing which for my part I like better, Cephalus, than conversing with aged men; for I regard them as travellers who have gone a journey which I too may have to go, and of whom I ought to enquire, whether the way is smooth and easy, or rugged and difficult. And this is a question which I should like to ask of you who have arrived at that time which the poets call the "threshold of old age": – Is life harder towards the end, or what report do you give of it?'

'I will tell you, Socrates,' he said, 'what my own feeling is. Men of my age flock together; we are birds of a feather, as the old proverb says; and at our meetings the tale of my acquaintance commonly is – I cannot eat, I cannot drink; the pleasures of youth and love are fled away: there was a good time once, but now that is gone, and life is no longer life. Some complain of the slights which are put upon them by relations, and they will tell you sadly of how many evils their old age is the cause. But to me, Socrates, these complainers seem to blame that which is not really in fault. For if old age were the cause, I too being old, and every other old man, would have felt as they do. But this is not my own experience, nor that of others whom I have known. How well I remember the aged poet Sophocles, when in answer to the question, "How does love suit with age, Sophocles – are you still the man you were?" "Peace," he replied; "most gladly have I escaped the thing of which you speak; I feel as if I had escaped from a mad and furious master." His words have often occurred to my mind since, and they seem as good to me now as at the time when he uttered them. For certainly old age has a great sense of calm and freedom; when the passions relax their hold, then, as Sophocles says, we are freed from the grasp not of one mad master only, but of many. The truth is, Socrates, that these regrets, and also the complaints about relations, are to be attributed to the same cause, which is not old age, but men's characters and tempers; for he who is of a calm and happy nature will hardly feel the pressure of age, but to him who is of an opposite disposition youth and age are equally a burden.'

I listened in admiration, and wanting to draw him out, that he might go on – 'Yes, Cephalus,' I said: 'but I rather suspect that people in general are not convinced by you when you speak thus; they think that old age sits lightly upon you, not because of your happy disposition, but because you are rich, and wealth is well known to be a great comforter.'

'You are right,' he replied; 'they are not convinced: and there is something in what they say; not, however, so much as they imagine. I might answer them as Themistocles answered the Seriphian who was abusing him and saying that he was famous, not for his own merits but because he was an Athenian: "If you had been a native of my country or I of yours, neither of us would have been famous." And to those who are not rich and are impatient of old age, the same reply may be made; for to the good poor man old age cannot be a light burden, nor can a bad rich man ever have peace with himself.'

'May I ask, Cephalus, whether your fortune was for the most part inherited or acquired by you?'

'Acquired! Socrates, do you want to know how much I acquired? In the art of making money I have been midway between my father and grandfather: for my grandfather, whose name I bear, doubled and trebled the value of his patrimony, that which he inherited being much what I possess now; but my father Lysanias reduced the property below what it is at present; and I shall be satisfied if I leave to these my sons not less but a little more than I received.'

'That was why I asked you the question,' I replied, 'because I see that you are indifferent about money, which is a characteristic rather of those who have inherited their fortunes than of those who have acquired them; the makers of fortunes have a second love of money as a creation of their own, resembling the affection of authors for their own poems, or of parents for their children, besides that natural love of it for the sake of use and profit which is common to them and all men. And hence they are very bad company, for they can talk about nothing but the praises of wealth.'

'That is true,' he said.

'Yes, that is very true, but may I ask another question? What do you consider to be the greatest blessing which you have reaped from your wealth?'

'One', he said, 'of which I could not expect easily to convince others. For let me tell you, Socrates, that when a man thinks himself to be near death, fears and cares enter into his mind which he never had before; the tales of a world below and the punishment which is exacted there of deeds done here were once a laughing matter to him, but now he is tormented with the thought that they may be true: either from the weakness of age, or because he is now drawing nearer to that other place, he has a clearer view of these things; suspicions and alarms crowd thickly upon him, and he begins to reflect and consider what wrongs he has done to others. And when he finds that the sum of his transgressions is great he will many a time like a child start up in his sleep for fear, and he is filled with dark forebodings. But to him who is conscious of no sin, sweet hope, as Pindar charmingly says, is the kind nurse of his age:

> "Hope", he says, "cherishes the soul of him who lives in justice and holiness and is the nurse of his age and the companion of his journey; – hope which is mightiest to sway the restless soul of man."

How admirable are his words! And the great blessing of riches, I do not say to every man, but to a good man, is, that he has had no occasion to deceive or to defraud others, either intentionally or unintentionally; and when he departs to the world below he is not in any apprehension about offerings due to the gods or debts which he owes to men. Now to this peace of mind the possession of wealth greatly contributes; and therefore I say, that, setting one thing against another, of the many advantages which wealth has to give, to a man of sense this is in my opinion the greatest.'

'Well said, Cephalus,' I replied; 'but as concerning justice, what is it? – to speak the truth and to pay your debts – no more than this? And even to this are there not exceptions? Suppose that a friend when in his right mind has deposited arms with me and he asks for them when he is not in his right mind, ought I to give them back to him? No one would say that I ought or that I should be right in doing so, any more than they would say that I ought always to speak the truth to one who is in his condition.'

'You are quite right,' he replied.

'But then,' I said, 'speaking the truth and paying your debts is not a correct definition of justice.'

'Quite correct, Socrates, if Simonides is to be believed,' said Polemarchus interposing.

'I fear', said Cephalus, 'that I must go now, for I have to look after the sacrifices, and I hand over the argument to Polemarchus and the company.'

'Is not Polemarchus your heir?' I said.

'To be sure,' he answered, and went away laughing to the sacrifices.

'Tell me then, O thou heir of the argument, what did Simonides say, and according to you truly say, about justice?'

'He said that the repayment of a debt is just, and in saying so he appears to me to be right.'

'I should be sorry to doubt the word of such a wise and inspired man, but his meaning, though probably clear to you, is the reverse of clear to me. For he certainly does not mean, as we were now saying, that I ought to return a deposit of arms or of anything else to one who asks for it when he is not in his right senses; and yet a deposit cannot be denied to be a debt.'

'True.'

'Then when the person who asks me is not in his right mind I am by no means to make the return?'

'Certainly not.'

'When Simonides said that the repayment of a debt was justice, he did not mean to include that case?'

'Certainly not; for he thinks that a friend ought always to do good to a friend and never evil.'

'You mean that the return of a deposit of gold which is to the injury of the receiver, if the two parties are friends, is not the repayment of a debt – that is what you would imagine him to say?'

'Yes.'

'And are enemies also to receive what we owe to them?'

'To be sure,' he said, 'they are to receive what we owe them, and an enemy, as I take it, owes to an enemy that which is due or proper to him – that is to say, evil.'

'Simonides, then, after the manner of poets, would seem to have spoken darkly of the nature of justice; for he really meant to say that justice is the giving to each man what is proper to him, and this he termed a debt.'

'That must have been his meaning,' he said.

'By heaven!' I replied. 'And if we asked him what due or proper thing is given by medicine, and to whom, what answer do you think that he would make to us?'

'He would surely reply that medicine gives drugs and meat and drink to human bodies.'

'And what due or proper thing is given by cookery, and to what?'

'Seasoning to food.'

'And what is that which justice gives, and to whom?'

'If, Socrates, we are to be guided at all by the analogy of the preceding instances, then justice is the art which gives good to friends and evil to enemies.'

'That is his meaning then?'

'I think so.'

'And who is best able to do good to his friends and evil to his enemies in time of sickness?'

'The physician.'

'Or when they are on a voyage, amid the perils of the sea?'

'The pilot.'

'And in what sort of actions or with a view to what result is the just man most able to do harm to his enemy and good to his friends?'

'In going to war against the one and in making alliances with the other.'

'But when a man is well, my dear Polemarchus, there is no need of a physician?'

'No.'

'And he who is not on a voyage has no need of a pilot?'

'No.'

'Then in time of peace, justice will be of no use?'

'I am very far from thinking so.'

'You think that justice may be of use in peace as well as in war?'

'Yes.'

'Like husbandry for the acquisition of corn?'

'Yes.'

'Or like shoemaking for the acquisition of shoes – that is what you mean?'

'Yes.'

'And what similar use or power of acquisition has justice in time of peace?'

'In contracts, Socrates, justice is of use.'

'And by contracts you mean partnerships?'

'Exactly.'

'But is the just man or the skilful player a more useful and better partner at a game of draughts?'

'The skilful player.'

'And in the laying of bricks and stones is the just man a more useful or better partner than the builder?'

'Quite the reverse.'

'Then in what sort of partnership is the just man a better partner than the harp-player, as in playing the harp the harp-player is certainly a better partner than the just man?'

'In a money partnership.'

'Yes, Polemarchus, but surely not in the use of money; for you do not want a just man to be your counsellor the purchase or sale of a horse; a man who is knowing about horses would be better for that, would he not?'

'Certainly.'

'And when you want to buy a ship, the shipwright or the pilot would be better?'

'True.'

'Then what is that joint use of silver or gold in which the just man is to be preferred?'

'When you want a deposit to be kept safely.'

'You mean when money is not wanted, but allowed to lie?'

'Precisely.'

'That is to say, justice is useful when money is useless?'

'That is the inference.'

'And when you want to keep a pruning-hook safe, then justice is useful to the individual and to the state; but when you want to use it, then the art of the vine-dresser?'

'Clearly.'

'And when you want to keep a shield or a lyre, and not to use them, you would say that justice is useful; but when you want to use them, then the art of the soldier or of the musician?'

'Certainly.'

'And so of all the other things: – justice is useful when they are useless, and useless when they are useful?'

'That is the inference.'

'Then justice is not good for much. But let us consider this further point: Is not he who can best strike a blow in a boxing match or in any kind of fighting best able to ward off a blow?'

'Certainly.'

'And he who is most skilful in preventing or escaping from a disease is best able to create one?'

'True.'

'And he is the best guard of a camp who is best able to steal a march upon the enemy?'

'Certainly.'

'Then he who is a good keeper of anything is also a good thief?'

'That, I suppose, is to be inferred.'

'Then if the just man is good at keeping money, he is good at stealing it.'

'That is implied in the argument.'

'Then after all the just man has turned out to be a thief. And this is a lesson which I suspect you must have learnt out of Homer; for he, speaking of Autolycus, the maternal grandfather of Odysseus, who is a favourite of his, affirms that:

"He was excellent above all men in theft and perjury."

And so, you and Homer and Simonides are agreed that justice is an art of theft; to be practised, however, "for the good of friends and for the harm of enemies" – that was what you were saying?'

'No, certainly not that, though I do not now know what I did say; but I still stand by the latter words.'

'Well, there is another question: by friends and enemies do we mean those who are so really, or only in seeming?'

'Surely,' he said, 'a man may be expected to love those whom he thinks good, and to hate those whom he thinks evil.'

'Yes, but do not persons often err about good and evil: many who are not good seem to be so, and conversely?'

'That is true.'

'Then to them the good will be enemies and the evil will be their friends? True.'

'And in that case they will be right in doing good to the evil and evil to the good?'

'Clearly.'

'But the good are just and would not do an injustice?'

'True.'

'Then according to your argument it is just to injure those who do no wrong?'

'Nay, Socrates; the doctrine is immoral.'

'Then I suppose that we ought to do good to the just and harm to the unjust?

'I like that better.'

'But see the consequence:– many a man who is ignorant of human nature has friends who are bad friends, and in that case he ought to do harm to them; and he has good enemies whom he ought to benefit; but, if so, we shall be saying the very opposite of that which we affirmed to be the meaning of Simonides.'

'Very true,' he said. 'And I think that we had better correct an error into which we seem to have fallen in the use of the words "friend" and "enemy".'

'What was the error, Polemarchus?' I asked.

'We assumed that he is a friend who seems to be or who is thought good.'

'And how is the error to be corrected?'

'We should rather say that he is a friend who is, as well as seems, good; and that he who seems only, and is not, good, only seems to be and is not a friend; and of an enemy the same may be said.'

'You would argue that the good are our friends and the bad our enemies?'

'Yes.'

'And instead of saying simply as we did at first, that it is just to do good to our friends and harm to our enemies, we should further say: it is just to do good to our friends when they are good and harm to our enemies when they are evil?'

'Yes, that appears to me to be the truth.'

'But ought the just to injure anyone at all?'

'Undoubtedly he ought to injure those who are both wicked and his enemies.'

'When horses are injured, are they improved or deteriorated?'

'The latter.'

'Deteriorated, that is to say, in the good qualities of horses, not of dogs?'

'Yes, of horses.'

'And dogs are deteriorated in the good qualities of dogs, and not of horses?'

'Of course.'

'And will not men who are injured be deteriorated in that which is the proper virtue of man?'

'Certainly.'

'And that human virtue is justice?'

'To be sure.'

'Then men who are injured are of necessity made unjust?'

'That is the result.'

'But can the musician by his art make men unmusical?'

'Certainly not.'

'Or the horseman by his art make them bad horsemen?'

'Impossible.'

'And can the just by justice make men unjust, or speaking general can the good by virtue make them bad?'

'Assuredly not.'

'Any more than heat can produce cold?'

'It cannot.'

'Or drought moisture?'

'Clearly not.'

'Nor can the good harm anyone?'

'Impossible.'

'And the just is the good?'

'Certainly.'

'Then to injure a friend or anyone else is not the act of a just man, but of the opposite, who is the unjust?'

'I think that what you say is quite true, Socrates.'

'Then if a man says that justice consists in the repayment of debts, and that good is the debt which a man owes to his friends, and evil the debt which he owes to his enemies – to say this is not wise; for it is not true, if, as has been clearly shown, the injuring of another can be in no case just.'

'I agree with you, said Polemarchus.'

'Then you and I are prepared to take up arms against anyone who attributes such a saying to Simonides or Bias or Pittacus, or any other wise man or seer?'

'I am quite ready to do battle at your side,' he said.

'Shall I tell you whose I believe the saying to be?'

'Whose?'

'I believe that Periander or Perdiccas or Xerxes or Ismenias the Theban, or some other rich and mighty man, who had a great opinion of his own power, was the first to say that justice is "doing good to your friends and harm to your enemies".'

'Most true,' he said.

'Yes,' I said; 'but if this definition of justice also breaks down, what other can be offered?'

Several times in the course of the discussion Thrasymachus had made an attempt to get the argument into his own hands, and had been put down by the rest of the company, who wanted to hear the end. But when Polemarchus and I had done speaking and there was a pause, he could no longer hold his peace; and, gathering himself up, he came at us like a wild beast, seeking to devour us. We were quite panic-stricken at the sight of him.

He roared out to the whole company: 'What folly, Socrates, has taken possession of you all? And why, sillybillies, do you knock under to one another? I say that if you want really to know what justice is, you should not only ask but answer, and you should not seek honour to yourself from the refutation of an opponent, but have your own answer; for there is many a one who can ask and cannot answer. And now I will not have you say that justice is duty or advantage or profit or gain or interest, for this sort of nonsense will not do for me; I must have clearness and accuracy.'

I was panic-stricken at his words, and could not look at him without trembling. Indeed I believe that if I had not fixed my eye upon him, I should have been struck dumb: but when I saw his fury rising, I looked at him first, and was therefore able to reply to him.

'Thrasymachus,' I said, with a quiver, 'don't be hard upon us. Polemarchus and I may have been guilty of a little mistake in the argument, but I can assure you that the error was not intentional. If we were seeking for a piece of gold, you would not imagine that we were "knocking under to one another", and so losing our chance of finding it. And why, when we are seeking for justice, a thing more precious than many pieces of gold, do you say that we are weakly yielding to one another and not doing our utmost to get at the truth? Nay, my good friend, we are most willing and anxious to do so, but the fact is that we cannot. And if so, you people who know all things should pity us and not be angry with us.'

'How characteristic of Socrates!' he replied, with a bitter laugh; 'That's your ironical style! Did I not foresee – have I not already told you – that whatever he was asked he would refuse to answer, and try irony or any other shuffle, in order that he might avoid answering?'

'You are a philosopher, Thrasymachus,' I replied, 'and well know that if you ask a person what numbers make up twelve, taking care to prohibit him whom you ask from answering twice six, or three times four, or six times two, or four times three, "for this sort of nonsense will not do for me" – then obviously, that is your way of putting the question, no one can answer you. But suppose that he were to retort, "Thrasymachus, what do you mean? If one of these numbers which you interdict be the true answer to the question, am I falsely to say some other number which is not the right one? – Is that your meaning?" – How would you answer him?'

'Just as if the two cases were at all alike!' he said.

'Why should they not be?' I replied. 'And even if they are not, but only appear to be so to the person who is asked, ought he not to say what he thinks, whether you and I forbid him or not?'

'I presume, then, that you are going to make one of the interdicted answers?'

'I dare say that I may, notwithstanding the danger, if upon reflection I approve of any of them.'

'But what if I give you an answer about justice other and better', he said, 'than any of these? What do you deserve to have done to you?'

'Done to me! – As becomes the ignorant, I must learn from the wise – that is what I deserve to have done to me.'

'What, and no payment! A pleasant notion!'

'I will pay when I have the money,' I replied.

'But you have, Socrates,' said Glaucon: 'And you, Thrasymachus, need be under no anxiety about money, for we will all make a contribution for Socrates.'

'Yes,' he replied, 'and then Socrates will do as he always does – refuse to answer himself, but take and pull to pieces the answer of someone else.'

'Why, my good friend,' I said, 'how can anyone answer who knows, and says that he knows, just nothing; and who, even if he has some faint notions of his own, is told by a man of authority not to utter them? The natural thing is, that the speaker should be someone like yourself who professes to know and can tell what he knows. Will you then kindly answer, for the edification of the company and of myself?'

Glaucon and the rest of the company joined in my request and Thrasymachus, as anyone might see, was in reality eager to speak; for he thought that he had an excellent answer, and would distinguish himself. But at first he affected to insist on my answering; at length he consented to begin. 'Behold,' he said, 'the wisdom of Socrates; he refuses to teach himself, and goes about learning of others, to whom he never even says thank you.'

'That I learn of others,' I replied, is quite true; 'but that I am ungrateful I wholly deny. Money I have none, and therefore I pay in praise, which is all I have: and how ready I am to praise anyone who appears to me to speak well you will very soon find out when you answer; for I expect that you will answer well.'

'Listen, then,' he said; 'I proclaim that justice is nothing else than the interest of the stronger. And now why do you not praise me? But of course you won't.'

'Let me first understand you,' I replied. 'Justice, as you say, is the interest of the stronger. What, Thrasymachus, is the meaning of this? You cannot mean to say that because Polydamas, the pancratiast, is stronger than we are, and finds the eating of beef conducive to his bodily strength, that to eat beef is therefore equally for our good who are weaker than he is, and right and just for us?'

'That's abominable of you, Socrates; you take the words in the sense which is most damaging to the argument.'

'Not at all, my good sir,' I said; 'I am trying to understand them; and I wish that you would be a little clearer.'

'Well,' he said, 'have you never heard that forms of government differ; there are tyrannies, and there are democracies, and there are aristocracies?'

'Yes, I know.'

'And the government is the ruling power in each state?'

'Certainly.'

'And the different forms of government make laws democratical, aristocratical, tyrannical, with a view to their several interests; and these laws, which are made by them for their own interests, are the justice which they deliver to their subjects, and him who transgresses them they punish as a breaker of the law, and unjust. And that is what I mean when I say that in all states there is the same principle of justice, which is the interest of the government; and as the government must be supposed to have power, the only reasonable conclusion is, that everywhere there is one principle of justice, which is the interest of the stronger.'

'Now I understand you,' I said; 'and whether you are right or not I will try to discover. But let me remark, that in defining justice you have yourself used the word "interest" which you forbade me to use. It is true, however, that in your definition the words "of the stronger" are added.'

'A small addition, you must allow,' he said.

'Great or small, never mind about that: we must first enquire whether what you are saying is the truth. Now we are both agreed that justice is interest of some sort, but you go on to say "of the stronger"; about this addition I am not so sure, and must therefore consider further.'

'Proceed.'

'I will; and first tell me, do you admit that it is just for subjects to obey their rulers?'

'I do.'

'But are the rulers of states absolutely infallible, or are they sometimes liable to err?'

'To be sure,' he replied, 'they are liable to err.'

'Then in making their laws they may sometimes make them rightly, and sometimes not?'

'True.'

'When they make them rightly, they make them agreeably to their interest; when they are mistaken, contrary to their interest; you admit that?'

'Yes.'

'And the laws which they make must be obeyed by their subjects – and that is what you call justice?'

'Doubtless.'

'Then justice, according to your argument, is not only obedience to the interest of the stronger but the reverse?'

'What is that you are saying?' he asked.

'I am only repeating what you are saying, I believe. But let us consider:

Have we not admitted that the rulers may be mistaken about their own interest in what they command, and also that to obey them is justice? Has not that been admitted?'

'Yes.'

'Then you must also have acknowledged justice not to be for the interest of the stronger, when the rulers unintentionally command things to be done which are to their own injury. For if, as you say, justice is the obedience which the subject renders to their commands, in that case, O wisest of men, is there any escape from the conclusion that the weaker are commanded to do, not what is for the interest, but what is for the injury of the stronger?'

'Nothing can be clearer, Socrates,' said Polemarchus.

'Yes,' said Cleitophon, interposing, 'if you are allowed to be his witness.'

'But there is no need of any witness,' said Polemarchus, 'for Thrasymachus himself acknowledges that rulers may sometimes command what is not for their own interest, and that for subjects to obey them is justice.'

'Yes, Polemarchus – Thrasymachus said that for subjects to do what was commanded by their rulers is just.'

'Yes, Cleitophon, but he also said that justice is the interest of the stronger, and, while admitting both these propositions, he further acknowledged that the stronger may command the weaker who are his subjects to do what is not for his own interest; whence follows that justice is the injury quite as much as the interest of the stronger.'

'But', said Cleitophon, 'he meant by the interest of the stronger what the stronger thought to be his interest – this was what the weaker had to do; and this was affirmed by him to be justice.'

'Those were not his words,' rejoined Polemarchus.

'Never mind,' I replied. 'If he now says that they are, let us accept his statement. Tell me, Thrasymachus, I said, did you mean by justice what the stronger thought to be his interest, whether really so or not?'

'Certainly not,' he said. 'Do you suppose that I call him who is mistaken the stronger at the time when he is mistaken?'

'Yes,' I said, 'my impression was that you did so, when you admitted that the ruler was not infallible but might be sometimes mistaken.'

'You argue like an informer, Socrates. Do you mean, for example, that he who is mistaken about the sick is a physician in that he is mistaken? Or that he who errs in arithmetic or grammar is an arithmetician or grammarian at the time when he is making the mistake, in respect of the mistake? True, we say that the physician or arithmetician or grammarian has made a mistake, but this is only a way of speaking; for the fact is that neither the grammarian nor any other person of skill ever makes a mistake in so far as he is what his name implies; they none of them err unless their skill fails them, and then they cease to be skilled artists. No artist or sage or ruler errs at the time when he is what his name implies; though he is commonly said to err, and I adopted the common mode of speaking. But to be perfectly accurate, since you are such a lover of accuracy, we should say that the ruler, in so far as he is the ruler, is unerring, and, being unerring, always commands that which is for his own interest; and the subject is required to execute his commands; and therefore, as I said at first and now repeat, justice is the interest of the stronger.'

'Indeed, Thrasymachus, and do I really appear to you to argue like an informer?'

'Certainly,' he replied.

'And you suppose that I ask these questions with any design of injuring you in the argument?'

'Nay,' he replied, '"suppose" is not the word – I know it; but you will be found out, and by sheer force of argument you will never prevail.'

'I shall not make the attempt, my dear man; but to avoid any misunderstanding occurring between us in future, let me ask, in what sense do you speak of a ruler or stronger whose interest, as you were saying, he being the superior, it is just that the inferior should execute – is he a ruler in the popular or in the strict sense of the term?'

'In the strictest of all senses,' he said. 'And now cheat and play the informer if you can; I ask no quarter at your hands. But you never will be able, never.'

'And do you imagine', I said, 'that I am such a madman as to try and cheat, Thrasymachus? I might as well shave a lion.'

'Why,' he said, 'you made the attempt a minute ago, and you failed.'

'Enough', I said, 'of these civilities. It will be better that I should ask you a question: is the physician, taken in that strict sense of which you are speaking, a healer of the sick or a maker of money? And remember that I am now speaking of the true physician.'

'A healer of the sick,' he replied.

'And the pilot – that is to say, the true pilot – is he a captain of sailors or a mere sailor?'

'A captain of sailors.'

'The circumstance that he sails in the ship is not to be taken into account; neither is he to be called a sailor; the name pilot by which he is distinguished has nothing to do with sailing, but is significant of his skill and of his authority over the sailors.'

'Very true,' he said.

'Now,' I said, 'every art has an interest?'

'Certainly.'

'For which the art has to consider and provide?'

'Yes, that is the aim of art.'

'And the interest of any art is the perfection of it – this and nothing else?'

'What do you mean?'

'I mean what I may illustrate negatively by the example of the body. Suppose you were to ask me whether the body is self-sufficing or has wants, I should reply: certainly the body has wants; for the body may be ill and require to be cured, and has therefore interests to which the art of medicine ministers; and this is the origin and intention of medicine, as you will acknowledge. Am I not right?'

'Quite right,' he replied.

'But is the art of medicine or any other art faulty or deficient in any quality in the same way that the eye may be deficient in sight or the ear fail of hearing, and therefore requires another art to provide for the interests of seeing and hearing – has art in itself, I say, any similar liability to fault or defect, and does every art require another supplementary art to provide for its interests, and that another and another without end? Or have the arts to look only after their own interests? Or have they no need either of themselves or of another? – Having no faults or defects, they have no need to correct them, either by the exercise of their own art or of any other; they have only to consider the interest of their subject-matter. For every art remains pure and faultless while remaining true – that is to say, while perfect and unimpaired. Take the words in your precise sense, and tell me whether I am not right.'

'Yes, clearly.'

'Then medicine does not consider the interest of medicine, but the interest of the body?'

'True,' he said.

'Nor does the art of horsemanship consider the interests of the art of horsemanship, but the interests of the horse; neither do any other arts care for themselves, for they have no needs; they care only for that which is the subject of their art?'

'True,' he said.

'But surely, Thrasymachus, the arts are the superiors and rulers of their own subjects?'

To this he assented with a good deal of reluctance.

'Then', I said, 'no science or art considers or enjoins the interest of the stronger or superior, but only the interest of the subject and weaker?'

He made an attempt to contest this proposition also, but finally acquiesced.

'Then', I continued, 'no physician, in so far as he is a physician, considers his own good in what he prescribes, but the good of his patient; for the true physician is also a ruler having the human body as a subject, and is not a mere money-maker; that has been admitted?'

'Yes.'

'And the pilot likewise, in the strict sense of the term, is a ruler of sailors and not a mere sailor?'

'That has been admitted.'

'And such a pilot and ruler will provide and prescribe for the interest of the sailor who is under him, and not for his own or the ruler's interest?'

He gave a reluctant, 'Yes.'

'Then', I said, 'Thrasymachus, there is no one in any rule who, in so far as he is a ruler, considers or enjoins what is for his own interest, but always what is for the interest of his subject or suitable to his art; to that he looks, and that alone he considers in everything which he says and does.'

When we had got to this point in the argument, and everyone saw that the definition of justice had been completely upset, Thrasymachus, instead of replying to me, said: 'Tell me, Socrates, have you got a nurse?'

'Why do you ask such a question,' I said, 'when you ought rather to be answering?'

'Because she leaves you to snivel, and never wipes your nose: she has not even taught you to know the shepherd from the sheep.'

'What makes you say that?' I replied.

'Because you fancy that the shepherd or neatherd fattens or tends the sheep or oxen with a view to their own good and not to the good of himself or his master; and you further imagine that the rulers of states, if they are true rulers, never think of their subjects as sheep, and that they are not studying their own advantage day and night. Oh, no; and so entirely astray are you in your ideas about the just and unjust as not even to know that justice and the just are in reality another's good; that is to say, the interest of the ruler and stronger, and the loss of the subject and servant; and injustice the opposite; for the unjust is lord over the truly simple and just: he is the stronger, and his subjects do what is for his interest, and minister to his happiness, which is very far from being their own. Consider further, most foolish Socrates, that the just is always a loser in comparison with the unjust. First of all, in private contracts: wherever the unjust is the partner of the just you will find that, when the partnership is dissolved, the unjust man has always more and the just less. Secondly, in their dealings with the State: when there is an income tax, the just man will pay more and the unjust less on the same amount of income; and when there is anything to be received the one gains nothing and the other much. Observe also what happens when they take an office; there is the just man neglecting his affairs and perhaps suffering other losses, and getting nothing out of the public, because he is just; moreover he is hated by his friends and acquaintance for refusing to serve them in unlawful ways. But all this is reversed in the case of the unjust man. I am speaking, as before, of injustice on a large scale in which the advantage of the unjust is more apparent; and my meaning will be most clearly seen if we turn to that highest form of injustice in which the criminal is the happiest of men, and the sufferers or those who refuse to do injustice are the most miserable – that is to say tyranny, which by fraud and force takes away the property of others, not little by little but wholesale; comprehending in one, things sacred as well as profane, private and public; for which acts of wrong, if he were detected perpetrating any one of them singly, he would be punished and incur great disgrace – they who do such wrong in particular cases are called robbers of temples, and man-stealers and burglars and swindlers and thieves. But when a man besides taking away the money of the citizens has made slaves of them, then, instead of these names of reproach, he is termed happy and blessed, not only by the citizens but by all who hear of his having achieved the consummation of injustice. For mankind censure injustice, fearing that they may be the victims of it and not because they shrink from committing it. And thus, as I have shown, Socrates, injustice, when on a sufficient scale, has more strength and freedom and mastery than justice; and, as I said at first, justice is the interest of the stronger, whereas injustice is a man's own profit and interest.'

Thrasymachus, when he had thus spoken, having, like a bathman, deluged our ears with his words, had a mind to go away. But the company would not let him; they insisted that he should remain and defend his position; and I myself added my own humble request that he would not leave us. 'Thrasymachus,' I said to him, 'excellent man, how suggestive are your remarks! And are you going to run away before you have fairly taught or learned whether they are true or not? Is the attempt to determine the way of man's life so small a matter in your eyes – to determine how life may be passed by each one of us to the greatest advantage?'

'And do I differ from you,' he said, 'as to the importance of the enquiry?'

'You appear rather', I replied, 'to have no care or thought about us, Thrasymachus – whether we live better or worse from not knowing what you say you know, is to you a matter of indifference. Prithee, friend, do not keep your knowledge to yourself; we are a large party; and any benefit which you confer upon us will be amply rewarded. For my own part I openly declare that

I am not convinced, and that I do not believe injustice to be more gainful than justice, even if uncontrolled and allowed to have free play. For, granting that there may be an unjust man who is able to commit injustice either by fraud or force, still this does not convince me of the superior advantage of injustice, and there may be others who are in the same predicament with myself. Perhaps we may be wrong; if so, you in your wisdom should convince us that we are mistaken in preferring justice to injustice.'

'And how am I to convince you,' he said, 'if you are not already convinced by what I have just said; what more can I do for you? Would you have me put the proof bodily into your souls?'

'Heaven forbid!' I said; 'I would only ask you to be consistent; or, if you change, change openly and let there be no deception. For I must remark, Thrasymachus, if you will recall what was previously said, that although you began by defining the true physician in an exact sense, you did not observe a like exactness when speaking of the shepherd; you thought that the shepherd as a shepherd tends the sheep not with a view to their own good, but like a mere diner or banqueter with a view to the pleasures of the table; or, again, as a trader for sale in the market, and not as a shepherd. Yet surely the art of the shepherd is concerned only with the good of his subjects; he has only to provide the best for them, since the perfection of the art is already ensured whenever all the requirements of it are satisfied. And that was what I was saying just now about the ruler. I conceived that the art of the ruler, considered as ruler, whether in a state or in private life, could only regard the good of his flock or subjects; whereas you seem to think that the rulers in states, that is to say, the true rulers, like being in authority.'

'Think! Nay, I am sure of it.'

'Then why in the case of lesser offices do men never take them willingly without payment, unless under the idea that they govern for the advantage not of themselves but of others? Let me ask you a question: are not the several arts different, by reason of their each having a separate function? And, my dear illustrious friend, do say what you think, that we may make a little progress.'

'Yes, that is the difference,' he replied.

'And each art gives us a particular good and not merely a general one – medicine, for example, gives us health; navigation, safety at sea, and so on?'

'Yes,' he said.

'And the art of payment has the special function of giving pay: but we do not confuse this with other arts, any more than the art of the pilot is to be confused with the art of medicine, because the health of the pilot may be improved by a sea voyage. You would not be inclined to say, would you, that navigation is the art of medicine, at least if we are to adopt your exact use of language?'

'Certainly not.'

'Or because a man is in good health when he receives pay you would not say that the art of payment is medicine?'

'I should say not.'

'Nor would you say that medicine is the art of receiving pay because a man takes fees when he is engaged in healing?'

'Certainly not.'

'And we have admitted', I said, 'that the good of each art is specially confined to the art?'

'Yes.'

'Then, if there be any good which all artists have in common, that is to be attributed to something of which they all have the common use?'

'True,' he replied.

'And when the artist is benefited by receiving pay the advantage is gained by an additional use of the art of pay, which is not the art professed by him?'

He gave a reluctant assent to this.

'Then the pay is not derived by the several artists from their respective arts. But the truth is, that while the art of medicine gives health, and the art of the builder builds a house, another art attends them which is the art of pay. The various arts may be doing their own business and benefiting that over which they preside, but would the artist receive any benefit from his art unless he were paid as well?'

'I suppose not.'

'But does he therefore confer no benefit when he works for nothing?'

'Certainly, he confers a benefit.'

'Then now, Thrasymachus, there is no longer any doubt that neither arts nor governments provide for their own interests; but, as we were before saying, they rule and provide for the interests of their subjects who are the weaker and not the stronger – to their good they attend and not to the good of the superior.

'And this is the reason, my dear Thrasymachus, why, as I was just now saying, no one is willing to govern; because no one likes to take in hand the reformation of evils which are not his concern without remuneration. For, in the execution of his work, and in giving his orders to another, the true artist does not regard his own interest, but always that of his subjects; and therefore in order that rulers may be willing to rule, they must be paid in one of three modes of payment: money, or honour, or a penalty for refusing.'

'What do you mean, Socrates?' said Glaucon. 'The first two modes of payment are intelligible enough, but what the penalty is I do not understand, or how a penalty can be a payment.'

'You mean that you do not understand the nature of this payment which to the best men is the great inducement to rule? Of course you know that ambition and avarice are held to be, as indeed they are, a disgrace?'

'Very true.'

'And for this reason,' I said, 'money and honour have no attraction for them; good men do not wish to be openly demanding payment for governing and so to get the name of hirelings, nor by secretly helping themselves out of the public revenues to get the name of thieves. And not being ambitious they do not care about honour. Wherefore necessity must be laid upon them, and they must be induced to serve from the fear of punishment. And this, as I imagine, is the reason why the forwardness to take office, instead of waiting to be compelled, has been deemed dishonourable. Now the worst part of the punishment is that he who refuses to rule is liable to be ruled by one who is worse than himself. And the fear of this, as I conceive, induces the good to take office, not because they would, but because they cannot help – not under the idea that they are going to have any benefit or enjoyment themselves, but as a necessity, and because they are not able to commit the task of ruling to anyone who is better than themselves, or indeed as good. For there is reason to think that if a city were composed entirely of good men, then to avoid office would be as much an object of contention as to obtain office is at present; then we should have plain proof that the true ruler is not meant by nature to regard his own interest, but that of his subjects; and everyone who knew this would choose rather to receive a benefit from another than to have the trouble of conferring one. So far am I from agreeing with Thrasymachus that justice is the interest of the stronger. This latter question need not be further discussed at present; but when Thrasymachus says that the life of the unjust is more advantageous than that of the just, his new statement appears to me to be of a far more serious character. Which of us has spoken truly? And which sort of life, Glaucon, do you prefer?'

'I for my part deem the life of the just to be the more advantageous,' he answered.

'Did you hear all the advantages of the unjust which Thrasymachus was rehearsing?'

'Yes, I heard him,' he replied, 'but he has not convinced me.'

'Then shall we try to find some way of convincing him, if we can, that he is saying what is not true?'

'Most certainly,' he replied.

'If', I said, 'he makes a set speech and we make another recounting all the advantages of being just, and he answers and we rejoin, there must be a numbering and measuring of the goods which are claimed on either side, and in the end we shall want judges to decide; but if we proceed in our enquiry as we lately did, by making admissions to one another, we shall unite the offices of judge and advocate in our own persons.'

'Very good,' he said.

'And which method do I understand you to prefer?' I said.

'That which you propose.'

'Well, then, Thrasymachus,' I said, 'suppose you begin at the beginning and answer me. You say that perfect injustice is more gainful than perfect justice?'

'Yes, that is what I say, and I have given you my reasons.'

'And what is your view about them? Would you call one of them virtue and the other vice?'

'Certainly.'

'I suppose that you would call justice virtue and injustice vice?'

'What a charming notion! So likely too, seeing that I affirm injustice to be profitable and justice not.'

'What else then would you say?'

'The opposite,' he replied.

'And would you call justice vice?'

'No, I would rather say sublime simplicity.'

'Then would you call injustice malignity?'

'No; I would rather say discretion.'

'And do the unjust appear to you to be wise and good?'

'Yes,' he said. 'At any rate those of them who are able to be perfectly unjust, and who have the power of subduing states and nations; but perhaps you imagine me to be talking of cutpurses.'

'Even this profession if undetected has advantages, though they are not to be compared with those of which I was just now speaking.'

'I do not think that I misapprehend your meaning, Thrasymachus,' I replied; 'but still I cannot hear without amazement that you class injustice with wisdom and virtue, and justice with the opposite.'

'Certainly I do so class them.'

'Now,' I said, 'you are on more substantial and almost unanswerable ground; for if the injustice which you were maintaining to be profitable had been admitted by you as by others to be vice and deformity, an answer might have been given to you on received principles; but now I perceive that you will call injustice honourable and strong, and to the unjust you will attribute all the qualities which were attributed by us before to the just, seeing that you do not hesitate to rank injustice with wisdom and virtue.'

'You have guessed most infallibly,' he replied.

'Then I certainly ought not to shrink from going through with the argument so long as I have reason to think that you, Thrasymachus, are speaking your real mind; for I do believe that you are now in earnest and are not amusing yourself at our expense.'

'I may be in earnest or not, but what is that to you? – To refute the argument is your business.'

'Very true,' I said; 'that is what I have to do. But will you be so good as answer yet one more question? Does the just man try to gain any advantage over the just?'

'Far otherwise; if he did, he would not be the simple, amusing creature which he is.'

'And would he try to go beyond just action?'

'He would not.'

'And how would he regard the attempt to gain an advantage over the unjust; would that be considered by him as just or unjust?'

'He would think it just, and would try to gain the advantage; but he would not be able.'

'Whether he would or would not be able', I said, 'is not to the point. My question is only whether the just man, while refusing to have more than another just man, would wish and claim to have more than the unjust?'

'Yes, he would.'

'And what of the unjust – does he claim to have more than the just man and to do more than is just?

'Of course,' he said, 'for he claims to have more than all men.'

'And the unjust man will strive and struggle to obtain more than the unjust man or action, in order that he may have more than all?'

'True.'

'We may put the matter thus,' I said. 'The just does not desire more than his like but more than his unlike, whereas the unjust desires more than both his like and his unlike?'

'Nothing', he said, 'can be better than that statement.'

'And the unjust is good and wise, and the just is neither?'

'Good again,' he said.

'And is not the unjust like the wise and good and the just unlike them?'

'Of course,' he said, 'he who is of a certain nature, is like those who are of a certain nature; he who is not, not.'

'Each of them', I said, 'is such as his like is?'

'Certainly,' he replied.

'Very good, Thrasymachus,' I said; 'and now to take the case of the arts: you would admit that one man is a musician and another not a musician?'

'Yes.'

'And which is wise and which is foolish?'

'Clearly the musician is wise, and he who is not a musician is foolish.'

'And he is good in as far as he is wise, and bad in as far as he is foolish?'

'Yes.'

'And you would say the same sort of thing of the physician?'

'Yes.'

'And do you think, my excellent friend, that a musician when he adjusts the lyre would desire or claim to exceed or go beyond a musician in the tightening and loosening the strings?'

'I do not think that he would.'

'But he would claim to exceed the non-musician?'

'Of course.'

'And what would you say of the physician? In prescribing meats and drinks would he wish to go beyond another physician or beyond the practice of medicine?'

'He would not.'

'But he would wish to go beyond the non-physician?'

'Yes.'

'And about knowledge and ignorance in general; see whether you think that any man who has knowledge ever would wish to have the choice of saying or doing more than another man who has knowledge. Would he not rather say or do the same as his like in the same case?'

'That, I suppose, can hardly be denied.'

'And what of the ignorant? Would he not desire to have more than either the knowing or the ignorant?'

'I dare say.'

'And the knowing is wise?'

'Yes.'

'And the wise is good?'

'True.'

'Then the wise and good will not desire to gain more than his like, but more than his unlike and opposite?'

'I suppose so.'

'Whereas the bad and ignorant will desire to gain more than both?'

'Yes.'

'But did we not say, Thrasymachus, that the unjust goes beyond both his like and unlike? Were not these your words?'

'They were.'

'And you also said that the lust will not go beyond his like but his unlike?'

'Yes.'

'Then the just is like the wise and good, and the unjust like the evil and ignorant?'

'That is the inference.'

'And each of them is such as his like is?'

'That was admitted.'

'Then the just has turned out to be wise and good and the unjust evil and ignorant.'

Thrasymachus made all these admissions, not fluently, as I repeat them, but with extreme reluctance; it was a hot summer's day, and the perspiration poured from him in torrents; and then I saw what I had never seen before, Thrasymachus blushing. As we were now agreed that justice was virtue and wisdom, and injustice vice and ignorance, I proceeded to another point:

'Well,' I said, 'Thrasymachus, that matter is now settled; but were we not also saying that injustice had strength; do you remember?'

'Yes, I remember,' he said, 'but do not suppose that I approve of what you are saying or have no answer; if, however, I were to answer, you would be quite certain to accuse me of haranguing; therefore either permit me to have my say out, or if you would rather ask, do so, and I will answer "Very good", as they say to story-telling old women, and will nod "Yes" and "No".'

'Certainly not,' I said, 'if contrary to your real opinion.'

'Yes,' he said, 'I will, to please you, since you will not let me speak. What else would you have?'

'Nothing in the world,' I said; 'and if you are so disposed I will ask and you shall answer.'

'Proceed.'

'Then I will repeat the question which I asked before, in order that our examination of the relative nature of justice and injustice may be carried on regularly. A statement was made that injustice is stronger and more powerful than justice, but now justice, having been identified with wisdom and virtue, is easily shown to be stronger than injustice, if injustice is ignorance; this can no longer be questioned by anyone. But I want to view the matter, Thrasymachus, in a different way: you would not deny that a state may be unjust and may be unjustly attempting to enslave other states, or may have already enslaved them, and may be holding many of them in subjection?'

'True,' he replied; 'and I will add the best and perfectly unjust state will be most likely to do so.'

'I know', I said, 'that such was your position; but what I would further consider is, whether this power which is possessed by the superior state can exist or be exercised without justice.'

'If you are right in you view, and justice is wisdom, then only with justice; but if I am right, then without justice.'

'I am delighted, Thrasymachus, to see you not only nodding assent and dissent, but making answers which are quite excellent.'

'That is out of civility to you,' he replied.

'You are very kind,' I said. 'And would you have the goodness also to inform me, whether you think that a state, or an army, or a band of robbers and thieves, or any other gang of evil-doers could act at all if they injured one another?'

'No indeed,' he said, 'they could not.'

'But if they abstained from injuring one another, then they might act together better?'

'Yes.'

'And this is because injustice creates divisions and hatreds and fighting, and justice imparts harmony and friendship; is not that true, Thrasymachus?'

'I agree,' he said, 'because I do not wish to quarrel with you.'

'How good of you,' I said. 'But I should like to know also whether injustice, having this tendency to arouse hatred, wherever existing, among slaves or among freemen, will not make them hate one another and set them at variance and render them incapable of common action?'

'Certainly.'

'And even if injustice be found in two only, will they not quarrel and fight, and become enemies to one another and to the just?'

'They will.'

'And suppose injustice abiding in a single person, would your wisdom say that she loses or that she retains her natural power?'

'Let us assume that she retains her power.'

'Yet is not the power which injustice exercises of such a nature that wherever she takes up her abode, whether in a city, in an army, in a family, or in any other body, that body is, to begin with, rendered incapable of united action by reason of sedition and distraction; and does it not become its own enemy and at variance with all that opposes it, and with the just? Is not this the case?'

'Yes, certainly.'

'And is not injustice equally fatal when existing in a single person; in the first place rendering him incapable of action because he is not at unity with himself, and in the second place making him an enemy to himself and the just? Is not that true, Thrasymachus?'

'Yes.'

'And O my friend,' I said, 'surely the gods are just?'

'Granted that they are.'

'But if so, the unjust will be the enemy of the gods, and the just will be their friend?'

'Feast away in triumph, and take your fill of the argument; I will not oppose you, lest I should displease the company.'

'Well then, proceed with your answers, and let me have the remainder of my repast. For we have already shown that the just are clearly wiser and better and abler than the unjust, and that the unjust are incapable of common action; nay more, that to speak as we did of men who are evil acting at any time vigorously together, is not strictly true, for if they had been perfectly evil, they would have laid hands upon one another; but it is evident that there must have been some remnant of justice in them, which enabled them to combine; if there had not been they would have injured one another as well as their victims; they were but half – villains in their enterprises; for had they been whole villains, and utterly unjust, they would have been utterly incapable of action. That, as I believe, is the truth of the matter, and not what you said at first. But whether the just have a better and happier life than the unjust is a further question which we also proposed to consider. I think that they have, and for the reasons which to have given; but still I should like to examine further, for no light matter is at stake, nothing less than the rule of human life.'

'Proceed.'

'I will proceed by asking a question: Would you not say that a horse has some end?'

'I should.'

'And the end or use of a horse or of anything would be that which could not be accomplished, or not so well accomplished, by any other thing?'

'I do not understand,' he said.

'Let me explain: can you see, except with the eye?'

'Certainly not.'

'Or hear, except with the ear?'

'No.'

'These then may be truly said to be the ends of these organs?'

'They may.'

'But you can cut off a vine-branch with a dagger or with a chisel, and in many other ways?'

'Of course.'

'And yet not so well as with a pruning-hook made for the purpose?'

'True.'

'May we not say that this is the end of a pruning-hook?'

'We may.'

'Then now I think you will have no difficulty in understanding my meaning when I asked the question whether the end of anything would be that which could not be accomplished, or not so well accomplished, by any other thing?'

'I understand your meaning,' he said, 'and assent.'

'And that to which an end is appointed has also an excellence? Need I ask again whether the eye has an end?'

'It has.'

'And has not the eye an excellence?'

'Yes.'

'And the ear has an end and an excellence also?'

'True.'

'And the same is true of all other things; they have each of them an end and a special excellence?'

'That is so.'

'Well, and can the eyes fulfil their end if they are wanting in their own proper excellence and have a defect instead?'

'How can they,' he said, 'if they are blind and cannot see?

'You mean to say, if they have lost their proper excellence, which is sight; but I have not arrived at that point yet. I would rather ask the question more generally, and only enquire whether the things which fulfil their ends fulfil them by their own proper excellence, and fall of fulfilling them by their own defect?'

'Certainly,' he replied.

'I might say the same of the ears; when deprived of their own proper excellence they cannot fulfil their end?'

'True.'

'And the same observation will apply to all other things?'

'I agree.'

'Well; and has not the soul an end which nothing else can fulfil? For example, to superintend and command and deliberate and the like. Are not these functions proper to the soul, and can they rightly be assigned to any other?'

'To no other.'

'And is not life to be reckoned among the ends of the soul?'

'Assuredly,' he said.

'And has not the soul an excellence also?'

'Yes.'

'And can she or can she not fulfil her own ends when deprived of that excellence?'

'She cannot.'

'Then an evil soul must necessarily be an evil ruler and superintendent, and the good soul a good ruler?'

'Yes, necessarily.'

'And we have admitted that justice is the excellence of the soul, and injustice the defect of the soul?'

'That has been admitted.'

'Then the just soul and the just man will live well, and the unjust man will live ill?'

'That is what your argument proves.'

'And he who lives well is blessed and happy, and he who lives ill the reverse of happy?'

'Certainly.'

'Then the just is happy, and the unjust miserable?'

'So be it.'

'But happiness and not misery is profitable.'

'Of course.'

'Then, my blessed Thrasymachus, injustice can never be more profitable than justice.'

'Let this, Socrates,' he said, 'be your entertainment at the Bendidea.'

'For which I am indebted to you,' I said, 'now that you have grown gentle towards me and have left off scolding. Nevertheless, I have not been well entertained; but that was my own fault and not yours. As an epicure snatches a taste of every dish which is successively brought to table, he not having allowed himself time to enjoy the one before, so have I gone from one subject to another without having discovered what I sought at first, the nature of justice. I left that enquiry and turned away to consider whether justice is virtue and wisdom or evil and folly; and when there arose a further question about the comparative advantages of justice and injustice, I could not refrain from passing on to that. And the result of the whole discussion has been that I know nothing at all. For I know not what justice is, and therefore I am not likely to know whether it is or is not a virtue, nor can I say whether the just man is happy or unhappy.'

Book II

With these words I was thinking that I had made an end of the discussion; but the end, in truth, proved to be only a beginning. For Glaucon, who is always the most pugnacious of men, was dissatisfied at Thrasymachus's retirement; he wanted to have the battle out. So he said to me: 'Socrates, do you wish really to persuade us, or only to seem to have persuaded us, that to be just is always better than to be unjust?'

'I should wish really to persuade you,' I replied, 'if I could.'

'Then you certainly have not succeeded. Let me ask you now:– how would you arrange goods – are there not some which we welcome for their own sakes, and independently of their consequences, as, for example, harmless pleasures and enjoyments, which delight us at the time, although nothing follows from them?'

'I agree in thinking that there is such a class,' I replied.

'Is there not also a second class of goods, such as knowledge, sight, health, which are desirable not only in themselves, but also for their results?'

'Certainly,' I said.

'And would you not recognise a third class, such as gymnastics, and the care of the sick, and the physician's art; also the various ways of money-making – these do us good but we regard them as disagreeable; and no one would choose them for their own sakes, but only for the sake of some reward or result which flows from them?'

'There is', I said, 'this third class also. But why do you ask?'

'Because I want to know in which of the three classes you would place justice?'

'In the highest class,' I replied, '– among those goods which he who would be happy desires both for their own sake and for the sake of their results.'

'Then the many are of another mind; they think that justice is to be reckoned in the troublesome class, among goods which are to be pursued for the sake of rewards and of reputation, but in themselves are disagreeable and rather to be avoided.'

'I know', I said, 'that this is their manner of thinking, and that this was the thesis which Thrasymachus was maintaining just now, when he censured justice and praised injustice. But I am too stupid to be convinced by him.'

'I wish', he said, 'that you would hear me as well as him, and then I shall see whether you and I agree. For Thrasymachus seems to me, like a snake, to have been charmed by your voice sooner than he ought to have been; but to my mind the nature of justice and injustice have not yet been made clear. Setting aside their rewards and results, I want to know what they are in themselves, and how they inwardly work in the soul. If you please, then, I will revive the argument of Thrasymachus. And first I will speak of the nature and origin of justice according to the common view of them. Secondly, I will show that all men who practise justice do so against their will, of necessity, but not as a good. And thirdly, I will argue that there is reason in this view, for the life of the unjust is after all better far than the life of the just – if what they say is true, Socrates, since I myself am not of their opinion. But still I acknowledge that I am perplexed when I hear the voices of Thrasymachus and myriads of others dinning in my ears; and, on the other hand, I have never yet heard the superiority of justice to injustice maintained by anyone in a satisfactory way. I want to hear justice praised in respect of itself; then I shall be satisfied, and you are the person from whom I think that I am most likely to hear this; and therefore I will praise the unjust life to the utmost of my power, and my manner of speaking will indicate the manner in which I desire to hear you too praising justice and censuring injustice. Will you say whether you approve of my proposal?'

'Indeed I do; nor can I imagine any theme about which a man of sense would oftener wish to converse.'

'I am delighted', he replied, 'to hear you say so, and shall begin by speaking, as I proposed, of the nature and origin of justice.

'They say that to do injustice is, by nature, good; to suffer injustice, evil; but that the evil is greater than the good. And so when men have both done and suffered injustice and have had experience of both, not being able to avoid the one and obtain the other, they think that they had better agree among themselves to have neither; hence there arise laws and mutual covenants; and that which is ordained by law is termed by them lawful and just. This they affirm to be the origin and nature of justice; – it is a mean or compromise, between the best of all, which is to do injustice and not be punished, and the worst of all, which is to suffer injustice without the power of retaliation; and justice, being at a middle point between the two, is tolerated not as a good, but as the lesser evil, and honoured by reason of the inability of men to do injustice. For no man who is worthy to be called a man would ever submit to such an agreement if he were able to resist; he would be mad if he did. Such is the received account, Socrates, of the nature and origin of justice.

'Now that those who practise justice do so involuntarily and because they have not the power to be unjust will best appear if we imagine something of this kind: having given both to the just and the unjust power to do what they will, let us watch and see whither desire will lead them; then we shall discover in the very act the just and unjust man to be proceeding along the same road, following their interest, which all natures deem to be their good, and are only diverted into the path of justice by the force of law. The liberty which we are supposing may be most completely given to them in the form of such a power as is said to have been possessed by Gyges the ancestor of Croesus the Lydian. According to the tradition, Gyges was a shepherd in the service of the king of Lydia; there was a great storm, and an earthquake made an opening in the earth at the place where he was feeding his flock. Amazed at the sight, he descended into the opening, where, among other marvels, he beheld a hollow brazen horse, having doors, at which he stooping and looking in saw a dead body of stature, as appeared to him, more than human, and having nothing on but a gold ring; this he took from the finger of the dead and reascended. Now the shepherds met together, according to custom, that they might send their monthly report about the flocks to the king; into their assembly he came having the ring on his finger, and as he was sitting among them he chanced to turn the collet of the ring inside his hand, when instantly he became invisible to the rest of the company and they began to speak of him as if he were no longer present. He was astonished at this, and again touching the ring he turned the collet outwards and reappeared; he made several trials of the ring, and always with the same result – when he turned the collet inwards he became invisible, when outwards he reappeared. Whereupon he contrived to be chosen one of the messengers who were sent to the court; where as soon as he arrived he seduced the queen, and with her help conspired against the king and slew him, and took the kingdom. Suppose now that there were two such magic rings, and the just put on one of them and the unjust the other; no man can be imagined to be of such an iron nature that he would stand fast in justice. No man would keep his hands off what was not his own when he could safely take what he liked out of the market, or go into houses and lie with anyone at his pleasure, or kill or release from prison whom he would, and in all respects be like a God among men. Then the actions of the just would be as the actions of the unjust; they would both come at last to the same point. And this we may truly affirm to be a great proof that a man is just, not willingly or because he thinks that justice is any good to him individually, but of necessity, for wherever anyone thinks that he can safely be unjust, there he is unjust. For all men believe in their hearts that injustice is far more profitable to the individual than justice, and he who argues as I have been supposing, will say that they are right. If you could imagine anyone obtaining this power of becoming invisible, and never doing any wrong or touching what was another's, he would be thought by the lookers-on to be a most wretched idiot, although they would praise him to one another's faces, and keep up appearances with one another from a fear that they too might suffer injustice. Enough of this.

'Now, if we are to form a real judgment of the life of the just and unjust, we must isolate them; there is no other way; and how is the isolation to be effected? I answer: let the unjust man be entirely unjust, and the just man entirely just; nothing is to be taken away from either of them, and both are to be perfectly furnished for the work of their respective lives. First, let the unjust be like other distinguished masters of craft; like the skilful pilot or physician, who knows intuitively his own powers and keeps within their limits, and who, if he fails at any point, is able to recover himself. So let the unjust make his unjust attempts in the right way, and lie hidden if he means to be great in his injustice (he who is found out is nobody): for the highest reach of injustice is: to be deemed just when you are not. Therefore I say that in the perfectly unjust man we must assume the most perfect injustice; there is to be no deduction, but we must allow him, while doing the most unjust acts, to have acquired the greatest reputation for justice. If he has taken a false step he must be able to recover himself; he must be one who can speak with effect, if any of his deeds come to light, and who can force his way where force is required by his courage and strength, and command of money and friends. And at his side let us place the just man in his nobleness and simplicity, wishing, as Aeschylus says, to be and not to seem good. There must be no seeming, for if he seem to be just he will be honoured and rewarded, and then we shall not know whether he is just for the sake of justice or for the sake of honours and rewards; therefore, let him be clothed in justice only, and have no other covering; and he must be imagined in a state of life the opposite of the former. Let him be the best of men, and let him be thought the worst; then he will have been put to the proof; and we shall see whether he will be affected by the fear of infamy and its consequences. And let him continue thus to the hour of death; being just and seeming to be unjust. When both have reached the uttermost extreme, the one of justice and the other of injustice, let judgment be given which of them is the happier of the two.'

'Heavens! My dear Glaucon,' I said, 'how energetically you polish them up for the decision, first one and then the other, as if they were two statues.'

'I do my best,' he said. 'And now that we know what they are like there is no difficulty in tracing out the sort of life which awaits either of them. This I will proceed to describe; but as you may think the description a little too coarse, I ask you to suppose, Socrates, that the words which follow are not mine. Let me put them into the mouths of the eulogists of injustice: They will tell you that the just man who is thought unjust will be scourged, racked, bound – will have his eyes burnt out; and, at last, after suffering every kind of evil, he will be impaled. Then he will understand that he ought to seem only, and not to be, just; the words of Aeschylus may be more truly spoken of the unjust than of the just. For the unjust is pursuing a reality; he does not live with a view to appearances – he wants to be really unjust and not to seem only:–

"His mind has a soil deep and fertile,
Out of which spring his prudent counsels."

In the first place, he is thought just, and therefore bears rule in the city; he can marry whom he will, and give in marriage to whom he will; also he can trade and deal where he likes, and always to his own advantage, because he has no misgivings about injustice and at every contest, whether in public or private, he gets the better of his antagonists, and gains at their expense, and is rich, and out of his gains he can benefit his friends, and harm his enemies; moreover, he can offer sacrifices, and dedicate gifts to the gods abundantly and magnificently, and can honour the gods or any man whom he wants to honour in a far better style than the just, and therefore he is likely to be dearer than they are to the gods. And thus, Socrates, gods and men are said to unite in making the life of the unjust better than the life of the just.'

I was going to say something in answer to Glaucon, when Adeimantus, his brother, interposed: 'Socrates,' he said, 'you do not suppose that there is nothing more to be urged?'

'Why, what else is there?' I answered.

'The strongest point of all has not been even mentioned,' he replied.

'Well, then, according to the proverb, "Let brother help brother" – if he fails in any part do you assist him; although I must confess that Glaucon has already said quite enough to lay me in the dust, and take from me the power of helping justice.'

'Nonsense,' he replied. 'But let me add something more: There is another side to Glaucon's argument about the praise and censure of justice and injustice, which is equally required in order to bring out what I believe to be his meaning. Parents and tutors are always telling their sons and their wards that they are to be just; but why? Not for the sake of justice, but for the sake of character and reputation; in the hope of obtaining for him who is reputed just some of those offices, marriages, and the like which Glaucon has enumerated among the advantages accruing to the unjust from the reputation of justice. More, however, is made of appearances by this class of persons than by the others; for they throw in the good opinion of the gods, and will tell you of a shower of benefits which the heavens, as they say, rain upon the pious; and this accords with the testimony of the noble Hesiod and Homer, the first of whom says that the gods make the oaks of the just –

"To bear acorns at their summit, and bees in the middle;
And the sheep bowed down with their fleeces,"

and many other blessings of a like kind are provided for them. And Homer has a very similar strain; for he speaks of one whose fame is –

"As the fame of some blameless king who, like a god,
Maintains justice to whom the black earth brings forth
Wheat and barley, whose trees are bowed with fruit,
And his sheep never fail to bear, and the sea gives him fish."

'Still grander are the gifts of heaven which Musaeus and his son vouchsafe to the just; they take them down into the world below, where they have the saints lying on couches at a feast, everlastingly drunk, crowned with garlands; their idea seems to be that an immortality of drunkenness is the highest meed of virtue. Some extend their rewards yet further; the posterity, as they say, of the faithful and just shall survive to the third and fourth generation. This is the style in which they praise justice. But about the wicked there is another strain; they bury them in a slough in Hades, and make them carry water in a sieve; also while they are yet living they bring them to infamy, and inflict upon them the punishments which Glaucon described as the portion of the just who are reputed to be unjust; nothing else does their invention supply. Such is their manner of praising the one and censuring the other.

'Once more, Socrates, I will ask you to consider another way of speaking about justice and injustice, which is not confined to the poets, but is found in prose writers. The universal voice of mankind is always declaring that justice and virtue are honourable, but grievous and toilsome; and that the pleasures of vice and injustice are easy of attainment, and are only censured by law and opinion. They say also that honesty is for the most part less profitable than dishonesty; and they are quite ready to call wicked men happy, and to honour them both in public and private when they are rich or in any other way influential, while they despise and overlook those who may be weak and poor, even though acknowledging them to be better than the others. But most extraordinary of all is their mode of speaking about virtue and the gods: they say that the gods apportion calamity and misery to many good men, and good and happiness to the wicked. And mendicant prophets go to rich men's doors and persuade them that they have a power committed to them by the gods of making an atonement for a man's own or his ancestor's sins by sacrifices or charms, with rejoicings and feasts; and they promise to harm an enemy, whether just or unjust, at a small cost; with magic arts and incantations binding heaven, as they say, to execute their will. And the poets are the authorities to whom they appeal, now smoothing the path of vice with the words of Hesiod: –

> "Vice may be had in abundance without trouble; the way is smooth and her dwelling-place is near. But before virtue the gods have set toil,"

and a tedious and uphill road; then citing Homer as a witness that the gods may be influenced by men, for he also says:–

> "The gods, too, may be turned from their purpose; and men pray to them and avert their wrath by sacrifices and soothing entreaties, and by libations and the odour of fat, when they have sinned and transgressed."

And they produce a host of books written by Musaeus and Orpheus, who were children of the Moon and the Muses – that is what they say – according to which they perform their ritual, and persuade not only individuals, but whole cities, that expiations and atonements for sin may be made by sacrifices and amusements which fill a vacant hour, and are equally at the service of the living and the dead; the latter sort they call mysteries, and they redeem us from the pains of hell, but if we neglect them no one knows what awaits us.'

He proceeded: 'And now when the young hear all this said about virtue and vice, and the way in which gods and men regard them, how are their minds likely to be affected, my dear Socrates – those of them, I mean, who are quickwitted, and, like bees on the wing, light on every flower, and from all that they hear are prone to draw conclusions as to what manner of persons they should be and in what way they should walk if they would make the best of life? Probably the youth will say to himself in the words of Pindar –

> "Can I by justice or by crooked ways of deceit ascend a loftier tower which may be a fortress to me all my days?"

For what men say is that, if I am really just and am not also thought just profit there is none, but the pain and loss on the other hand are unmistakable. But if, though unjust, I acquire the reputation of justice, a heavenly life is promised to me. Since then, as philosophers prove, appearance tyrannises over truth and is lord of happiness, to appearance I must devote myself. I will describe around me a picture and shadow of virtue to be the vestibule and exterior of my house;

behind I will trail the subtle and crafty fox, as Archilochus, greatest of sages, recommends. But I hear someone exclaiming that the concealment of wickedness is often difficult; to which I answer, Nothing great is easy. Nevertheless, the argument indicates this, if we would be happy, to be the path along which we should proceed. With a view to concealment we will establish secret brotherhoods and political clubs. And there are professors of rhetoric who teach the art of persuading courts and assemblies; and so, partly by persuasion and partly by force, I shall make unlawful gains and not be punished. Still I hear a voice saying that the gods cannot be deceived, neither can they be compelled. But what if there are no gods? or, suppose them to have no care of human things – why in either case should we mind about concealment? And even if there are gods, and they do care about us, yet we know of them only from tradition and the genealogies of the poets; and these are the very persons who say that they may be influenced and turned by "sacrifices and soothing entreaties and by offerings." Let us be consistent then, and believe both or neither. If the poets speak truly, why then we had better be unjust, and offer of the fruits of injustice; for if we are just, although we may escape the vengeance of heaven, we shall lose the gains of injustice; but, if we are unjust, we shall keep the gains, and by our sinning and praying, and praying and sinning, the gods will be propitiated, and we shall not be punished. "But there is a world below in which either we or our posterity will suffer for our unjust deeds." Yes, my friend, will be the reflection, but there are mysteries and atoning deities, and these have great power. That is what mighty cities declare; and the children of the gods, who were their poets and prophets, bear a like testimony.

'On what principle, then, shall we any longer choose justice rather than the worst injustice? when, if we only unite the latter with a deceitful regard to appearances, we shall fare to our mind both with gods and men, in life and after death, as the most numerous and the highest authorities tell us. Knowing all this, Socrates, how can a man who has any superiority of mind or person or rank or wealth, be willing to honour justice; or indeed to refrain from laughing when he hears justice praised? And even if there should be someone who is able to disprove the truth of my words, and who is satisfied that justice is best, still he is not angry with the unjust, but is very ready to forgive them, because he also knows that men are not just of their own free will; unless, peradventure, there be someone whom the divinity within him may have inspired with a hatred of injustice, or who has attained knowledge of the truth – but no other man. He only blames injustice who, owing to cowardice or age or some weakness, has not the power of being unjust. And this is proved by the fact that when he obtains the power, he immediately becomes unjust as far as he can be.

'The cause of all this, Socrates, was indicated by us at the beginning of the argument, when my brother and I told you how astonished we were to find that of all the professing panegyrists of justice – beginning with the ancient heroes of whom any memorial has been preserved to us, and ending with the men of our own time – no one has ever blamed injustice or praised justice except with a view to the glories, honours, and benefits which flow from them. No one has ever adequately described either in verse or prose the true essential nature of either of them abiding in the soul, and invisible to any human or divine eye; or shown that of all the things of a man's soul which he has within him, justice is the greatest good, and injustice the greatest evil. Had this been the universal strain, had you sought to persuade us of this from our youth upwards, we should not have been on the watch to keep one another from doing wrong, but everyone would have been his own watchman, because afraid, if he did wrong, of harbouring in himself the greatest of evils. I dare say that Thrasymachus and others would seriously hold the language which I have been merely repeating, and words even stronger than these about justice and injustice, grossly, as I conceive, perverting their true nature. But I speak in this vehement manner, as I must frankly confess to you, because I want to hear from you the opposite side; and I would ask you to show not only the superiority which justice has over injustice, but what effect they have on the possessor of them which makes the one to be a good and the other an evil to him. And please, as Glaucon requested of you, to exclude reputations; for unless you take away from each of them his true reputation and add on the false, we shall say that you do not praise justice, but the appearance of it; we shall think that you are only exhorting us to keep injustice dark, and that you really agree with Thrasymachus in thinking that justice is another's good and the interest of the stronger, and that injustice is a man's own profit and interest, though injurious to the weaker. Now as you have admitted that justice is one of that highest class of goods which are desired indeed for their results, but in a far greater degree for their own sakes – like sight or hearing or knowledge or health, or any other real and natural and not merely conventional good – I would ask you in your praise of justice to regard one point only: I mean the essential good and evil which justice and injustice work in the possessors of them. Let others praise justice and censure injustice, magnifying the rewards and honours of the one and abusing the other; that is a manner of arguing which, coming from them, I am ready to tolerate, but from you who have spent your whole life in the consideration of this question, unless I hear the contrary from your own lips, I expect something better. And therefore, I say, not only prove to us that justice is better than injustice, but show what they either of them do to the possessor of them, which makes the one to be a good and the other an evil, whether seen or unseen by gods and men.'

I had always admired the genius of Glaucon and Adeimantus, but on hearing these words I was quite delighted, and said: 'Sons of an illustrious father, that was not a bad beginning of the Elegiac verses which the admirer of Glaucon made in honour of you after you had distinguished yourselves at the battle of Megara: –

"Sons of Ariston," he sang, "divine offspring of an illustrious hero."

The epithet is very appropriate, for there is something truly divine in being able to argue as you have done for the superiority of injustice, and remaining unconvinced by your own arguments. And I do believe that you are not convinced – this I infer from your general character, for had I judged only from your speeches I should have mistrusted you. But now, the greater my confidence in you, the greater is my difficulty in knowing what to say. For I am in a strait between two; on the one hand I feel that I am unequal to the task; and my inability is brought home to me by the fact that you were not satisfied with the answer which I made to Thrasymachus, proving, as I thought, the superiority which justice has over injustice. And yet I cannot refuse to help, while breath and speech remain to me; I am afraid that there would be an impiety in being present when justice is evil spoken of and not lifting up a hand in her defence. And therefore I had best give such help as I can.'

Glaucon and the rest entreated me by all means not to let the question drop, but to proceed in the investigation. They wanted to arrive at the truth, first, about the nature of justice and injustice, and secondly, about their relative advantages. I told them, what I really thought, that the enquiry would be of a serious nature, and would require very good eyes. 'Seeing, then,' I said, 'that we are no great wits, I think that we had better adopt a method which I may illustrate thus; suppose that a short-sighted person had been asked by someone to read small letters from a distance; and it occurred to someone else that they might be found in another place which was larger and in which the letters were larger – if they were the same and he could read the larger letters first, and then proceed to the lesser – this would have been thought a rare piece of good fortune.'

'Very true,' said Adeimantus; 'but how does the illustration apply to our enquiry?'

'I will tell you,' I replied. 'Justice, which is the subject of our enquiry, is, as you know, sometimes spoken of as the virtue of an individual, and sometimes as the virtue of a State.'

'True,' he replied.

'And is not a State larger than an individual?'

'It is.'

'Then in the larger, the quantity of justice is likely to be larger and more easily discernible. I propose therefore that we enquire into the nature of justice and injustice, first as they appear in the State, and secondly in the individual, proceeding from the greater to the lesser and comparing them.'

'That', he said, 'is an excellent proposal.'

'And if we imagine the State in process of creation, we shall see the justice and injustice of the State in process of creation also.'

'I dare say.'

'When the State is completed there may be a hope that the object of our search will be more easily discovered.'

'Yes, far more easily.'

'But ought we to attempt to construct one?' I said. 'For to do so, as I am inclined to think, will be a very serious task. Reflect therefore.'

'I have reflected,' said Adeimantus, 'and am anxious that you should proceed.'

'A State', I said, 'arises, as I conceive, out of the needs of mankind; no one is self-sufficing, but all of us have many wants. Can any other origin of a State be imagined?'

'There can be no other.'

'Then, as we have many wants, and many persons are needed to supply them, one takes a helper for one purpose and another for another; and when these partners and helpers are gathered together in one habitation the body of inhabitants is termed a State.'

'True,' he said.

'And they exchange with one another, and one gives, and another receives, under the idea that the exchange will be for their good.'

'Very true.'

'Then,' I said, 'let us begin and create in idea a State; and yet the true creator is necessity, who is the mother of our invention.'

'Of course,' he replied.

'Now the first and greatest of necessities is food, which is the condition of life and existence.'

'Certainly.'

'The second is a dwelling, and the third clothing and the like.'

'True.'

'And now let us see how our city will be able to supply this great demand: We may suppose that one man is a husbandman, another a builder, someone else a weaver – shall we add to them a shoemaker, or perhaps some other purveyor to our bodily wants?'

'Quite right.'

'The barest notion of a State must include four or five men.'

'Clearly.'

'And how will they proceed? Will each bring the result of his labours into a common stock? – The individual husbandman, for example, producing for four, and labouring four times as long and as much as he need in the provision of food with which he supplies others as well as himself; or will he have nothing to do with others and not be at the trouble of producing for them, but provide for himself alone a fourth of the food in a fourth of the time, and in the remaining three-fourths of his time be employed in making a house or a coat or a pair of shoes, having no partnership with others, but supplying himself all his own wants?'

Adeimantus thought that he should aim at producing food only and not at producing everything.

'Probably,' I replied, 'that would be the better way; and when I hear you say this, I am myself reminded that we are not all alike; there are diversities of natures among us which are adapted to different occupations.'

'Very true.'

'And will you have a work better done when the workman has many occupations, or when he has only one?'

'When he has only one.'

'Further, there can be no doubt that a work is spoilt when not done at the right time?'

'No doubt.'

'For business is not disposed to wait until the doer of the business is at leisure; but the doer must follow up what he is doing, and make the business his first object.'

'He must.'

'And if so, we must infer that all things are produced more plentifully and easily and of a better quality when one man does one thing which is natural to him and does it at the right time, and leaves other things.'

'Undoubtedly.'

'Then more than four citizens will be required; for the husbandman will not make his own plough or mattock, or other implements of agriculture, if they are to be good for anything. Neither will the builder make his tools – and he too needs many; and in like manner the weaver and shoemaker.'

'True.'

'Then carpenters, and smiths, and many other artisans, will be sharers in our little State, which is already beginning to grow?'

'True.'

'Yet even if we add neatherds, shepherds, and other herdsmen, in order that our husbandmen may have oxen to plough with, and builders as well as husbandmen may have draught cattle, and curriers and weavers fleeces and hides – still our State will not be very large.'

'That is true; yet neither will it be a very small State which contains all these.'

'Then, again, there is the situation of the city – to find a place where nothing need be imported is well-nigh impossible.'

'Impossible.'

'Then there must be another class of citizens who will bring the required supply from another city?'

'There must.'

'But if the trader goes empty-handed, having nothing which they require who would supply his need, he will come back empty-handed.'

'That is certain.'

'And therefore what they produce at home must be not only enough for themselves, but such both in quantity and quality as to accommodate those from whom their wants are supplied.'

'Very true.'

'Then more husbandmen and more artisans will be required?'

'They will.'

'Not to mention the importers and exporters, who are called merchants?'

'Yes.'

'Then we shall want merchants?'

'We shall.'

'And if merchandise is to be carried over the sea, skilful sailors will also be needed, and in considerable numbers?'

'Yes, in considerable numbers.'

'Then, again, within the city, how will they exchange their productions? To secure such an exchange was, as you will remember, one of our principal objects when we formed them into a society and constituted a State.'

'Clearly they will buy and sell.'

'Then they will need a market-place, and a money-token for purposes of exchange.'

'Certainly.'

'Suppose now that a husbandman, or an artisan, brings some production to market, and he comes at a time when there is no one to exchange with him, – is he to leave his calling and sit idle in the market-place?'

'Not at all; he will find people there who, seeing the want, undertake the office of salesmen. In well-ordered States they are commonly those who are the weakest in bodily strength, and therefore of little use for any other purpose; their duty is to be in the market, and to give money in exchange for goods to those who desire to sell and to take money from those who desire to buy.'

'This want, then, creates a class of retail-traders in our State. Is not "retailer" the term which is applied to those who sit in the market-place engaged in buying and selling, while those who wander from one city to another are called merchants?'

'Yes,' he said.

'And there is another class of servants, who are intellectually hardly on the level of companionship; still they have plenty of bodily strength for labour, which accordingly they sell, and are called, if I do not mistake, hirelings, hire being the name which is given to the price of their labour.'

'True.'

'Then hirelings will help to make up our population?'

'Yes.'

'And now, Adeimantus, is our State matured and perfected?'

'I think so.'

'Where, then, is justice, and where is injustice, and in what part of the State did they spring up?'

'Probably in the dealings of these citizens with one another. I cannot imagine that they are more likely to be found anywhere else.'

'I dare say that you are right in your suggestion,' I said; 'we had better think the matter out, and not shrink from the enquiry.'

'Let us then consider, first of all, what will be their way of life, now that we have thus established them. Will they not produce corn, and wine, and clothes, and shoes, and build houses for themselves? And when they are housed, they will work, in summer, commonly, stripped and barefoot, but in winter substantially clothed and shod. They will feed on barley-meal and flour of wheat, baking and kneading them, making noble cakes and loaves; these they will serve up on a mat of reeds or on clean leaves, themselves reclining the while upon beds strewn with yew or myrtle. And they and their children will feast, drinking of the wine which they have made, wearing garlands on their heads, and hymning the praises of the gods, in happy converse with one another. And they will take care that their families do not exceed their means; having an eye to poverty or war.'

'But,' said Glaucon, 'interposing, you have not given them a relish to their meal.'

'True,' I replied, 'I had forgotten; of course they must have a relish-salt, and olives, and cheese, and they will boil roots and herbs such as country people prepare; for a dessert we shall give them figs, and peas, and beans; and they will roast myrtle-berries and acorns at the fire, drinking in moderation. And with such a diet they may be expected to live in peace and health to a good old age, and bequeath a similar life to their children after them.'

'Yes, Socrates,' he said, 'and if you were providing for a city of pigs, how else would you feed the beasts?'

'But what would you have, Glaucon?' I replied.

'Why,' he said, 'you should give them the ordinary conveniences of life. People who are to be comfortable are accustomed to lie on sofas, and dine off tables, and they should have sauces and sweets in the modern style.'

'Yes,' I said, 'now I understand: the question which you would have me consider is, not only how a State, but how a luxurious State is created; and possibly there is no harm in this, for in such a State we shall be more likely to see how justice and injustice originate. In my opinion the true and healthy constitution of the State is the one which I have described. But if you wish also to see a State at fever heat, I have no objection. For I suspect that many will not be satisfied with the simpler way of life. They will be for adding sofas, and tables, and other furniture; also dainties, and perfumes, and incense, and courtesans, and cakes, all these not of one sort only, but in every variety; we must go beyond the necessaries of which I was at first speaking, such as houses, and clothes, and shoes: the arts of the painter and the embroiderer will have to be set in motion, and gold and ivory and all sorts of materials must be procured.'

'True,' he said.

'Then we must enlarge our borders; for the original healthy State is no longer sufficient. Now will the city have to fill and swell with a multitude of callings which are not required by any natural want; such as the whole tribe of hunters and actors, of whom one large class have to do with forms and colours; another will be the votaries of music – poets and their attendant train of rhapsodists, players, dancers, contractors; also makers of divers kinds of articles, including women's dresses. And we shall want more servants. Will not tutors be also in request, and nurses wet and dry, tirewomen and barbers, as well as confectioners and cooks; and swineherds, too, who were not needed and therefore had no place in the former edition of our State, but are needed now? They must not be forgotten: and there will be animals of many other kinds, if people eat them.'

'Certainly.'

'And living in this way we shall have much greater need of physicians than before?'

'Much greater.'

'And the country which was enough to support the original inhabitants will be too small now, and not enough?'

'Quite true.'

'Then a slice of our neighbours' land will be wanted by us for pasture and tillage, and they will want a slice of ours, if, like ourselves, they exceed the limit of necessity, and give themselves up to the unlimited accumulation of wealth?'

'That, Socrates, will be inevitable.'

'And so we shall go to war, Glaucon. Shall we not?'

'Most certainly,' he replied.

'Then without determining as yet whether war does good or harm, thus much we may affirm, that now we have discovered war to be derived from causes which are also the causes of almost all the evils in States, private as well as public.'

'Undoubtedly.'

'And our State must once more enlarge; and this time the enlargement will be nothing short of a whole army, which will have to go out and fight with the invaders for all that we have, as well as for the things and persons whom we were describing above.'

'Why?' he said; 'Are they not capable of defending themselves?'

'No,' I said; 'not if we were right in the principle which was acknowledged by all of us when we were framing the State: the principle, as you will remember, was that one man cannot practise many arts with success.'

'Very true,' he said.

'But is not war an art?'

'Certainly.'

'And an art requiring as much attention as shoemaking?'

'Quite true.'

'And the shoemaker was not allowed by us to be husbandman, or a weaver, a builder – in order that we might have our shoes well made; but to him and to every other worker was assigned one work for which he was by nature fitted, and at that he was to continue working all his life long and at no other; he was not to let opportunities slip, and then he would become a good workman. Now nothing can be more important than that the work of a soldier should be well done. But is war an art so easily acquired that a man may be a warrior who is also a husbandman, or shoemaker, or other artisan; although no one in the world would be a good dice or draught player who merely took up the game as a recreation, and had not from his earliest years devoted himself to this and nothing else?'

'No tools will make a man a skilled workman, or master of defence, nor be of any use to him who has not learned how to handle them, and has never bestowed any attention upon them. How, then, will he who takes up a shield or other implement of war become a good fighter all in a day, whether with heavy-armed or any other kind of troops?'

'Yes,' he said, 'the tools which would teach men their own use would be beyond price.'

'And the higher the duties of the guardian,' I said, 'the more time, and skill, and art, and application will be needed by him?'

'No doubt,' he replied.

'Will he not also require natural aptitude for his calling?'

'Certainly.'

'Then it will be our duty to select, if we can, natures which are fitted for the task of guarding the city?'

'It will.'

'And the selection will be no easy matter,' I said; 'but we must be brave and do our best.'

'We must.'

'Is not the noble youth very like a well-bred dog in respect of guarding and watching?'

'What do you mean?'

'I mean that both of them ought to be quick to see, and swift to overtake the enemy when they see him; and strong too if, when they have caught him, they have to fight with him.'

'All these qualities, he replied, will certainly be required by them.'

'Well, and your guardian must be brave if he is to fight well?'

'Certainly.'

'And is he likely to be brave who has no spirit, whether horse or dog or any other animal? Have you never observed how invincible and unconquerable is spirit and how the presence of it makes the soul of any creature to be absolutely fearless and indomitable?'

'I have.'

'Then now we have a clear notion of the bodily qualities which are required in the guardian.'

'True.'

'And also of the mental ones; his soul is to be full of spirit?'

'Yes.'

'But are not these spirited natures apt to be savage with one another, and with everybody else?'

'A difficulty by no means easy to overcome,' he replied.

'Whereas,' I said, 'they ought to be dangerous to their enemies, and gentle to their friends; if not, they will destroy themselves without waiting for their enemies to destroy them.'

'True,' he said.

'What is to be done, then?' I said; 'How shall we find a gentle nature which has also a great spirit, for the one is the contradiction of the other?'

'True.'

'He will not be a good guardian who is wanting in either of these two qualities; and yet the combination of them appears to be impossible; and hence we must infer that to be a good guardian is impossible.'

'I am afraid that what you say is true,' he replied.

Here, feeling perplexed, I began to think over what had preceded. 'My friend,' I said, 'no wonder that we are in a perplexity; for we have lost sight of the image which we had before us.'

'What do you mean?' he said.

'I mean to say that there do exist natures gifted with those opposite qualities.'

'And where do you find them?'

'Many animals', I replied, 'furnish examples of them; our friend the dog is a very good one: you know that well-bred dogs are perfectly gentle to their familiars and acquaintances, and the reverse to strangers.'

'Yes, I know.'

'Then there is nothing impossible or out of the order of nature in our finding a guardian who has a similar combination of qualities?'

'Certainly not.'

'Would not he who is fitted to be a guardian, besides the spirited nature, need to have the qualities of a philosopher?'

'I do not apprehend your meaning.'

'The trait of which I am speaking,' I replied, 'may be also seen in the dog, and is remarkable in the animal.'

'What trait?'

'Why, a dog, whenever he sees a stranger, is angry; when an acquaintance, he welcomes him, although the one has never done him any harm, nor the other any good. Did this never strike you as curious?'

'The matter never struck me before; but I quite recognise the truth of your remark.'

'And surely this instinct of the dog is very charming – your dog is a true philosopher.'

'Why?'

'Why, because he distinguishes the face of a friend and of an enemy only by the criterion of knowing and not knowing. And must not an animal be a lover of learning who determines what he likes and dislikes by the test of knowledge and ignorance?'

'Most assuredly.'

'And is not the love of learning the love of wisdom, which is philosophy?'

'They are the same,' he replied.

'And may we not say confidently of man also, that he who is likely to be gentle to his friends and acquaintances, must by nature be a lover of wisdom and knowledge?'

'That we may safely affirm.'

'Then he who is to be a really good and noble guardian of the State will require to unite in himself philosophy and spirit and swiftness and strength?'

'Undoubtedly.'

'Then we have found the desired natures; and now that we have found them, how are they to be reared and educated? Is not this an enquiry which may be expected to throw light on the greater enquiry which is our final end – How do justice and injustice grow up in States? For we do not want either to omit what is to the point or to draw out the argument to an inconvenient length.'

Adeimantus thought that the enquiry would be of great service to us.

'Then,' I said, 'my dear friend, the task must not be given up, even if somewhat long.'

'Certainly not.'

'Come then, and let us pass a leisure hour in story-telling, and our story shall be the education of our heroes.'

'By all means.'

'And what shall be their education? Can we find a better than the traditional sort? – And this has two divisions, gymnastics for the body, and music for the soul.'

'True.'

'Shall we begin education with music, and go on to gymnastics afterwards?'

'By all means.'

'And when you speak of music, do you include literature or not?'

'I do.'

'And literature may be either true or false?'

'Yes.'

'And the young should be trained in both kinds, and we begin with the false?'

'I do not understand your meaning,' he said.

'You know', I said, 'that we begin by telling children stories which, though not wholly destitute of truth, are in the main fictitious; and these stories are told them when they are not of an age to learn gymnastics.'

'Very true.'

'That was my meaning when I said that we must teach music before gymnastics.'

'Quite right,' he said.

'You know also that the beginning is the most important part of any work, especially in the case of a young and tender thing; for that is the time at which the character is being formed and the desired impression is more readily taken.'

'Quite true.'

'And shall we just carelessly allow children to hear any casual tales which may be devised by casual persons, and to receive into their minds ideas for the most part the very opposite of those which we should wish them to have when they are grown up?'

'We cannot.'

'Then the first thing will be to establish a censorship of the writers of fiction, and let the censors receive any tale of fiction which is good, and reject the bad; and we will desire mothers and nurses to tell their children the authorised ones only. Let them fashion the mind with such tales, even more fondly than they mould the body with their hands; but most of those which are now in use must be discarded.'

'Of what tales are you speaking?' he said.

'You may find a model of the lesser in the greater,' I said. 'For they are necessarily of the same type, and there is the same spirit in both of them.'

'Very likely,' he replied; 'but I do not as yet know what you would term the greater.'

'Those', I said, 'which are narrated by Homer and Hesiod, and the rest of the poets, who have ever been the great story-tellers of mankind.'

'But which stories do you mean,' he said; 'and what fault do you find with them?'

'A fault which is most serious,' I said; 'the fault of telling a lie, and, what is more, a bad lie.'

'But when is this fault committed?'

'Whenever an erroneous representation is made of the nature of gods and heroes – as when a painter paints a portrait not having the shadow of a likeness to the original.'

'Yes,' he said, 'that sort of thing is certainly very blamable; but what are the stories which you mean?'

'First of all,' I said, 'there was that greatest of all lies, in high places, which the poet told about Uranus, and which was a bad lie too – I mean what Hesiod says that Uranus did, and how Cronus retaliated to him. The doings of Cronus, and the sufferings which in turn his son inflicted upon him, even if they were true, ought certainly not to be lightly told to young and thoughtless persons; if possible, they had better be buried in silence. But if there is an absolute necessity for their mention, a chosen few might hear them in a mystery, and they should sacrifice not a common [Eleusinian] pig, but some huge and unprocurable victim; and then the number of the hearers will be very few indeed.'

'Why, yes,' said he, 'those stories are extremely objectionable.'

'Yes, Adeimantus, they are stories not to be repeated in our State; the young man should not be told that in committing the worst of crimes he is far from doing anything outrageous; and that even if he chastises his father when does wrong, in whatever manner, he will only be following the example of the first and greatest among the gods.'

'I entirely agree with you,' he said; 'in my opinion those stories are quite unfit to be repeated.'

'Neither, if we mean our future guardians to regard the habit of quarrelling among themselves as of all things the basest, should any word be said to them of the wars in heaven, and of the plots and fightings of the gods against one another, for they are not true. No, we shall never mention the battles of the giants, or let them be embroidered on garments; and we shall be silent about the innumerable other quarrels of gods and heroes with their friends and relatives. If they would only believe us we would tell them that quarrelling is unholy, and that never up to this time has there been any quarrel between citizens; this is what old men and old women should begin by telling children; and when they grow up, the poets also should be told to compose for them in a similar spirit. But the narrative of Hephaestus binding Hera his mother, or how on another occasion Zeus sent him flying for taking her part when she was being beaten, and all the battles of the gods in Homer – these tales must not be admitted into our State, whether they are supposed to have an allegorical meaning or not. For a young person cannot judge what is allegorical and what is literal; anything that he receives into his mind at that age is likely to become indelible and unalterable; and therefore it is most important that the tales which the young first hear should be models of virtuous thoughts.'

'There you are right,' he replied. 'But if anyone asks where are such models to be found and of what tales are you speaking – how shall we answer him?'

I said to him, 'You and I, Adeimantus, at this moment are not poets, but founders of a State: now the founders of a State ought to know the general forms in which poets should cast their tales, and the limits which must be observed by them, but to make the tales is not their business.'

'Very true,' he said; 'but what are these forms of theology which you mean?

'Something of this kind,' I replied: – 'God is always to be represented as he truly is, whatever be the sort of poetry, epic, lyric or tragic, in which the representation is given.'

'Right.'

'And is he not truly good? And must he not be represented as such?'

'Certainly.'

'And no good thing is hurtful?'

'No, indeed.'

'And that which is not hurtful hurts not?'

'Certainly not.'

'And that which hurts not does no evil?'

'No.'

'And can that which does no evil be a cause of evil?'

'Impossible.'

'And the good is advantageous?'

'Yes.'

'And therefore the cause of wellbeing?'

'Yes.'

'It follows therefore that the good is not the cause of all things, but of the good only?'

'Assuredly.'

'Then God, if he be good, is not the author of all things, as many assert, but he is the cause of a few things only, and not of most things that occur to men. For few are the goods of human life, and many are the evils, and the good is to be attributed to God alone; of the evils the causes are to be sought elsewhere, and not in him.'

'That appears to me to be most true,' he said.

'Then we must not listen to Homer or to any other poet who is guilty of the folly of saying that two casks

> "lie at the threshold of Zeus, full of lots, one of good, the other of evil lots,"

and that he to whom Zeus gives a mixture of the two

> "sometimes meets with evil fortune, at other times with good;"

but that he to whom is given the cup of unmingled ill,

> "him wild hunger drives o'er the beauteous earth".

And again –

"Zeus, who is the dispenser of good and evil to us".

And if anyone asserts that the violation of oaths and treaties, which was really the work of Pandarus, was brought about by Athene and Zeus, or that the strife and contention of the gods was instigated by Themis and Zeus, he shall not have our approval; neither will we allow our young men to hear the words of Aeschylus, that

"God plants guilt among men when he desires utterly to destroy a house."

'And if a poet writes of the sufferings of Niobe – the subject of the tragedy in which these iambic verses occur – or of the house of Pelops, or of the Trojan war or on any similar theme, either we must not permit him to say that these are the works of God, or if they are of God, he must devise some explanation of them such as we are seeking; he must say that God did what was just and right, and they were the better for being punished; but that those who are punished are miserable, and that God is the author of their misery – the poet is not to be permitted to say; though he may say that the wicked are miserable because they require to be punished, and are benefited by receiving punishment from God; but that God being good is the author of evil to anyone is to be strenuously denied, and not to be said or sung or heard in verse or prose by anyone whether old or young in any well-ordered commonwealth. Such a fiction is suicidal, ruinous, impious.'

'I agree with you,' he replied, 'and am ready to give my assent to the law.'

'Let this then be one of our rules and principles concerning the gods, to which our poets and reciters will be expected to conform – that God is not the author of all things, but of good only.'

'That will do,' he said.

'And what do you think of a second principle? Shall I ask you whether God is a magician, and of a nature to appear insidiously now in one shape, and now in another – sometimes himself changing and passing into many forms, sometimes deceiving us with the semblance of such transformations; or is he one and the same immutably fixed in his own proper image?'

'I cannot answer you,' he said, 'without more thought.'

'Well,' I said; 'but if we suppose a change in anything, that change must be effected either by the thing itself, or by some other thing?'

'Most certainly.'

'And things which are at their best are also least liable to be altered or discomposed; for example, when healthiest and strongest, the human frame is least liable to be affected by meats and drinks, and the plant which is in the fullest vigour also suffers least from winds or the heat of the sun or any similar causes.'

'Of course.'

'And will not the bravest and wisest soul be least confused or deranged by any external influence?'

'True.'

'And the same principle, as I should suppose, applies to all composite things – furniture, houses, garments; when good and well made, they are least altered by time and circumstances.'

'Very true.'

'Then everything which is good, whether made by art or nature, or both, is least liable to suffer change from without?'

'True.'

'But surely God and the things of God are in every way perfect?'

'Of course they are.'

'Then he can hardly be compelled by external influence to take many shapes?'

'He cannot.'

'But may he not change and transform himself?'

'Clearly,' he said, 'that must be the case if he is changed at all.'

'And will he then change himself for the better and fairer, or for the worse and more unsightly?'

'If he change at all he can only change for the worse, for we cannot suppose him to be deficient either in virtue or beauty.'

'Very true, Adeimantus; but then, would anyone, whether God or man, desire to make himself worse?'

'Impossible.'

'Then it is impossible that God should ever be willing to change; being, as is supposed, the fairest and best that is conceivable, every god remains absolutely and for ever in his own form.'

'That necessarily follows,' he said, 'in my judgment.'

'Then,' I said, 'my dear friend, let none of the poets tell us that

> "The gods, taking the disguise of strangers from other lands, walk up and down cities in all sorts of forms;"

and let no one slander Proteus and Thetis, neither let anyone, either in tragedy or in any other kind of poetry, introduce Hera disguised in the likeness of a priestess asking an alms

> "For the life-giving daughters of Inachus the river of Argos;"

– let us have no more lies of that sort. Neither must we have mothers under the influence of the poets scaring their children with a bad version of these myths – telling how certain gods, as they say, "go about by night in the likeness of so many strangers and in divers forms"; but let them take heed lest they make cowards of their children, and at the same time speak blasphemy against the gods.'

'Heaven forbid,' he said.

'But although the gods are themselves unchangeable, still by witchcraft and deception they may make us think that they appear in various forms?'

'Perhaps,' he replied.

'Well, but can you imagine that God will be willing to lie, whether in word or deed, or to put forth a phantom of himself?'

'I cannot say,' he replied.

'Do you not know', I said, 'that the true lie, if such an expression may be allowed, is hated of gods and men?'

'What do you mean?' he said.

'I mean that no one is willingly deceived in that which is the truest and highest part of himself, or about the truest and highest matters; there, above all, he is most afraid of a lie having possession of him.'

'Still,' he said, 'I do not comprehend you.'

'The reason is', I replied, 'that you attribute some profound meaning to my words; but I am only saying that deception, or being deceived or uninformed about the highest realities in the highest part of themselves, which is the soul, and in that part of them to have and to hold the lie, is what mankind least like; – that, I say, is what they utterly detest.'

'There is nothing more hateful to them.'

'And, as I was just now remarking, this ignorance in the soul of him who is deceived may be called the true lie; for the lie in words is only a kind of imitation and shadowy image of a previous affection of the soul, not pure unadulterated falsehood. Am I not right?'

'Perfectly right.'

'The true lie is hated not only by the gods, but also by men?'

'Yes.'

'Whereas the lie in words is in certain cases useful and not hateful; in dealing with enemies – that would be an instance; or again, when those whom we call our friends in a fit of madness or illusion are going to do some harm, then it is useful and is a sort of medicine or preventive; also in the tales of mythology, of which we were just now speaking – because we do not know the truth about ancient times, we make falsehood as much like truth as we can, and so turn it to account.'

'Very true,' he said.

'But can any of these reasons apply to God? Can we suppose that he is ignorant of antiquity, and therefore has recourse to invention?'

'That would be ridiculous,' he said.

'Then the lying poet has no place in our idea of God?'

'I should say not.'

'Or perhaps he may tell a lie because he is afraid of enemies?'

'That is inconceivable.'

'But he may have friends who are senseless or mad?'

'But no mad or senseless person can be a friend of God.'

'Then no motive can be imagined why God should lie?'

'None whatever.'

'Then the superhuman and divine is absolutely incapable of falsehood?'

'Yes.'

'Then is God perfectly simple and true both in word and deed; he changes not; he deceives not, either by sign or word, by dream or waking vision.'

'Your thoughts', he said, 'are the reflection of my own.'

'You agree with me then,' I said, 'that this is the second type or form in which we should write and speak about divine things. The gods are not magicians who transform themselves, neither do they deceive mankind in any way.'

'I grant that.'

'Then, although we are admirers of Homer, we do not admire the lying dream which Zeus sends to Agamemnon; neither will we praise the verses of Aeschylus in which Thetis says that Apollo at her nuptials

> "Was celebrating in song her fair progeny whose days were to he long, and to know no sickness. And when he had spoken of my lot as in all things blessed of heaven he raised a note of triumph and cheered my soul. And I thought that the word of Phoebus being divine and full of prophecy, would not fail. And now he himself who uttered the strain, he who was present at the banquet, and who said this – he it is who has slain my son."

These are the kind of sentiments about the gods which will arouse our anger; and he who utters them shall be refused a chorus; neither shall we allow teachers to make use of them in the instruction of the young, meaning, as we do, that our guardians, as far as men can be, should be true worshippers of the gods and like them.'

'I entirely agree,' he said, 'in these principles, and promise to make them my laws.'

Book III

'Such then', I said, 'are our principles of theology – some tales are to be told, and others are not to be told to our disciples from their youth upwards, if we mean them to honour the gods and their parents, and to value friendship with one another.'

'Yes; and I think that our principles are right,' he said.

'But if they are to be courageous, must they not learn other lessons besides these, and lessons of such a kind as will take away the fear of death? Can any man be courageous who has the fear of death in him?'

'Certainly not,' he said.

'And can he be fearless of death, or will he choose death in battle rather than defeat and slavery, who believes the world below to be real and terrible?'

'Impossible.'

'Then we must assume a control over the narrators of this class of tales as well as over the others, and beg them not simply to revile, but rather to commend the world below, intimating to them that their descriptions are untrue, and will do harm to our future warriors.'

'That will be our duty,' he said.

'Then,' I said, 'we shall have to obliterate many obnoxious passages, beginning with the verses

> "I would rather be a serf on the land of a poor and portionless man than rule over all the dead who have come to nought."

We must also expunge the verse which tells us how Pluto feared

> "Lest the mansions grim and squalid which the gods abhor should be seen both of mortals and immortals".

And again:

> "O heavens! Verily in the house of Hades there is soul and ghostly form but no mind at all!"

Again of Tiresias:

> "[To him even after death did Persephone grant mind,] that he alone should be wise; but the other souls are flitting shades."

Again:

> "The soul flying from the limbs had gone to Hades, lamenting her fate, leaving manhood and youth."

Again:

> "And the soul, with shrilling cry, passed like smoke beneath the earth."

And,

> "As bats in hollow of mystic cavern, whenever any of them has dropped out of the string and falls from the rock, fly shrilling and cling to one another, so did they with shrilling cry hold together as they moved."

And we must beg Homer and the other poets not to be angry if we strike out these and similar passages, not because they are unpoetical, or unattractive to the popular ear, but because the greater the poetical charm of them, the less are they meet for the ears of boys and men who are meant to be free, and who should fear slavery more than death.'

'Undoubtedly.'

'Also we shall have to reject all the terrible and appalling names which describe the world below – Cocytus and Styx, ghosts under the earth, and sapless shades, and any similar words of which the very mention causes a shudder to pass through the inmost soul of him who hears them. I do not say that these horrible stories may not have a use of some kind; but there is a danger that the nerves of our guardians may be rendered too excitable and effeminate by them.'

'There is a real danger,' he said.

'Then we must have no more of them.'

'True.

'Another and a nobler strain must be composed and sung by us.'

'Clearly.'

'And shall we proceed to get rid of the weepings and wailings of famous men?'

'They will go with the rest.'

'But shall we be right in getting rid of them? Reflect: our principle is that the good man will not consider death terrible to any other good man who is his comrade.'

'Yes; that is our principle.'

'And therefore he will not sorrow for his departed friend as though he had suffered anything terrible?'

'He will not.'

'Such a one, as we further maintain, is sufficient for himself and his own happiness, and therefore is least in need of other men.'

'True,' he said.

'And for this reason the loss of a son or brother, or the deprivation of fortune, is to him of all men least terrible.'

'Assuredly.'

'And therefore he will be least likely to lament, and will bear with the greatest equanimity any misfortune of this sort which may befall him.'

'Yes, he will feel such a misfortune far less than another.'

'Then we shall be right in getting rid of the lamentations of famous men, and making them over to women (and not even to women who are good for anything), or to men of a baser sort, that those who are being educated by us to be the defenders of their country may scorn to do the like.'

'That will be very right.'

'Then we will once more entreat Homer and the other poets not to depict Achilles, who is the son of a goddess, first lying on his side, then on his back, and then on his face; then starting up and sailing in a frenzy along the shores of the barren sea; now taking the sooty ashes in both his hands and pouring them over his head, or weeping and wailing in the various modes which Homer has delineated. Nor should he describe Priam the kinsman of the gods as praying and beseeching,

> "Rolling in the dirt, calling each man loudly by his name".

Still more earnestly will we beg of him at all events not to introduce the gods lamenting and saying,

> "Alas! My misery! Alas! That I bore the harvest to my sorrow."

But if he must introduce the gods, at any rate let him not dare so completely to misrepresent the greatest of the gods as to make him say –

> "O heavens! With my eyes verily I behold a dear friend of mine chased round and round the city, and my heart is sorrowful."

Or again: –

> "Woe is me that I am fated to have Sarpedon, dearest of men to me, subdued at the hands of Patroclus the son of Menoetius."

For if, my sweet Adeimantus, our youth seriously listen to such unworthy representations of the gods, instead of laughing at them as they ought, hardly will any of them deem that he himself, being but a man, can be dishonoured by similar actions; neither will he rebuke any inclination which may arise in his mind to say and do the like. And instead of having any shame or self-control, he will be always whining and lamenting on slight occasions.'

'Yes,' he said, 'that is most true.'

'Yes,' I replied. 'But that surely is what ought not to be, as the argument has just proved to us; and by that proof we must abide until it is disproved by a better.'

'It ought not to be.'

'Neither ought our guardians to be given to laughter. For a fit of laughter which has been indulged to excess almost always produces a violent reaction.'

'So I believe.'

'Then persons of worth, even if only mortal men, must not be represented as overcome by laughter, and still less must such a representation of the gods be allowed.'

'Still less of the gods, as you say,' he replied.

'Then we shall not suffer such an expression to be used about the gods as that of Homer when he describes how

> "Inextinguishable laughter arose among the blessed gods, when they saw
> Hephaestus bustling about the mansion."

On your views, we must not admit them.'

'On my views, if you like to father them on me; that we must not admit them is certain.'

'Again, truth should be highly valued; if, as we were saying, a lie is useless to the gods, and useful only as a medicine to men, then the use of such medicines should be restricted to physicians; private individuals have no business with them.'

'Clearly not,' he said.

'Then if anyone at all is to have the privilege of lying, the rulers of the State should be the persons; and they, in their dealings either with enemies or with their own citizens, may be allowed to lie for the public good. But nobody else should meddle with anything of the kind; and although the rulers have this privilege, for a private man to lie to them in return is to be deemed a more heinous fault than for the patient or the pupil of a gymnasium not to speak the truth about his own bodily illnesses to the physician or to the trainer, or for a sailor not to tell the captain what is happening about the ship and the rest of the crew, and how things are going with himself or his fellow sailors.'

'Most true,' he said.

'If, then, the ruler catches anybody beside himself lying in the State,

> "Any of the craftsmen, whether he be priest or physician or carpenter,"

he will punish him for introducing a practice which is equally subversive and destructive of ship or State.'

'Most certainly,' he said, 'if our idea of the State is ever carried out.'

'In the next place our youth must be temperate?'

'Certainly.'

'Are not the chief elements of temperance, speaking generally, obedience to commanders and self-control in sensual pleasures?'

'True.'

'Then we shall approve such language as that of Diomede in Homer,

> "Friend, sit still and obey my word,"

and the verses which follow,

> "The Greeks marched breathing prowess
> ...in silent awe of their leaders,"

and other sentiments of the same kind.'

'We shall.'

'What of this line,

> "O heavy with wine, who hast the eyes of a dog and the heart of a stag,"

and of the words which follow? Would you say that these, or any similar impertinences which private individuals are supposed to address to their rulers, whether in verse or prose, are well or ill spoken?'

'They are ill spoken.'

'They may very possibly afford some amusement, but they do not conduce to temperance. And therefore they are likely to do harm to our young men – you would agree with me there?'

'Yes.'

'And then, again, to make the wisest of men say that nothing in his opinion is more glorious than

> "When the tables are full of bread and meat, and the cup-bearer carries round wine which he draws from the bowl and pours into the cups,"

is it fit or conducive to temperance for a young man to hear such words? Or the verse

> "The saddest of fates is to die and meet destiny from hunger"?

What would you say again to the tale of Zeus, who, while other gods and men were asleep and he the only person awake, lay devising plans, but forgot them all in a moment through his lust, and was so completely overcome at the sight of Hera that he would not even go into the hut, but wanted to lie with her on the ground, declaring that he had never been in such a state of rapture before, even when they first met one another

"without the knowledge of their parents";

or that other tale of how Hephaestus, because of similar goings-on, cast a chain around Ares and Aphrodite?'

'Indeed,' he said, 'I am strongly of opinion that they ought not to hear that sort of thing.'

'But any deeds of endurance which are done or told by famous men, these they ought to see and hear; as, for example, what is said in the verses,

"He smote his breast, and thus reproached his heart,
Endure, my heart; far worse hast thou endured!"

'Certainly,' he said.

'In the next place, we must not let them be receivers of gifts or lovers of money.'

'Certainly not.'

'Neither must we sing to them of

"Gifts persuading gods, and persuading reverend kings."

Neither is Phoenix, the tutor of Achilles, to be approved or deemed to have given his pupil good counsel when he told him that he should take the gifts of the Greeks and assist them; but that without a gift he should not lay aside his anger. Neither will we believe or acknowledge Achilles himself to have been such a lover of money that he took Agamemnon's or that when he had received payment he restored the dead body of Hector, but that without payment he was unwilling to do so.'

'Undoubtedly,' he said, 'these are not sentiments which can be approved.'

'Loving Homer as I do, I hardly like to say that in attributing these feelings to Achilles, or in believing that they are truly to him, he is guilty of downright impiety. As little can I believe the narrative of his insolence to Apollo, where he says,

"Thou hast wronged me, O far-darter, most abominable of deities. Verily
I would be even with thee, if I had only the power,"

or his insubordination to the river-god, on whose divinity he is ready to lay hands; or his offering to the dead Patroclus of his own hair, which had been previously dedicated to the other river-god Spercheius, and that he actually performed this vow; or that he dragged Hector round the tomb of Patroclus, and slaughtered the captives at the pyre; of all this I cannot believe that he was guilty, any more than I can allow our citizens to believe that he, the wise Cheiron's pupil, the son of a goddess and of Peleus who was the gentlest of men and third in descent from Zeus, was so disordered in his wits as to be at one time the slave of two seemingly inconsistent passions, meanness, not untainted by avarice, combined with overweening contempt of gods and men.'

'You are quite right,' he replied.

'And let us equally refuse to believe, or allow to be repeated, the tale of Theseus son of Poseidon, or of Peirithous son of Zeus, going forth as they did to perpetrate a horrid rape; or of any other hero or son of a god daring to do such impious and dreadful things as they falsely ascribe to them in our day: and let us further compel the poets to declare either that these acts were not done by them, or that they were not the sons of gods; – both in the same breath they shall not be permitted to affirm. We will not have them trying to persuade our youth that the gods are the authors of evil, and that heroes are no better than men – sentiments which, as we were saying, are neither pious nor true, for we have already proved that evil cannot come from the gods.'

'Assuredly not.'

'And further they are likely to have a bad effect on those who hear them; for everybody will begin to excuse his own vices when he is convinced that similar wickednesses are always being perpetrated by

> "The kindred of the gods, the relatives of Zeus, whose ancestral altar, the altar of Zeus, is aloft in air on the peak of Ida, and who have the blood of deities yet flowing in their veins."

And therefore let us put an end to such tales, lest they engender laxity of morals among the young.'

'By all means,' he replied.

'But now that we are determining what classes of subjects are or are not to be spoken of, let us see whether any have been omitted by us. The manner in which gods and demigods and heroes and the world below should be treated has been already laid down.'

'Very true.'

'And what shall we say about men? That is clearly the remaining portion of our subject.'

'Clearly so.'

'But we are not in a condition to answer this question at present, my friend.'

'Why not?'

'Because, if I am not mistaken, we shall have to say that about men poets and story-tellers are guilty of making the gravest misstatements when they tell us that wicked men are often happy, and the good miserable; and that injustice is profitable when undetected, but that justice is a man's own loss and another's gain – these things we shall forbid them to utter, and command them to sing and say the opposite.'

'To be sure we shall,' he replied.

'But if you admit that I am right in this, then I shall maintain that you have implied the principle for which we have been all along contending.'

'I grant the truth of your inference.'

'That such things are or are not to be said about men is a question which we cannot determine until we have discovered what justice is, and how naturally advantageous to the possessor, whether he seems to be just or not.'

'Most true,' he said.

'Enough of the subjects of poetry: let us now speak of the style; and when this has been considered, both matter and manner will have been completely treated.'

'I do not understand what you mean,' said Adeimantus.

'Then I must make you understand; and perhaps I may be more intelligible if I put the matter in this way. You are aware, I suppose, that all mythology and poetry is a narration of events, either past, present, or to come?'

'Certainly,' he replied.

'And narration may be either simple narration, or imitation, or a union of the two?'

'That again', he said, 'I do not quite understand.'

'I fear that I must be a ridiculous teacher when I have so much difficulty in making myself apprehended. Like a bad speaker, therefore, I will not take the whole of the subject, but will break a piece off in illustration of my meaning. You know the first lines of the *Iliad*, in which the poet says that Chryses prayed Agamemnon to release his daughter, and that Agamemnon flew into a passion with him; whereupon Chryses, failing of his object, invoked the anger of the God against the Achaeans. Now as far as these lines,

> "And he prayed all the Greeks, but especially the two sons of Atreus, the chiefs of the people,"

the poet is speaking in his own person; he never leads us to suppose that he is anyone else. But in what follows he takes the person of Chryses, and then he does all that he can to make us believe that the speaker is not Homer but the aged priest himself. And in this double form he has cast the entire narrative of the events which occurred at Troy and in Ithaca and throughout the *Odyssey*.'

'Yes.'

'And a narrative it remains both in the speeches which the poet recites from time to time and in the intermediate passages?'

'Quite true.'

'But when the poet speaks in the person of another, may we not say that he assimilates his style to that of the person who, as he informs you, is going to speak?'

'Certainly.'

'And this assimilation of himself to another, either by the use of voice or gesture, is the imitation of the person whose character he assumes?'

'Of course.'

'Then in this case the narrative of the poet may be said to proceed by way of imitation?'

'Very true.'

'Or, if the poet everywhere appears and never conceals himself, then again the imitation is dropped, and his poetry becomes simple narration. However, in order that I may make my meaning quite clear, and that you may no more say, "I don't understand," I will show how the change might be effected. If Homer had said, "The priest came, having his daughter's ransom in his hands, supplicating the Achaeans, and above all the kings;" and then if, instead of speaking in the person of Chryses, he had continued in his own person, the words would have been not imitation but simple narration. The passage would have run as follows (I am no poet, and therefore I drop the metre), "The priest came and prayed the gods on behalf of the Greeks that they might capture Troy and return safely home, but begged that they would give him back his daughter, and take the ransom which he brought, and respect the god. Thus he spoke, and the other Greeks revered the priest and assented. But Agamemnon was wroth, and bade him depart and not come again, lest the staff and chaplets of the god should be of no avail to him – the daughter of Chryses should not be released, he said – she should grow old with him in Argos. And then he told him to go away and not to provoke him, if he intended to get home unscathed. And the old man went away in fear and silence, and, when he had left the camp, he called upon Apollo by his many names, reminding him of everything which he had done pleasing to him, whether in building his temples, or in offering sacrifice, and praying that his good deeds might be returned to him, and that the Achaeans might expiate his tears by the arrows of the god," – and so on. In this way the whole becomes simple narrative.'

'I understand,' he said.

'Or you may suppose the opposite case – that the intermediate passages are omitted, and the dialogue only left.'

'That also', he said, 'I understand; you mean, for example, as in tragedy.'

'You have conceived my meaning perfectly; and if I mistake not, what you failed to apprehend before is now made clear to you, that poetry and mythology are, in some cases, wholly imitative – instances of this are supplied by tragedy and comedy; there is likewise the opposite style, in which the poet is the only speaker – of this the dithyramb affords the best example; and the combination of both is found in epic, and in several other styles of poetry. Do I take you with me?'

'Yes,' he said; 'I see now what you meant.'

'I will ask you to remember also what I began by saying, that we had done with the subject and might proceed to the style.'

'Yes, I remember.'

'In saying this, I intended to imply that we must come to an understanding about the mimetic art – whether the poets, in narrating their stories, are to be allowed by us to imitate, and if so, whether in whole or in part, and if the latter, in what parts; or should all imitation be prohibited?'

'You mean, I suspect, to ask whether tragedy and comedy shall be admitted into our State?'

'Yes,' I said; 'but there may be more than this in question: I really do not know as yet, but whither the argument may blow, thither we go.'

'And go we will,' he said.

'Then, Adeimantus, let me ask you whether our guardians ought to be imitators; or rather, has not this question been decided by the rule already laid down that one man can only do one thing well, and not many; and that if he attempt many, he will altogether fall of gaining much reputation in any?'

'Certainly.'

'And this is equally true of imitation; no one man can imitate many things as well as he would imitate a single one?'

'He cannot.'

'Then the same person will hardly be able to play a serious part in life, and at the same time to be an imitator and imitate many other parts as well; for even when two species of imitation are nearly allied, the same persons cannot succeed in both, as, for example, the writers of tragedy and comedy – did you not just now call them imitations?'

'Yes, I did; and you are right in thinking that the same persons cannot succeed in both.'

'Any more than they can be rhapsodists and actors at once?'

'True.'

'Neither are comic and tragic actors the same; yet all these things are but imitations.'

'They are so.'

'And human nature, Adeimantus, appears to have been coined into yet smaller pieces, and to be as incapable of imitating many things well, as of performing well the actions of which the imitations are copies.'

'Quite true,' he replied.

'If then we adhere to our original notion and bear in mind that our guardians, setting aside every other business, are to dedicate themselves wholly to the maintenance of freedom in the State, making this their craft, and engaging in no work which does not bear on this end, they ought not to practise or imitate anything else; if they imitate at all, they should imitate from youth upward only those characters which are suitable to their profession – the courageous, temperate, holy, free, and the like; but they should not depict or be skilful at imitating any kind of illiberality or baseness, lest from imitation they should come to be what they imitate. Did you never observe how imitations, beginning in early youth and continuing far into life, at length grow into habits and become a second nature, affecting body, voice, and mind?'

'Yes, certainly,' he said.

'Then,' I said, 'we will not allow those for whom we profess a care and of whom we say that they ought to be good men, to imitate a woman, whether young or old, quarrelling with her husband, or striving and vaunting against the gods in conceit of her happiness, or when she is in affliction, or sorrow, or weeping; and certainly not one who is in sickness, love, or labour.'

'Very right,' he said.

'Neither must they represent slaves, male or female, performing the offices of slaves?'

'They must not.'

'And surely not bad men, whether cowards or any others, who do the reverse of what we have just been prescribing, who scold or mock or revile one another in drink or out of drink, or who in any other manner sin against themselves and their neighbours in word or deed, as the manner of such is. Neither should they be trained to imitate the action or speech of men or women who are mad or bad; for madness, like vice, is to be known but not to be practised or imitated.'

'Very true,' he replied.

'Neither may they imitate smiths or other artificers, or oarsmen, or boatswains, or the like?'

'How can they,' he said, 'when they are not allowed to apply their minds to the callings of any of these?'

'Nor may they imitate the neighing of horses, the bellowing of bulls, the murmur of rivers and roll of the ocean, thunder, and all that sort of thing?'

'Nay,' he said, 'if madness be forbidden, neither may they copy the behaviour of madmen.'

'You mean,' I said, 'if I understand you aright, that there is one sort of narrative style which may be employed by a truly good man when he has anything to say, and that another sort will be used by a man of an opposite character and education.'

'And which are these two sorts?' he asked.

'Suppose,' I answered, 'that a just and good man in the course of a narration comes on some saying or action of another good man – I should imagine that he will like to personate him, and will not be ashamed of this sort of imitation: he will be most ready to play the part of the good man when he is acting firmly and wisely; in a less degree when he is overtaken by illness or love or drink, or has met with any other disaster. But when he comes to a character which is unworthy of him, he will not make a study of that; he will disdain such a person, and will assume his likeness, if at all, for a moment only when he is performing some good action; at other times he will be ashamed to play a part which he has never practised, nor will he like to fashion and frame himself after the baser models; he feels the employment of such an art, unless in jest, to be beneath him, and his mind revolts at it.'

'So I should expect,' he replied.

'Then he will adopt a mode of narration such as we have illustrated out of Homer, that is to say, his style will be both imitative and narrative; but there will be very little of the former, and a great deal of the latter. Do you agree?'

'Certainly,' he said; 'that is the model which such a speaker must necessarily take.'

'But there is another sort of character who will narrate anything, and, the worse he is, the more unscrupulous he will be; nothing will be too bad for him: and he will be ready to imitate anything, not as a joke, but in right good earnest, and before a large company. As I was just now saying, he will attempt to represent the roll of thunder, the noise of wind and hall, or the creaking of wheels, and pulleys, and the various sounds of flutes; pipes, trumpets, and all sorts of instruments: he will bark like a dog, bleat like a sheep, or crow like a cock; his entire art will consist in imitation of voice and gesture, and there will be very little narration.'

'That, he said, will be his mode of speaking.'

'These, then, are the two kinds of style?'

'Yes.'

'And you would agree with me in saying that one of them is simple and has but slight changes; and if the harmony and rhythm are also chosen for their simplicity, the result is that the speaker, if he speaks correctly, is always pretty much the same in style, and he will keep within the limits of a single harmony (for the changes are not great), and in like manner he will make use of nearly the same rhythm?'

'That is quite true,' he said.

'Whereas the other requires all sorts of harmonies and all sorts of rhythms, if the music and the style are to correspond, because the style has all sorts of changes.'

'That is also perfectly true,' he replied.

'And do not the two styles, or the mixture of the two, comprehend all poetry, and every form of expression in words? No one can say anything except in one or other of them or in both together.'

'They include all,' he said.

'And shall we receive into our State all the three styles, or one only of the two unmixed styles? Or would you include the mixed?'

'I should prefer only to admit the pure imitator of virtue.'

'Yes,' I said, 'Adeimantus, but the mixed style is also very charming: and indeed the pantomimic, which is the opposite of the one chosen by you, is the most popular style with children and their attendants, and with the world in general.'

'I do not deny it.'

'But I suppose you would argue that such a style is unsuitable to our State, in which human nature is not twofold or manifold, for one man plays one part only?'

'Yes; quite unsuitable. '

'And this is the reason why in our State, and in our State only, we shall find a shoemaker to be a shoemaker and not a pilot also, and a husbandman to be a husbandman and not a dicast also, and a soldier a soldier and not a trader also, and the same throughout?'

'True,' he said.

'And therefore when any one of these pantomimic gentlemen, who are so clever that they can imitate anything, comes to us, and makes a proposal to exhibit himself and his poetry, we will fall down and worship him as a sweet and holy and wonderful being; but we must also inform him that in our State such as he are not permitted to exist; the law will not allow them. And so when we have anointed him with myrrh, and set a garland of wool upon his head, we shall send him away to another city. For we mean to employ for our souls' health the rougher and severer poet or story-teller, who will imitate the style of the virtuous only, and will follow those models which we prescribed at first when we began the education of our soldiers.'

'We certainly will,' he said, 'if we have the power.'

'Then now, my friend,' I said, 'that part of music or literary education which relates to the story or myth may be considered to be finished; for the matter and manner have both been discussed.'

'I think so too,' he said.

'Next in order will follow melody and song.'

'That is obvious.'

'Everyone can see already what we ought to say about them, if we are to be consistent with ourselves.'

'I fear', said Glaucon, laughing, 'that the word "everyone" hardly includes me, for I cannot at the moment say what they should be; though I may guess.'

'At any rate you can tell that a song or ode has three parts – the words, the melody, and the rhythm; that degree of knowledge I may presuppose?'

'Yes,' he said; 'so much as that you may.'

'And as for the words, there surely be no difference between words which are and which are not set to music; both will conform to the same laws, and these have been already determined by us?'

'Yes.'

'And the melody and rhythm will depend upon the words?'

'Certainly.'

'We were saying, when we spoke of the subject-matter, that we had no need of lamentations and strains of sorrow?'

'True.'

'And which are the harmonies expressive of sorrow? You are musical, and can tell me.'

'The harmonies which you mean are the mixed or tenor Lydian, and the full-toned or bass Lydian, and such like.'

'These then,' I said, 'must be banished; even to women who have a character to maintain they are of no use, and much less to men.'

'Certainly.'

'In the next place, drunkenness and softness and indolence are utterly unbecoming the character of our guardians.'

'Utterly unbecoming.'

'And which are the soft or drinking harmonies?'

'The Ionian', he replied, 'and the Lydian; they are termed "relaxed".'

'Well, and are these of any military use?'

'Quite the reverse,' he replied. 'And if so, the Dorian and the Phrygian are the only ones which you have left.'

I answered: 'Of the harmonies I know nothing, but I want to have one warlike, to sound the note or accent which a brave man utters in the hour of danger and stern resolve, or when his cause is failing, and he is going to wounds or death or is overtaken by some other evil, and at every such crisis meets the blows of fortune with firm step and a determination to endure; and another to be used by him in times of peace and freedom of action, when there is no pressure of necessity, and he is seeking to persuade God by prayer, or man by instruction and admonition, or on the other hand, when he is expressing his willingness to yield to persuasion or entreaty or admonition, and which represents him when by prudent conduct he has attained his end, not carried away by his success, but acting moderately and wisely under the circumstances, and acquiescing in the event. These two harmonies I ask you to leave; the strain of necessity and the strain of freedom, the strain of the unfortunate and the strain of the fortunate, the strain of courage, and the strain of temperance; these, I say, leave.'

'And these,' he replied, 'are the Dorian and Phrygian harmonies of which I was just now speaking.'

'Then,' I said, 'if these and these only are to be used in our songs and melodies, we shall not want multiplicity of notes or a panharmonic scale?'

'I suppose not.'

'Then we shall not maintain the artificers of lyres with three corners and complex scales, or the makers of any other many-stringed curiously harmonised instruments?'

'Certainly not.'

'But what do you say to flute-makers and flute-players? Would you admit them into our State when you reflect that in this composite use of harmony the flute is worse than all the stringed instruments put together; even the panharmonic music is only an imitation of the flute?'

'Clearly not.'

'There remain then only the lyre and the harp for use in the city, and the shepherds may have a pipe in the country.'

'That is surely the conclusion to be drawn from the argument.'

'The preferring of Apollo and his instruments to Marsyas and his instruments is not at all strange,' I said.

'Not at all,' he replied.

'And so, by the dog of Egypt, we have been unconsciously purging the State, which not long ago we termed luxurious.'

'And we have done wisely,' he replied.

'Then let us now finish the purgation,' I said. 'Next in order to harmonies, rhythms will naturally follow, and they should be subject to the same rules, for we ought not to seek out complex systems of metre, or metres of every kind, but rather to discover what rhythms are the expressions of a courageous and harmonious life; and when we have found them, we shall adapt the foot and the melody to words having a like spirit, not the words to the foot and melody. To say what these rhythms are will be your duty – you must teach me them, as you have already taught me the harmonies.'

'But, indeed,' he replied, 'I cannot tell you. I only know that there are some three principles of rhythm out of which metrical systems are framed, just as in sounds there are four notes out of which all the harmonies are composed; that is an observation which I have made. But of what sort of lives they are severally the imitations I am unable to say.'

'Then,' I said, 'we must take Damon into our counsels; and he will tell us what rhythms are expressive of meanness, or insolence, or fury, or other unworthiness, and what are to be reserved for the expression of opposite feelings. And I think that I have an indistinct recollection of his mentioning a complex Cretic rhythm; also a dactylic or heroic, and he arranged them in some manner which I do not quite understand, making the rhythms equal in the rise and fall of the foot, long and short alternating; and, unless I am mistaken, he spoke of an iambic as well as of a trochaic rhythm, and assigned to them short and long quantities. Also in some cases he appeared to praise or censure the movement of the foot quite as much as the rhythm; or perhaps a combination of the two; for I am not certain what he meant. These matters, however, as I was saying, had better be referred to Damon himself, for the analysis of the subject would be difficult, you know.'

'Rather so, I should say.'

'But there is no difficulty in seeing that grace or the absence of grace is an effect of good or bad rhythm.'

'None at all.'

'And also that good and bad rhythm naturally assimilate to a good and bad style; and that harmony and discord in like manner follow style; for our principle is that rhythm and harmony are regulated by the words, and not the words by them.'

'Just so,' he said, 'they should follow the words.'

'And will not the words and the character of the style depend on the temper of the soul?'

'Yes.'

'And everything else on the style?'

'Yes.'

'Then beauty of style and harmony and grace and good rhythm depend on simplicity – I mean the true simplicity of a rightly and nobly ordered mind and character, not that other simplicity which is only an euphemism for folly?'

'Very true,' he replied.

'And if our youth are to do their work in life, must they not make these graces and harmonies their perpetual aim?'

'They must.'

'And surely the art of the painter and every other creative and constructive art are full of them – weaving, embroidery, architecture, and every kind of manufacture; also nature, animal and vegetable – in all of them there is grace or the absence of grace. And ugliness and discord and inharmonious motion are nearly allied to ill words and ill nature, as grace and harmony are the twin sisters of goodness and virtue and bear their likeness.'

'That is quite true,' he said.

'But shall our superintendence go no further, and are the poets only to be required by us to express the image of the good in their works, on pain, if they do anything else, of expulsion from our State? Or is the same control to be extended to other artists, and are they also to be prohibited from exhibiting the opposite forms of vice and intemperance and meanness and indecency in sculpture and building and the other creative arts; and is he who cannot conform to this rule of ours to be prevented from practising his art in our State, lest the taste of our citizens be corrupted by him? We would not have our guardians grow up amid images of moral deformity, as in some noxious pasture, and there browse and feed upon many a baneful herb and flower day by day, little by little, until they silently gather a festering mass of corruption in their own soul. Let our artists rather be those who are gifted to discern the true nature of the beautiful and graceful; then will our youth dwell in a land of health, amid fair sights and sounds, and receive the good in everything; and beauty, the effluence of fair works, shall flow into the eye and ear, like a health-giving breeze from a purer region, and insensibly draw the soul from earliest years into likeness and sympathy with the beauty of reason.'

'There can be no nobler training than that,' he replied.

'And therefore,' I said, 'Glaucon, musical training is a more potent instrument than any other, because rhythm and harmony find their way into the inward places of the soul, on which they mightily fasten, imparting grace, and making the soul of him who is rightly educated graceful, or of him who is ill-educated ungraceful; and also because he who has received this true education of the inner being will most shrewdly perceive omissions or faults in art and nature, and with a true taste, while he praises and rejoices over and receives into his soul the good, and becomes noble and good, he will justly blame and hate the bad, now in the days of his youth, even before he is able to know the reason why; and when reason comes he will recognise and salute the friend with whom his education has made him long familiar.'

'Yes,' he said, 'I quite agree with you in thinking that our youth should be trained in music and on the grounds which you mention.'

'Just as in learning to read,' I said, 'we were satisfied when we knew the letters of the alphabet, which are very few, in all their recurring sizes and combinations; not slighting them as unimportant whether they occupy a space large or small, but everywhere eager to make them out; and not thinking ourselves perfect in the art of reading until we recognise them wherever they are found.'

'True –'

'Or, as we recognise the reflection of letters in the water, or in a mirror, only when we know the letters themselves; the same art and study giving us the knowledge of both.'

'Exactly –'

'Even so, as I maintain, neither we nor our guardians, whom we have to educate, can ever become musical until we and they know the essential forms, in all their combinations, and can recognise them and their images wherever they are found, not slighting them either in small things or great, but believing them all to be within the sphere of one art and study.'

'Most assuredly.'

'And when a beautiful soul harmonises with a beautiful form, and the two are cast in one mould, that will be the fairest of sights to him who has an eye to see it?'

'The fairest indeed.'

'And the fairest is also the loveliest?'

'That may be assumed.'

'And the man who has the spirit of harmony will be most in love with the loveliest; but he will not love him who is of an inharmonious soul?'

'That is true,' he replied, 'if the deficiency be in his soul; but if there be any merely bodily defect in another he will be patient of it, and will love all the same.'

'I perceive', I said, 'that you have or have had experiences of this sort, and I agree. But let me ask you another question: has excess of pleasure any affinity to temperance?'

'How can that be?' he replied. 'Pleasure deprives a man of the use of his faculties quite as much as pain.'

'Or any affinity to virtue in general?'

'None whatever.'

'Any affinity to wantonness and intemperance?'

'Yes, the greatest.'

'And is there any greater or keener pleasure than that of sensual love?'

'No, nor a madder.'

'Whereas true love is a love of beauty and order – temperate and harmonious?'

'Quite true,' he said.

'Then no intemperance or madness should be allowed to approach true love?'

'Certainly not.'

'Then mad or intemperate pleasure must never be allowed to come near the lover and his beloved; neither of them can have any part in it if their love is of the right sort?

'No, indeed, Socrates, it must never come near them.'

'Then I suppose that in the city which we are founding you would make a law to the effect that a friend should use no other familiarity to his love than a father would use to his son, and then only for a noble purpose, and he must first have the other's consent; and this rule is to limit him in all his intercourse, and he is never to be seen going further, or, if he exceeds, he is to be deemed guilty of coarseness and bad taste.'

'I quite agree,' he said.

'Thus much of music, which makes a fair ending; for what should be the end of music if not the love of beauty?'

'I agree,' he said.

'After music comes gymnastics, in which our youth are next to be trained.'

'Certainly.'

'Gymnastics as well as music should begin in early years; the training in it should be careful and should continue through life. Now my belief is – and this is a matter upon which I should like to have your opinion in confirmation of my own, but my own belief is – not that the good body by any bodily excellence improves the soul, but, on the contrary, that the good soul, by her own excellence, improves the body as far as this may be possible. What do you say?'

'Yes, I agree.'

'Then, to the mind when adequately trained, we shall be right in handing over the more particular care of the body; and in order to avoid prolixity we will now only give the general outlines of the subject.'

'Very good.'

'That they must abstain from intoxication has been already remarked by us; for of all persons a guardian should be the last to get drunk and not know where in the world he is.'

'Yes,' he said; 'that a guardian should require another guardian to take care of him is ridiculous indeed.'

'But next, what shall we say of their food; for the men are in training for the great contest of all – are they not?'

'Yes,' he said.

'And will the habit of body of our ordinary athletes be suited to them?'

'Why not?'

'I am afraid', I said, 'that a habit of body such as they have is but a sleepy sort of thing, and rather perilous to health. Do you not observe that these athletes sleep away their lives, and are liable to most dangerous illnesses if they depart, in ever so slight a degree, from their customary regimen?'

'Yes, I do.'

'Then', I said, 'a finer sort of training will be required for our warrior athletes, who are to be like wakeful dogs, and to see and hear with the utmost keenness; amid the many changes of water and also of food, of summer heat and winter cold, which they will have to endure when on a campaign, they must not be liable to break down in health.'

'That is my view.'

'The really excellent gymnastics is twin sister of that simple music which we were just now describing.'

'How so?'

'Why, I conceive that there is a gymnastics which, like our music, is simple and good; and especially the military gymnastics.'

'What do you mean?'

'My meaning may be learned from Homer; he, you know, feeds his heroes at their feasts, when they are campaigning, on soldiers' fare; they have no fish, although they are on the shores of the Hellespont, and they are not allowed boiled meats but only roast, which is the food most convenient for soldiers, requiring only that they should light a fire, and not involving the trouble of carrying about pots and pans.'

'True.'

'And I can hardly be mistaken in saying that sweet sauces are nowhere mentioned in Homer. In proscribing them, however, he is not singular; all professional athletes are well aware that a man who is to be in good condition should take nothing of the kind.'

'Yes,' he said; 'and knowing this, they are quite right in not taking them.'

'Then you would not approve of Syracusan dinners, and the refinements of Sicilian cookery?'

'I think not.'

'Nor, if a man is to be in condition, would you allow him to have a Corinthian girl as his fair friend?'

'Certainly not.'

'Neither would you approve of the delicacies, as they are thought, of Athenian confectionery?'

'Certainly not.'

'All such feeding and living may be rightly compared by us to melody and song composed in the panharmonic style, and in all the rhythms.'

'Exactly.'

'There complexity engendered licence, and here disease; whereas simplicity in music was the parent of temperance in the soul; and simplicity in gymnastics of health in the body.'

'Most true,' he said.

'But when intemperance and disease multiply in a State, halls of justice and medicine are always being opened; and the arts of the doctor and the lawyer give themselves airs, finding how keen is the interest which not only the slaves but the freemen of a city take about them.'

'Of course.'

'And yet what greater proof can there be of a bad and disgraceful state of education than this, that not only artisans and the meaner sort of people need the skill of first-rate physicians and judges, but also those who would profess to have had a liberal education? Is it not disgraceful, and a great sign of want of good-breeding, that a man should have to go abroad for his law and physic because he has none of his own at home, and must therefore surrender himself into the hands of other men whom he makes lords and judges over him?'

'Of all things', he said, 'the most disgraceful.'

'Would you say "most",' I replied, 'when you consider that there is a further stage of the evil in which a man is not only a life-long litigant, passing all his days in the courts, either as plaintiff or defendant, but is actually led by his bad taste to pride himself on his litigiousness; he imagines that he is a master in dishonesty; able to take every crooked turn, and wriggle into and out of every hole, bending like a withy and getting out of the way of justice: and all for what? – In order to gain small points not worth mentioning, he not knowing that so to order his life as to be able to do without a napping judge is a far higher and nobler sort of thing. Is not that still more disgraceful?'

'Yes,' he said, 'that is still more disgraceful.'

'Well,' I said, 'and to require the help of medicine, not when a wound has to be cured, or on occasion of an epidemic, but just because, by indolence and a habit of life such as we have been describing, men fill themselves with waters and winds, as if their bodies were a marsh, compelling the ingenious sons of Asclepius to find more names for diseases, such as flatulence and catarrh; is not this, too, a disgrace?'

'Yes,' he said, 'they do certainly give very strange and newfangled names to diseases.'

'Yes,' I said, 'and I do not believe that there were any such diseases in the days of Asclepius; and this I infer from the circumstance that the hero Eurypylus, after he has been wounded in Homer, drinks a posset of Pramnian wine well besprinkled with barley-meal and grated cheese, which are certainly inflammatory, and yet the sons of Asclepius who were at the Trojan war do not blame the damsel who gives him the drink, or rebuke Patroclus, who is treating his case.'

'Well,' he said, 'that was surely an extraordinary drink to be given to a person in his condition.'

'Not so extraordinary,' I replied, 'if you bear in mind that in former days, as is commonly said, before the time of Herodicus, the guild of Asclepius did not practise our present system of medicine, which may be said to educate diseases. But Herodicus, being a trainer, and himself of a sickly constitution, by a combination of training and doctoring found out a way of torturing first and chiefly himself, and secondly the rest of the world.'

'How was that?' he said.

'By the invention of lingering death; for he had a mortal disease which he perpetually tended, and as recovery was out of the question, he passed his entire life as a valetudinarian; he could do nothing but attend upon himself, and he was in constant torment whenever he departed in anything from his usual regimen, and so dying hard, by the help of science he struggled on to old age.'

'A rare reward of his skill!'

'Yes,' I said; 'a reward which a man might fairly expect who never understood that, if Asclepius did not instruct his descendants in valetudinarian arts, the omission arose, not from ignorance or inexperience of such a branch of medicine, but because he knew that in all well-ordered states every individual has an occupation to which he must attend, and has therefore no leisure to spend in continually being ill. This we remark in the case of the artisan, but, ludicrously enough, do not apply the same rule to people of the richer sort.'

'How do you mean?' he said.

'I mean this: when a carpenter is ill he asks the physician for a rough and ready cure: an emetic or a purge or a cautery or the knife – these are his remedies. And if someone prescribes for him a course of dietetics, and tells him that he must swathe and swaddle his head, and all that sort of thing, he replies at once that he has no time to be ill, and that he sees no good in a life which is spent in nursing his disease to the neglect of his customary employment; and therefore bidding good-bye to this sort of physician, he resumes his ordinary habits, and either gets well and lives and does his business, or, if his constitution falls, he dies and has no more trouble.'

'Yes,' he said, 'and a man in his condition of life ought to use the art of medicine thus far only.'

'Has he not', I said, 'an occupation; and what profit would there be in his life if he were deprived of his occupation?'

'Quite true,' he said.

'But with the rich man this is otherwise; of him we do not say that he has any specially appointed work which he must perform, if he would live.'

'He is generally supposed to have nothing to do.'

'Then you never heard of the saying of Phocylides, that as soon as a man has a livelihood he should practise virtue?'

'Nay,' he said, 'I think that he had better begin somewhat sooner.'

'Let us not have a dispute with him about this,' I said; 'but rather ask ourselves: is the practice of virtue obligatory on the rich man, or can he live without it? And if obligatory on him, then let us raise a further question, whether this dieting of disorders which is an impediment to the application of the mind in carpentering and the mechanical arts, does not equally stand in the way of the sentiment of Phocylides?'

'Of that,' he replied, 'there can be no doubt; such excessive care of the body, when carried beyond the rules of gymnastics, is most inimical to the practice of virtue.'

'Yes,' indeed, 'I replied, and equally incompatible with the management of a house, an army, or an office of state; and, what is most important of all, irreconcilable with any kind of study or thought or self-reflection – there is a constant suspicion that headache and giddiness are to be ascribed to philosophy, and hence all practising or making trial of virtue in the higher sense is absolutely stopped; for a man is always fancying that he is being made ill, and is in constant anxiety about the state of his body.'

'Yes, likely enough.'

'And therefore our politic Asclepius may be supposed to have exhibited the power of his art only to persons who, being generally of healthy constitution and habits of life, had a definite ailment; such as these he cured by purges and operations, and bade them live as usual, herein consulting the interests of the State; but bodies which disease had penetrated through and through he would not have attempted to cure by gradual processes of evacuation and infusion: he did not want to lengthen out good-for-nothing lives, or to have weak fathers begetting weaker sons; – if a man was not able to live in the ordinary way he had no business to cure him; for such a cure would have been of no use either to himself, or to the State.'

'Then,' he said, 'you regard Asclepius as a statesman.'

'Clearly; and his character is further illustrated by his sons. Note that they were heroes in the days of old and practised the medicines of which I am speaking at the siege of Troy: You will remember how, when Pandarus wounded Menelaus, they

"Sucked the blood out of the wound, and sprinkled soothing remedies,"

'but they never prescribed what the patient was afterwards to eat or drink in the case of Menelaus, any more than in the case of Eurypylus; the remedies, as they conceived, were enough to heal any man who before he was wounded was healthy and regular in habits; and even though he did happen to drink a posset of Pramnian wine, he might get well all the same. But they would have nothing to do with unhealthy and intemperate subjects, whose lives were of no use either to themselves or others; the art of medicine was not designed for their good, and though they were as rich as Midas, the sons of Asclepius would have declined to attend them.'

'They were very acute persons, those sons of Asclepius.'

'Naturally so,' I replied. 'Nevertheless, the tragedians and Pindar disobeying our behests, although they acknowledge that Asclepius was the son of Apollo, say also that he was bribed into healing a rich man who was at the point of death, and for this reason he was struck by lightning. But we, in accordance with the principle already affirmed by us, will not believe them when they tell us both; – if he was the son of a god, we maintain that he was not avaricious; or, if he was avaricious he was not the son of a god.'

'All that, Socrates, is excellent; but I should like to put a question to you: Ought there not to be good physicians in a State, and are not the best those who have treated the greatest number of constitutions good and bad? and are not the best judges in like manner those who are acquainted with all sorts of moral natures?'

'Yes,' I said, 'I too would have good judges and good physicians. But do you know whom I think good?'

'Will you tell me?'

'I will, if I can. Let me however note that in the same question you join two things which are not the same.'

'How so? he asked.

'Why,' I said, 'you join physicians and judges. Now the most skilful physicians are those who, from their youth upwards, have combined with the knowledge of their art the greatest experience of disease; they had better not be robust in health, and should have had all manner of diseases in their own persons. For the body, as I conceive, is not the instrument with which they cure the body; in that case we could not allow them ever to be or to have been sickly; but they cure the body with the mind, and the mind which has become and is sick can cure nothing.'

'That is very true,' he said.

'But with the judge it is otherwise; since he governs mind by mind; he ought not therefore to have been trained among vicious minds, and to have associated with them from youth upwards, and to have gone through the whole calendar of crime, only in order that he may quickly infer the crimes of others as he might their bodily diseases from his own self-consciousness; the honourable mind which is to form a healthy judgment should have had no experience or contamination of evil habits when young. And this is the reason why in youth good men often appear to be simple, and are easily practised upon by the dishonest, because they have no examples of what evil is in their own souls.'

'Yes,' he said, 'they are far too apt to be deceived.'

'Therefore,' I said, 'the judge should not be young; he should have learned to know evil, not from his own soul, but from late and long observation of the nature of evil in others: knowledge should be his guide, not personal experience.'

'Yes,' he said, 'that is the ideal of a judge.

'Yes,' I replied, 'and he will be a good man (which is my answer to your question); for he is good who has a good soul. But the cunning and suspicious nature of which we spoke – he who has committed many crimes, and fancies himself to be a master in wickedness, when he is amongst his fellows, is wonderful in the precautions which he takes, because he judges of them by himself: but when he gets into the company of men of virtue, who have the experience of age, he appears to be a fool again, owing to his unseasonable suspicions; he cannot recognise an honest man, because he has no pattern of honesty in himself; at the same time, as the bad are more numerous than the good, and he meets with them oftener, he thinks himself, and is by others thought to be, rather wise than foolish.'

'Most true,' he said.

'Then the good and wise judge whom we are seeking is not this man, but the other; for vice cannot know virtue too, but a virtuous nature, educated by time, will acquire a knowledge both of virtue and vice: the virtuous, and not the vicious, man has wisdom – in my opinion.'

'And in mine also.'

'This is the sort of medicine, and this is the sort of law, which you sanction in your State. They will minister to better natures, giving health both of soul and of body; but those who are diseased in their bodies they will leave to die, and the corrupt and incurable souls they will put an end to themselves.'

'That is clearly the best thing both for the patients and for the State.'

'And thus our youth, having been educated only in that simple music which, as we said, inspires temperance, will be reluctant to go to law.'

'Clearly.'

'And the musician, who, keeping to the same track, is content to practise the simple gymnastics, will have nothing to do with medicine unless in some extreme case.'

'That I quite believe.'

'The very exercises and tolls which he undergoes are intended to stimulate the spirited element of his nature, and not to increase his strength; he will not, like common athletes, use exercise and regimen to develop his muscles.'

'Very right,' he said.

'Neither are the two arts of music and gymnastics really designed, as is often supposed, the one for the training of the soul, the other for the training of the body.'

'What then is the real object of them?'

'I believe', I said, 'that the teachers of both have in view chiefly the improvement of the soul.'

'How can that be?' he asked.

'Did you never observe', I said, 'the effect on the mind itself of exclusive devotion to gymnastics, or the opposite effect of an exclusive devotion to music?'

'In what way shown?' he said.

'The one producing a temper of hardness and ferocity, the other of softness and effeminacy,' I replied.

'Yes,' he said, 'I am quite aware that the mere athlete becomes too much of a savage, and that the mere musician is melted and softened beyond what is good for him.'

'Yet surely,' I said, 'this ferocity only comes from spirit, which, if rightly educated, would give courage, but, if too much intensified, is liable to become hard and brutal.'

'That I quite think.'

'On the other hand, the philosopher will have the quality of gentleness. And this also, when too much indulged, will turn to softness, but, if educated rightly, will be gentle and moderate.'

'True.'

'And in our opinion the guardians ought to have both these qualities?'

'Assuredly.'

'And both should be in harmony?'

'Beyond question.'

'And the harmonious soul is both temperate and courageous?'

'Yes.'

'And the inharmonious is cowardly and boorish?'

'Very true.'

'And, when a man allows music to play upon him and to pour into his soul through the funnel of his ears those sweet and soft and melancholy airs of which we were just now speaking, and his whole life is passed in warbling and the delights of song; in the first stage of the process the passion or spirit which is in him is tempered like iron, and made useful, instead of brittle and useless. But, if he carries on the softening and soothing process, in the next stage he begins to melt and waste, until he has wasted away his spirit and cut out the sinews of his soul; and he becomes a feeble warrior.'

'Very true.'

'If the element of spirit is naturally weak in him the change is speedily accomplished, but if he has a good deal, then the power of music weakening the spirit renders him excitable – on the least provocation he flames up at once, and is speedily extinguished; instead of having spirit he grows irritable and passionate and is quite impracticable.'

'Exactly.'

'And so in gymnastics, if a man takes violent exercise and is a great feeder, and the reverse of a great student of music and philosophy, at first the high condition of his body fills him with pride and spirit, and he becomes twice the man that he was.'

'Certainly.'

'And what happens? If he do nothing else, and holds no converse with the Muses, does not even that intelligence which there may be in him, having no taste of any sort of learning or enquiry or thought or culture, grow feeble and dull and blind, his mind never waking up or receiving nourishment, and his senses not being purged of their mists?'

'True,' he said.

'And he ends by becoming a hater of philosophy, uncivilised, never using the weapon of persuasion – he is like a wild beast, all violence and fierceness, and knows no other way of dealing; and he lives in all ignorance and evil conditions, and has no sense of propriety and grace.'

'That is quite true,' he said.

'And as there are two principles of human nature, one the spirited and the other the philosophical, some God, as I should say, has given mankind two arts answering to them (and only indirectly to the soul and body), in order that these two principles (like the strings of an instrument) may be relaxed or drawn tighter until they are duly harmonised.'

'That appears to be the intention.'

'And he who mingles music with gymnastics in the fairest proportions, and best attempers them to the soul, may be rightly called the true musician and harmonist in a far higher sense than the tuner of the strings.'

'You are quite right, Socrates.'

'And such a presiding genius will be always required in our State if the government is to last.'

'Yes, he will be absolutely necessary.'

'Such, then, are our principles of nurture and education: where would be the use of going into further details about the dances of our citizens, or about their hunting and coursing, their gymnastic and equestrian contests? For these all follow the general principle, and having found that, we shall have no difficulty in discovering them.'

'I dare say that there will be no difficulty.'

'Very good,' I said. 'Then what is the next question? Must we not ask who are to be rulers and who subjects?'

'Certainly.'

'There can be no doubt that the elder must rule the younger.'

'Clearly.'

'And that the best of these must rule.'

'That is also clear.'

'Now, are not the best husbandmen those who are most devoted to husbandry?'

'Yes.'

'And as we are to have the best of guardians for our city, must they not be those who have most the character of guardians?'

'Yes.'

'And to this end they ought to be wise and efficient, and to have a special care of the State?'

'True.'

'And a man will be most likely to care about that which he loves?'

'To be sure.'

'And he will be most likely to love that which he regards as having the same interests with himself, and that of which the good or evil fortune is supposed by him at any time most to affect his own?'

'Very true,' he replied.

'Then there must be a selection. Let us note among the guardians those who in their whole life show the greatest eagerness to do what is for the good of their country, and the greatest repugnance to do what is against her interests.'

'Those are the right men.'

'And they will have to be watched at every age, in order that we may see whether they preserve their resolution, and never, under the influence either of force or enchantment, forget or cast off their sense of duty to the State.'

'How cast off?' he said.

'I will explain to you,' I replied. 'A resolution may go out of a man's mind either with his will or against his will; with his will when he gets rid of a falsehood and learns better, against his will whenever he is deprived of a truth.'

'I understand', he said, 'the willing loss of a resolution; the meaning of the unwilling I have yet to learn.'

'Why,' I said, 'do you not see that men are unwillingly deprived of good, and willingly of evil? Is not to have lost the truth an evil, and to possess the truth a good? And you would agree that to conceive things as they are is to possess the truth?'

'Yes,' he replied; 'I agree with you in thinking that mankind are deprived of truth against their will.'

'And is not this involuntary deprivation caused either by theft, or force, or enchantment?'

'Still,' he replied, 'I do not understand you.'

'I fear that I must have been talking darkly, like the tragedians. I only mean that some men are changed by persuasion and that others forget; argument steals away the hearts of one class, and time of the other; and this I call theft. Now you understand me?'

'Yes.'

'Those again who are forced are those whom the violence of some pain or grief compels to change their opinion.'

'I understand,' he said, 'and you are quite right.'

'And you would also acknowledge that the enchanted are those who change their minds either under the softer influence of pleasure, or the sterner influence of fear?'

'Yes,' he said; 'everything that deceives may be said to enchant.'

'Therefore, as I was just now saying, we must enquire who are the best guardians of their own conviction that what they think the interest of the State is to be the rule of their lives. We must watch them from their youth upwards, and make them perform actions in which they are most likely to forget or to be deceived, and he who remembers and is not deceived is to be selected, and he who falls in the trial is to be rejected. That will be the way?'

'Yes.'

'And there should also be toils and pains and conflicts prescribed for them, in which they will be made to give further proof of the same qualities.'

'Very right,' he replied.

'And then,' I said, 'we must try them with enchantments that are the third sort of test – and see what will be their behaviour: like those who take colts amid noise and tumult to see if they are of a timid nature, so must we take our youth amid terrors of some kind, and again pass them into pleasures, and prove them more thoroughly than gold is proved in the furnace, that we may discover whether they are armed against all enchantments, and of a noble bearing always, good guardians of themselves and of the music which they have learned, and retaining under all circumstances a rhythmical and harmonious nature, such as will be most serviceable to the individual and to the State. And he who at every age, as boy and youth and in mature life, has come out of the trial victorious and pure, shall be appointed a ruler and guardian of the State; he shall be honoured in life and death, and shall receive sepulture and other memorials of honour, the greatest that we have to give. But him who fails, we must reject. I am inclined to think that this is the sort of way in which our rulers and guardians should be chosen and appointed. I speak generally, and not with any pretension to exactness.'

'And, speaking generally, I agree with you,' he said.

'And perhaps the word "guardian" in the fullest sense ought to be applied to this higher class only who preserve us against foreign enemies and maintain peace among our citizens at home, that the one may not have the will, or the others the power, to harm us. The young men whom we before called guardians may be more properly designated auxiliaries and supporters of the principles of the rulers.'

'I agree with you,' he said.

'How then may we devise one of those needful falsehoods of which we lately spoke – just one royal lie which may deceive the rulers, if that be possible, and at any rate the rest of the city?'

'What sort of lie?' he said.

'Nothing new,' I replied. 'Only an old Phoenician tale of what has often occurred before now in other places (as the poets say, and have made the world believe), though not in our time, and I do not know whether such an event could ever happen again, or could now even be made probable, if it did.'

'How your words seem to hesitate on your lips!'

'You will not wonder', I replied, 'at my hesitation when you have heard.'

'Speak,' he said, 'and fear not.'

'Well then, I will speak, although I really know not how to look you in the face, or in what words to utter the audacious fiction, which I propose to communicate gradually, first to the rulers, then to the soldiers, and lastly to the people. They are to be told that their youth was a dream, and the education and training which they received from us, an appearance only; in reality during all that time they were being formed and fed in the womb of the earth, where they themselves and their arms and appurtenances were manufactured; when they were completed, the earth, their mother, sent them up; and so, their country being their mother and also their nurse, they are bound to advise for her good, and to defend her against attacks, and her citizens they are to regard as children of the earth and their own brothers.'

'You had good reason', he said, 'to be ashamed of the lie which you were going to tell.'

'True,' I replied, 'but there is more coming; I have only told you half. Citizens, we shall say to them in our tale, you are brothers, yet God has framed you differently. Some of you have the power of command, and in the composition of these he has mingled gold, wherefore also they have the greatest honour; others he has made of silver, to be auxillaries; others again who are to be husbandmen and craftsmen he has composed of brass and iron; and the species will generally be preserved in the children. But as all are of the same original stock, a golden parent will sometimes have a silver son, or a silver parent a golden son. And God proclaims as a first principle to the rulers, and above all else, that there is nothing which they should so anxiously guard, or of which they are to be such good guardians, as of the purity of the race. They should observe what elements mingle in their offspring; for if the son of a golden or silver parent has an admixture of brass and iron, then nature orders a transposition of ranks, and the eye of the ruler must not be pitiful towards the child because he has to descend in the scale and become a husbandman or artisan, just as there may be sons of artisans who having an admixture of gold or silver in them are raised to honour, and become guardians or auxiliaries. For an oracle says that when a man of brass or iron guards the State, it will be destroyed. Such is the tale; is there any possibility of making our citizens believe in it?'

'Not in the present generation,' he replied; 'there is no way of accomplishing this; but their sons may be made to believe in the tale, and their sons' sons, and posterity after them.'

'I see the difficulty,' I replied; 'yet the fostering of such a belief will make them care more for the city and for one another. Enough, however, of the fiction, which may now fly abroad upon the wings of rumour, while we arm our earth-born heroes, and lead them forth under the command of their rulers. Let them look round and select a spot whence they can best suppress insurrection, if any prove refractory within, and also defend themselves against enemies, who like wolves may come down on the fold from without; there let them encamp, and when they have encamped, let them sacrifice to the proper Gods and prepare their dwellings.'

'Just so,' he said.

'And their dwellings must be such as will shield them against the cold of winter and the heat of summer.'

'I suppose that you mean houses,' he replied.

'Yes,' I said; 'but they must be the houses of soldiers, and not of shop-keepers.'

'What is the difference?' he said.

'That I will endeavour to explain,' I replied. 'To keep watchdogs, who, from want of discipline or hunger, or some evil habit, or evil habit or other, would turn upon the sheep and worry them, and behave not like dogs but wolves, would be a foul and monstrous thing in a shepherd?'

'Truly monstrous,' he said.

'And therefore every care must be taken that our auxiliaries, being stronger than our citizens, may not grow to be too much for them and become savage tyrants instead of friends and allies?'

'Yes, great care should be taken.'

'And would not a really good education furnish the best safeguard?'

'But they are well-educated already,' he replied.

'I cannot be so confident, my dear Glaucon,' I said; 'I am much certain that they ought to be, and that true education, whatever that may be, will have the greatest tendency to civilise and humanise them in their relations to one another, and to those who are under their protection.'

'Very true,' he replied.

'And not only their education, but their habitations, and all that belongs to them, should be such as will neither impair their virtue as guardians, nor tempt them to prey upon the other citizens. Any man of sense must acknowledge that.'

'He must.'

'Then let us consider what will be their way of life, if they are to realise our idea of them. In the first place, none of them should have any property of his own beyond what is absolutely necessary; neither should they have a private house or store closed against anyone who has a mind to enter; their provisions should be only such as are required by trained warriors, who are men of temperance and courage; they should agree to receive from the citizens a fixed rate of pay, enough to meet the expenses of the year and no more; and they will go and live together like soldiers in a camp. Gold and silver we will tell them that they have from God; the diviner metal is within them, and they have therefore no need of the dross which is current among men, and ought not to pollute the divine by any such earthly admixture; for that commoner metal has been the source of many unholy deeds, but their own is undefiled. And they alone of all the citizens may not touch or handle silver or gold, or be under the same roof with them, or wear them, or drink from them. And this will be their salvation, and they will be the saviours of the State. But should they ever acquire homes or lands or moneys of their own, they will become housekeepers and husbandmen instead of guardians, enemies and tyrants instead of allies of the other citizens; hating and being hated, plotting and being plotted against, they will pass their whole life in much greater terror of internal than of external enemies, and the hour of ruin, both to themselves and to the rest of the State, will be at hand. For all which reasons may we not say that thus shall our State be ordered, and that these shall be the regulations appointed by us for guardians concerning their houses and all other matters?'

'Yes,' said Glaucon.

Book IV

Here Adeimantus interposed a question: 'How would you answer, Socrates,' said he, 'if a person were to say that you are making these people miserable, and that they are the cause of their own unhappiness; the city in fact belongs to them, but they are none the better for it; whereas other men acquire lands, and build large and handsome houses, and have everything handsome about them, offering sacrifices to the gods on their own account, and practising hospitality; moreover, as you were saying just now, they have gold and silver, and all that is usual among the favourites of fortune; but our poor citizens are no better than mercenaries who are quartered in the city and are always mounting guard?'

'Yes,' I said; 'and you may add that they are only fed, and not paid in addition to their food, like other men; and therefore they cannot, if they would, take a journey of pleasure; they have no money to spend on a mistress or any other luxurious fancy, which, as the world goes, is thought to be happiness; and many other accusations of the same nature might be added.'

'But,' said he, 'let us suppose all this to be included in the charge.'

'You mean to ask,' I said, 'what will be our answer?'

'Yes.'

'If we proceed along the old path, my belief', I said, 'is that we shall find the answer. And our answer will be that, even as they are, our guardians may very likely be the happiest of men; but that our aim in founding the State was not the disproportionate happiness of any one class, but the greatest happiness of the whole; we thought that in a State which is ordered with a view to the good of the whole we should be most likely to find Justice, and in the ill-ordered State injustice; and, having found them, we might then decide which of the two is the happier. At present, I take it, we are fashioning the happy State, not piecemeal, or with a view of making a few happy citizens, but as a whole; and by-and-by we will proceed to view the opposite kind of State. Suppose that we were painting a statue, and someone came up to us and said, "Why do you not put the most beautiful colours on the most beautiful parts of the body – the eyes ought to be purple, but you have made them black?" – to him we might fairly answer, "Sir, you would not surely have us beautify the eyes to such a degree that they are no longer eyes; consider rather whether, by giving this and the other features their due proportion, we make the whole beautiful." And so I say to you, do not compel us to assign to the guardians a sort of happiness which will make them anything but guardians; for we too can clothe our husbandmen in royal apparel, and set crowns of gold on their heads, and bid them till the ground as much as they like, and no more. Our potters also might be allowed to repose on couches, and feast by the fireside, passing round the wine-cup, while their wheel is conveniently at hand, and working at pottery only as much as they like; in this way we might make every class happy – and then, as you imagine, the whole State would be happy. But do not put this idea into our heads; for, if we listen to you, the husbandman will be no longer a husbandman, the potter will cease to be a potter, and no one will have the character of any distinct class in the State. Now this is not of much consequence where the corruption of society, and pretension to be what you are not, is confined to cobblers; but when the guardians of the laws and of the government are only seemingly and not real guardians, then see how they turn the State upside down; and on the other hand they alone have the power of giving order and happiness to the State. We mean our guardians to be true saviours and not the destroyers of the State, whereas our opponent is thinking of peasants at a festival, who are enjoying a life of revelry, not of citizens who are doing their duty to the State. But, if so, we mean different things, and he is speaking of something which is not a State. And therefore we must consider whether in appointing our guardians we would look to their greatest happiness individually, or whether this principle of happiness does not rather reside in the State as a whole. But the latter be the truth, then the guardians and auxillaries, and all others equally with them, must be compelled or induced to do their own work in the best way. And thus the whole State will grow up in a noble order, and the several classes will receive the proportion of happiness which nature assigns to them.'

'I think that you are quite right.'

'I wonder whether you will agree with another remark which occurs to me.'

'What may that be?'

'There seem to be two causes of the deterioration of the arts.'

'What are they?'

'Wealth,' I said, 'and poverty.'

'How do they act?'

'The process is as follows: when a potter becomes rich, will he, think you, any longer take the same pains with his art?'

'Certainly not.'

'He will grow more and more indolent and careless?'

'Very true.'

'And the result will be that he becomes a worse potter?'

'Yes; he greatly deteriorates.'

'But, on the other hand, if he has no money, and cannot provide himself tools or instruments, he will not work equally well himself, nor will he teach his sons or apprentices to work equally well.'

'Certainly not.'

'Then, under the influence either of poverty or of wealth, workmen and their work are equally liable to degenerate?'

'That is evident.'

'Here, then, is a discovery of new evils,' I said, 'against which the guardians will have to watch, or they will creep into the city unobserved.'

'What evils?'

'Wealth,' I said, 'and poverty: the one is the parent of luxury and indolence, and the other of meanness and viciousness, and both of discontent.'

'That is very true,' he replied; 'but still I should like to know, Socrates, how our city will be able to go to war, especially against an enemy who is rich and powerful, if deprived of the sinews of war.'

'There would certainly be a difficulty,' I replied, 'in going to war with one such enemy; but there is no difficulty where there are two of them.'

'How so?' he asked.

'In the first place,' I said, 'if we have to fight, our side will be trained warriors fighting against an army of rich men.'

'That is true,' he said.

'And do you not suppose, Adeimantus, that a single boxer who was perfect in his art would easily be a match for two stout and well-to-do gentlemen who were not boxers?'

'Hardly, if they came upon him at once.'

'What, not', I said, 'if he were able to run away and then turn and strike at the one who first came up? And supposing he were to do this several times under the heat of a scorching sun, might he not, being an expert, overturn more than one stout personage?'

'Certainly,' he said, 'there would be nothing wonderful in that.'

'And yet rich men probably have a greater superiority in the science and practice of boxing than they have in military qualities.'

'Likely enough.'

'Then we may assume that our athletes will be able to fight with two or three times their own number?'

'I agree with you, for I think you right.'

'And suppose that, before engaging, our citizens send an embassy to one of the two cities, telling them what is the truth: silver and gold we neither have nor are permitted to have, but you may; do you therefore come and help us in war, and take the spoils of the other city. Who, on hearing these words, would choose to fight against lean wiry dogs, rather than, with the dogs on their side, against fat and tender sheep?'

'That is not likely; and yet there might be a danger to the poor State if the wealth of many States were to be gathered into one.'

'But how simple of you to use the term State at all of any but our own!'

'Why so?'

'You ought to speak of other States in the plural number; not one of them is a city, but many cities, as they say in the game. For indeed any city, however small, is in fact divided into two, one the city of the poor, the other of the rich; these are at war with one another; and in either there are many smaller divisions, and you would be altogether beside the mark if you treated them all as a single State. But if you deal with them as many, and give the wealth or power or persons of the one to the others, you will always have a great many friends and not many enemies. And your State, while the wise order which has now been prescribed continues to prevail in her, will be the greatest of States, I do not mean to say in reputation or appearance, but in deed and truth, though she number not more than a thousand defenders. A single State which is her equal you will hardly find, either among Hellenes or barbarians, though many that appear to be as great and many times greater.'

'That is most true,' he said.

'And what', I said, 'will be the best limit for our rulers to fix when they are considering the size of the State and the amount of territory which they are to include, and beyond which they will not go?'

'What limit would you propose?'

'I would allow the State to increase so far as is consistent with unity; that, I think, is the proper limit.'

'Very good,' he said.

'Here then', I said, 'is another order which will have to be conveyed to our guardians: Let our city be accounted neither large nor small, but one and self-sufficing.'

'And surely,' said he, 'this is not a very severe order which we impose upon them.'

'And the other', said I, 'of which we were speaking before is lighter still – I mean the duty of degrading the offspring of the guardians when inferior, and of elevating into the rank of guardians the offspring of the lower classes, when naturally superior. The intention was, that, in the case of the citizens generally, each individual should be put to the use for which nature which nature intended him, one to one work, and then every man would do his own business, and be one and not many; and so the whole city would be one and not many.'

'Yes,' he said; 'that is not so difficult.'

'The regulations which we are prescribing, my good Adeimantus, are not, as might be supposed, a number of great principles, but trifles all, if care be taken, as the saying is, of the one great thing – a thing, however, which I would rather call, not great, but sufficient for our purpose.'

'What may that be?' he asked.

'Education,' I said, 'and nurture: if our citizens are well educated, and grow into sensible men, they will easily see their way through all these, as well as other matters which I omit; such, for example, as marriage, the possession of women and the procreation of children, which will all follow the general principle that friends have all things in common, as the proverb says.'

'That will be the best way of settling them.'

'Also,' I said, 'the State, if once started well, moves with accumulating force like a wheel. For good nurture and education implant good constitutions, and these good constitutions taking root in a good education improve more and more, and this improvement affects the breed in man as in other animals.'

'Very possibly,' he said.

'Then to sum up: this is the point to which, above all, the attention of our rulers should be directed – that music and gymnastics be preserved in their original form, and no innovation made. They must do their utmost to maintain them intact. And when anyone says that mankind most regard

"The newest song which the singers have,"

they will be afraid that he may be praising, not new songs, but a new kind of song; and this ought not to be praised, or conceived to be the meaning of the poet; for any musical innovation is full of danger to the whole State, and ought to be prohibited. So Damon tells me, and I can quite believe him; he says that when modes of music change, the fundamental laws of the State always change with them.'

'Yes,' said Adeimantus; 'and you may add my suffrage to Damon's and your own.'

'Then', I said, 'our guardians must lay the foundations of their fortress in music?'

'Yes,' he said; 'the lawlessness of which you speak too easily steals in.'

'Yes,' I replied, 'in the form of amusement; and at first sight it appears harmless.'

'Why, yes,' he said, 'and there is no harm; were it not that little by little this spirit of licence, finding a home, imperceptibly penetrates into manners and customs; whence, issuing with greater force, it invades contracts between man and man, and from contracts goes on to laws and constitutions, in utter recklessness, ending at last, Socrates, by an overthrow of all rights, private as well as public.'

'Is that true?' I said.

'That is my belief,' he replied.

'Then, as I was saying, our youth should be trained from the first in a stricter system, for if amusements become lawless, and the youths themselves become lawless, they can never grow up into well-conducted and virtuous citizens.'

'Very true,' he said.

'And when they have made a good beginning in play, and by the help of music have gained the habit of good order, then this habit of order, in a manner how unlike the lawless play of the others, will accompany them in all their actions and be a principle of growth to them, and if there be any fallen places a principle in the State will raise them up again.'

'Very true,' he said.

'Thus educated, they will invent for themselves any lesser rules which their predecessors have altogether neglected.'

'What do you mean?'

'I mean such things as these: when the young are to be silent before their elders; how they are to show respect to them by standing and making them sit; what honour is due to parents; what garments or shoes are to be worn; the mode of dressing the hair; deportment and manners in general. You would agree with me?'

'Yes.'

'But there is, I think, small wisdom in legislating about such matters – I doubt if it is ever done; nor are any precise written enactments about them likely to be lasting.'

'Impossible.'

'It would seem, Adeimantus, that the direction in which education starts a man, will determine his future life. Does not like always attract like?'

'To be sure.'

'Until some one rare and grand result is reached which may be good, and may be the reverse of good?'

'That is not to be denied.'

'And for this reason,' I said, 'I shall not attempt to legislate further about them.'

'Naturally enough,' he replied.

'Well, and about the business of the agora, dealings and the ordinary dealings between man and man, or again about agreements with the commencement with artisans; about insult and injury, of the commencement of actions, and the appointment of juries, what would you say? There may also arise questions about any impositions and extractions of market and harbour dues which may be required, and in general about the regulations of markets, police, harbours, and the like. But, oh heavens! Shall we condescend to legislate on any of these particulars?'

'I think', he said, 'that there is no need to impose laws about them on good men; what regulations are necessary they will find out soon enough for themselves.'

'Yes,' I said, 'my friend, if God will only preserve to them the laws which we have given them.'

'And without divine help,' said Adeimantus, 'they will go on for ever making and mending their laws and their lives in the hope of attaining perfection.'

'You would compare them', I said, 'to those invalids who, having no self-restraint, will not leave off their habits of intemperance?'

'Exactly.'

'Yes,' I said; 'and what a delightful life they lead! They are always doctoring and increasing and complicating their disorders, and always fancying that they will be cured by any nostrum which anybody advises them to try.'

'Such cases are very common,' he said, 'with invalids of this sort.'

'Yes,' I replied; 'and the charming thing is that they deem him their worst enemy who tells them the truth, which is simply that, unless they give up eating and drinking and wenching and idling, neither drug nor cautery nor spell nor amulet nor any other remedy will avail.'

'Charming!' he replied. 'I see nothing charming in going into a passion with a man who tells you what is right.'

'These gentlemen', I said, 'do not seem to be in your good graces.'

'Assuredly not.'

'Nor would you praise the behaviour of States which act like the men whom

I was just now describing. For are there not ill-ordered States in which the citizens are forbidden under pain of death to alter the constitution; and yet he who most sweetly courts those who live under this regime and indulges them and fawns upon them and is skilful in anticipating and gratifying their humours is held to be a great and good statesman – do not these States resemble the persons whom I was describing?'

'Yes,' he said; 'the States are as bad as the men; and I am very far from praising them.'

'But do you not admire,' I said, 'the coolness and dexterity of these ready ministers of political corruption?'

'Yes,' he said, 'I do; but not of all of them, for there are some whom the applause of the multitude has deluded into the belief that they are really statesmen, and these are not much to be admired.'

'What do you mean?' I said. 'You should have more feeling for them. When a man cannot measure, and a great many others who cannot measure declare that he is four cubits high, can he help believing what they say?'

'Nay,' he said, 'certainly not in that case.'

'Well, then, do not be angry with them; for are they not as good as a play, trying their hand at paltry reforms such as I was describing; they are always fancying that by legislation they will make an end of frauds in contracts, and the other rascalities which I was mentioning, not knowing that they are in reality cutting off the heads of a hydra?'

'Yes,' he said; 'that is just what they are doing.'

'I conceive', I said, 'that the true legislator will not trouble himself with this class of enactments whether concerning laws or the constitution either in an ill-ordered or in a well-ordered State; for in the former they are quite useless, and in the latter there will be no difficulty in devising them; and many of them will naturally flow out of our previous regulations.'

'What, then,' he said, 'is still remaining to us of the work of legislation?'

'Nothing to us,' I replied; 'but to Apollo, the God of Delphi, there remains the ordering of the greatest and noblest and chiefest things of all.'

'Which are they?' he said.

'The institution of temples and sacrifices, and the entire service of gods, demigods, and heroes; also the ordering of the repositories of the dead, and the rites which have to be observed by him who would propitiate the inhabitants of the world below. These are matters of which we are ignorant ourselves, and as founders of a city we should be unwise in trusting them to any interpreter but our ancestral deity. He is the god who sits in the centre, on the navel of the earth, and he is the interpreter of religion to all mankind.'

'You are right, and we will do as you propose.'

'But where, amid all this, is justice? Son of Ariston, tell me where. Now that our city has been made habitable, light a candle and search, and get your brother and Polemarchus and the rest of our friends to help, and let us see where in it we can discover justice and where injustice, and in what they differ from one another, and which of them the man who would be happy should have for his portion, whether seen or unseen by gods and men.'

'Nonsense,' said Glaucon. 'Did you not promise to search yourself, saying that for you not to help justice in her need would be an impiety?'

'I do not deny that I said so, and as you remind me, I will be as good as my word; but you must join.'

'We will,' he replied.

'Well, then, I hope to make the discovery in this way: I mean to begin with the assumption that our State, if rightly ordered, is perfect.'

'That is most certain.'

'And being perfect, is therefore wise and valiant and temperate and just.'

'That is likewise clear.'

'And whichever of these qualities we find in the State, the one which is not found will be the residue?'

'Very good.'

'If there were four things, and we were searching for one of them, wherever it might be, the one sought for might be known to us from the first, and there would be no further trouble; or we might know the other three first, and then the fourth would clearly be the one left.'

'Very true,' he said.

'And is not a similar method to be pursued about the virtues, which are also four in number?'

'Clearly.'

'First among the virtues found in the State, wisdom comes into view, and in this I detect a certain peculiarity.'

'What is that?'

'The State which we have been describing is said to be wise as being good in counsel?'

'Very true.'

'And good counsel is clearly a kind of knowledge, for not by ignorance, but by knowledge, do men counsel well?'

'Clearly.'

'And the kinds of knowledge in a State are many and diverse?'

'Of course.'

'There is the knowledge of the carpenter; but is that the sort of knowledge which gives a city the title of wise and good in counsel?'

'Certainly not; that would only give a city the reputation of skill in carpentering.'

'Then a city is not to be called wise because possessing a knowledge which counsels for the best about wooden implements?'

'Certainly not.'

'Nor by reason of a knowledge which advises about brazen pots,' I said, 'nor as possessing any other similar knowledge?'

'Not by reason of any of them,' he said.

'Nor yet by reason of a knowledge which cultivates the earth; that would give the city the name of agricultural?'

'Yes.'

'Well,' I said, 'and is there any knowledge in our recently founded State among any of the citizens which advises, not about any particular thing in the State, but about the whole, and considers how a State can best deal with itself and with other States?'

'There certainly is.'

'And what is knowledge, and among whom is it found?' I asked.

'It is the knowledge of the guardians,' he replied, 'and found among those whom we were just now describing as perfect guardians.'

'And what is the name which the city derives from the possession of this sort of knowledge?'

'The name of good in counsel and truly wise.'

'And will there be in our city more of these true guardians or more smiths?'

'The smiths', he replied, 'will be far more numerous.'

'Will not the guardians be the smallest of all the classes who receive a name from the profession of some kind of knowledge?'

'Much the smallest.'

'And so by reason of the smallest part or class, and of the knowledge which resides in this presiding and ruling part of itself, the whole State, being thus constituted according to nature, will be wise; and this, which has the only knowledge worthy to be called wisdom, has been ordained by nature to be of all classes the least.'

'Most true.'

'Thus, then,' I said, 'the nature and place in the State of one of the four virtues has somehow or other been discovered.'

'And, in my humble opinion, very satisfactorily discovered,' he replied.

'Again,' I said, 'there is no difficulty in seeing the nature of courage; and in what part that quality resides which gives the name of courageous to the State.'

'How do you mean?'

'Why,' I said, 'everyone who calls any State courageous or cowardly will be thinking of the part which fights and goes out to war on the State's behalf.'

'No one', he replied, 'would ever think of any other.'

'Certainly not.'

'The rest of the citizens may be courageous or may be cowardly but their courage or cowardice will not, as I conceive, have the effect of making the city either the one or the other.'

'The city will be courageous in virtue of a portion of herself which preserves under all circumstances that opinion about the nature of things to be feared and not to be feared in which our legislator educated them; and this is what you term courage.'

'I should like to hear what you are saying once more, for I do not think that I perfectly understand you.'

'I mean that courage is a kind of salvation.'

'Salvation of what?'

'Of the opinion respecting things to be feared, what they are and of what nature, which the law implants through education; and I mean by the words 'under all circumstances' to intimate that in pleasure or in pain, or under the influence of desire or fear, a man preserves and does not lose this opinion. Shall I give you an illustration?'

'If you please.'

'You know', I said, 'that dyers, when they want to dye wool for making the true sea-purple, begin by selecting their white colour first; this they prepare and dress with much care and pains, in order that the white ground may take the purple hue in full perfection. The dyeing then proceeds; and whatever is dyed in this manner becomes a fast colour, and no washing either with lyes or without them can take away the bloom. But, when the ground has not been duly prepared, you will have noticed how poor is the look either of purple or of any other colour.'

'Yes,' he said; 'I know that they have a washed-out and ridiculous appearance.'

'Then now', I said, 'you will understand what our object was in selecting our soldiers, and educating them in music and gymnastics; we were contriving influences which would prepare them to take the dye of the laws in perfection, and the colour of their opinion about dangers and of every other opinion was to be indelibly fixed by their nurture and training, not to be washed away by such potent lyes as pleasure – mightier agent far in washing the soul than any soda or lye; or by sorrow, fear, and desire, the mightiest of all other solvents. And this sort of universal saving power of true opinion in conformity with law about real and false dangers I call and maintain to be courage, unless you disagree.'

'But I agree,' he replied; 'for I suppose that you mean to exclude mere uninstructed courage, such as that of a wild beast or of a slave – this, in your opinion, is not the courage which the law ordains, and ought to have another name.'

'Most certainly.'

'Then I may infer courage to be such as you describe?'

'Why, yes,' said I, 'you may, and if you add the words "of a citizen", you will not be far wrong – hereafter, if you like, we will carry the examination further, but at present we are seeking not for courage but justice; and for the purpose of our enquiry we have said enough.'

'You are right,' he replied.

'Two virtues remain to be discovered in the State – first temperance, and then justice, which is the end of our search.'

'Very true.'

'Now, can we find justice without troubling ourselves about temperance?'

'I do not know how that can be accomplished,' he said, 'nor do I desire that justice should be brought to light and temperance lost sight of; and therefore I wish that you would do me the favour of considering temperance first.'

'Certainly,' I replied, 'I should not be justified in refusing your request.'

'Then consider,' he said.

'Yes,' I replied; 'I will; and as far as I can at present see, the virtue of temperance has more of the nature of harmony and symphony than the preceding.'

'How so?' he asked.

'Temperance', I replied, 'is the ordering or controlling of certain pleasures and desires; this is curiously enough implied in the saying of "a man being his own master" and other traces of the same notion may be found in language.'

'No doubt,' he said.

'There is something ridiculous in the expression "master of himself"; for the master is also the servant and the servant the master; and in all these modes of speaking the same person is denoted.'

'Certainly.'

'The meaning is, I believe, that in the human soul there is a better and also a worse principle; and when the better has the worse under control, then a man is said to be master of himself; and this is a term of praise: but when, owing to evil education or association, the better principle, which is also the smaller, is overwhelmed by the greater mass of the worse – in this case he is blamed and is called the slave of self and unprincipled.'

'Yes, there is reason in that.'

'And now, I said, look at our newly created State, and there you will find one of these two conditions realised; for the State, as you will acknowledge, may be justly called master of itself, if the words "temperance" and "self-mastery" truly express the rule of the better part over the worse.'

'Yes,' he said, 'I see that what you say is true.'

'Let me further note that the manifold and complex pleasures and desires and pains are generally found in children and women and servants, and in the freemen so called who are of the lowest and more numerous class.'

'Certainly,' he said.

'Whereas the simple and moderate desires which follow reason, and are under the guidance of mind and true opinion, are to be found only in a few, and those the best born and best educated.'

'Very true.'

'These two, as you may perceive, have a place in our State; and the meaner desires of the many are held down by the virtuous desires and wisdom of the few.'

'That I perceive,' he said.

'Then if there be any city which may be described as master of its own pleasures and desires, and master of itself, ours may claim such a designation?'

'Certainly,' he replied.

'It may also be called temperate, and for the same reasons?'

'Yes.'

'And if there be any State in which rulers and subjects will be agreed as to the question who are to rule, that again will be our State?'

'Undoubtedly.'

'And the citizens being thus agreed among themselves, in which class will temperance be found – in the rulers or in the subjects?'

'In both, as I should imagine,' he replied.

'Do you observe that we were not far wrong in our guess that temperance was a sort of harmony?'

'Why so?'

'Why, because temperance is unlike courage and wisdom, each of which resides in a part only, the one making the State wise and the other valiant; not so temperance, which extends to the whole, and runs through all the notes of the scale, and produces a harmony of the weaker and the stronger and the middle class, whether you suppose them to be stronger or weaker in wisdom or power or numbers or wealth, or anything else. Most truly then may we deem temperance to be the agreement of the naturally superior and inferior, as to the right to rule of either, both in states and individuals.'

'I entirely agree with you.'

'And so,' I said, 'we may consider three out of the four virtues to have been discovered in our State. The last of those qualities which make a state virtuous must be justice, if we only knew what that was.'

'The inference is obvious.'

'The time then has arrived, Glaucon, when, like huntsmen, we should surround the cover, and look sharp that justice does not steal away, and pass out of sight and escape us; for beyond a doubt she is somewhere in this country: watch therefore and strive to catch a sight of her, and if you see her first, let me know.'

'Would that I could! But you should regard me rather as a follower who has just eyes enough to see what you show him – that is about as much as I am good for.'

'Offer up a prayer with me and follow.'

'I will, but you must show me the way.'

'Here is no path,' I said, 'and the wood is dark and perplexing; still we must push on.'

'Let us push on.'

'Here I saw something: halloo!' I said, 'I begin to perceive a track, and I believe that the quarry will not escape.'

'Good news,' he said.

'Truly,' I said, 'we are stupid fellows.

'Why so?'

'Why, my good sir, at the beginning of our enquiry, ages ago, there was justice tumbling out at our feet, and we never saw her; nothing could be more ridiculous. Like people who go about looking for what they have in their hands – that was the way with us – we looked not at what we were seeking, but at what was far off in the distance; and therefore, I suppose, we missed her.'

'What do you mean?'

'I mean to say that in reality for a long time past we have been talking of justice, and have failed to recognise her.'

'I grow impatient at the length of your exordium.'

'Well then, tell me,' I said, 'whether I am right or not: You remember the original principle which we were always laying down at the foundation of the State, that one man should practise one thing only, the thing to which his nature was best adapted; now justice is this principle or a part of it.'

'Yes, we often said that one man should do one thing only.'

'Further, we affirmed that justice was doing one's own business, and not being a busybody; we said so again and again, and many others have said the same to us.'

'Yes, we said so.'

'Then to do one's own business in a certain way may be assumed to be justice. Can you tell me whence I derive this inference?'

'I cannot, but I should like to be told.'

'Because I think that this is the only virtue which remains in the State when the other virtues of temperance and courage and wisdom are abstracted; and, that this is the ultimate cause and condition of the existence of all of them, and while remaining in them is also their preservative; and we were saying that if the three were discovered by us, justice would be the fourth or remaining one.'

'That follows of necessity.'

'If we are asked to determine which of these four qualities by its presence contributes most to the excellence of the State, whether the agreement of rulers and subjects, or the preservation in the soldiers of the opinion which the law ordains about the true nature of dangers, or wisdom and watchfulness in the rulers, or whether this other which I am mentioning, and which is found in children and women, slave and freeman, artisan, ruler, subject – the quality, I mean, of everyone doing his own work, and not being a busybody, would claim the palm – the question is not so easily answered.'

'Certainly,' he replied, 'there would be a difficulty in saying which.'

'Then the power of each individual in the State to do his own work appears to compete with the other political virtues, wisdom, temperance, courage.'

'Yes,' he said.

'And the virtue which enters into this competition is justice?'

'Exactly.'

'Let us look at the question from another point of view: are not the rulers in a State those to whom you would entrust the office of determining suits at law?'

'Certainly.'

'And are suits decided on any other ground but that a man may neither take what is another's, nor be deprived of what is his own?'

'Yes; that is their principle.'

'Which is a just principle?'

'Yes.'

'Then on this view also justice will be admitted to be the having and doing what is a man's own, and belongs to him?'

'Very true.'

'Think, now, and say whether you agree with me or not. Suppose a carpenter to be doing the business of a cobbler, or a cobbler of a carpenter; and suppose them to exchange their implements or their duties, or the same person to be doing the work of both, or whatever be the change; do you think that any great harm would result to the State?'

'Not much.'

'But when the cobbler or any other man whom nature designed to be a trader, having his heart lifted up by wealth or strength or the number of his followers, or any like advantage, attempts to force his way into the class of warriors, or a warrior into that of legislators and guardians, for which he is unfitted, and either to take the implements or the duties of the other; or when one man is trader, legislator, and warrior all in one, then I think you will agree with me in saying that this interchange and this meddling of one with another is the ruin of the State.'

'Most true.'

'Seeing then,' I said, 'that there are three distinct classes, any meddling of one with another, or the change of one into another, is the greatest harm to the State, and may be most justly termed evil-doing?'

'Precisely.'

'And the greatest degree of evil-doing to one's own city would be termed by you injustice?'

'Certainly.'

'This, then, is injustice; and on the other hand when the trader, the auxiliary, and the guardian each do their own business, that is justice, and will make the city just.'

'I agree with you.'

'We will not', I said, 'be over-positive as yet; but if, on trial, this conception of justice be verified in the individual as well as in the State, there will be no longer any room for doubt; if it be not verified, we must have a fresh enquiry. First let us complete the old investigation, which we began, as you remember, under the impression that, if we could previously examine justice on the larger scale, there would be less difficulty in discerning her in the individual. That larger example appeared to be the State, and accordingly we constructed as good a one as we could, knowing well that in the good State justice would be found. Let the discovery which we made be now applied to the individual – if they agree, we shall be satisfied; or, if there be a difference in the individual, we will come back to the State and have another trial of the theory. The friction of the two when rubbed together may possibly strike a light in which justice will shine forth, and the vision which is then revealed we will fix in our souls.'

'That will be in regular course; let us do as you say.'

'I proceeded to ask: when two things, a greater and less, are called by the same name, are they like or unlike in so far as they are called the same?'

'Like,' he replied.

'The just man then, if we regard the idea of justice only, will be like the just State?'

'He will.'

'And a State was thought by us to be just when the three classes in the State severally did their own business; and also thought to be temperate and valiant and wise by reason of certain other affections and qualities of these same classes?'

'True,' he said.

'And so of the individual; we may assume that he has the same three principles in his own soul which are found in the State; and he may be rightly described in the same terms, because he is affected in the same manner?'

'Certainly,' he said.

'Once more then, O my friend, we have alighted upon an easy question – whether the soul has these three principles or not?'

'An easy question! Nay, rather, Socrates, the proverb holds that hard is the good.'

'Very true;' I said, 'and I do not think that the method which we are employing is at all adequate to the accurate solution of this question; the true method is another and a longer one. Still we may arrive at a solution not below the level of the previous enquiry.'

'May we not be satisfied with that?' he said. 'Under the circumstances, I am quite content.'

'I too', I replied, 'shall be extremely well satisfied.'

'Then faint not in pursuing the speculation,' he said.

'Must we not acknowledge', I said, 'that in each of us there are the same principles and habits which there are in the State; and that from the individual they pass into the State? – How else can they come there? Take the quality of passion or spirit; it would be ridiculous to imagine that this quality, when found in States, is not derived from the individuals who are supposed to possess it, e.g. the Thracians, Scythians, and in general the northern nations; and the same may be said of the love of knowledge, which is the special characteristic of our part of the world; or of the love of money, which may, with equal truth, be attributed to the Phoenicians and Egyptians.'

'Exactly so,' he said.

'There is no difficulty in understanding this.'

'None whatever.'

'But the question is not quite so easy when we proceed to ask whether these principles are three or one; whether, that is to say, we learn with one part of our nature, are angry with another, and with a third part desire the satisfaction of our natural appetites; or whether the whole soul comes into play in each sort of action – to determine that is the difficulty.'

'Yes,' he said; 'there lies the difficulty.'

'Then let us now try and determine whether they are the same or different.'

'How can we?' he asked.

I replied as follows: 'The same thing clearly cannot act or be acted upon in the same part or in relation to the same thing at the same time, in contrary ways; and therefore whenever this contradiction occurs in things apparently the same, we know that they are really not the same, but different.'

'Good.'

'For example,' I said, 'can the same thing be at rest and in motion at the same time in the same part?'

'Impossible.'

'Still,' I said, 'let us have a more precise statement of terms, lest we should hereafter fall out by the way. Imagine the case of a man who is standing and also moving his hands and his head, and suppose a person to say that one and the same person is in motion and at rest at the same moment – to such a mode of speech we should object, and should rather say that one part of him is in motion while another is at rest.'

'Very true.'

'And suppose the objector to refine still further, and to draw the nice distinction that not only parts of tops, but whole tops, when they spin round with their pegs fixed on the spot, are at rest and in motion at the same time (and he may say the same of anything which revolves in the same spot), his objection would not be admitted by us, because in such cases things are not at rest and in motion in the same parts of themselves; we should rather say that they have both an axis and a circumference, and that the axis stands still, for there is no deviation from the perpendicular; and that the circumference goes round. But if, while revolving, the axis inclines either to the right or left, forwards or backwards, then in no point of view can they be at rest.'

'That is the correct mode of describing them,' he replied.

'Then none of these objections will confuse us, or incline us to believe that the same thing at the same time, in the same part or in relation to the same thing, can act or be acted upon in contrary ways.'

'Certainly not, according to my way of thinking.'

'Yet,' I said, 'that we may not be compelled to examine all such objections, and prove at length that they are untrue, let us assume their absurdity, and go forward on the understanding that hereafter, if this assumption turn out to be untrue, all the consequences which follow shall be withdrawn.'

'Yes,' he said, 'that will be the best way.'

'Well,' I said, 'would you not allow that assent and dissent, desire and aversion, attraction and repulsion, are all of them opposites, whether they are regarded as active or passive (for that makes no difference in the fact of their opposition)?'

'Yes,' he said, 'they are opposites.'

'Well,' I said, 'and hunger and thirst, and the desires in general, and again willing and wishing – all these you would refer to the classes already mentioned. You would say – would you not? – that the soul of him who desires is seeking after the object of his desires; or that he is drawing to himself the thing which he wishes to possess: or again, when a person wants anything to be given him, his mind, longing for the realisation of his desires, intimates his wish to have it by a nod of assent, as if he had been asked a question?'

'Very true.'

'And what would you say of unwillingness and dislike and the absence of desire; should not these be referred to the opposite class of repulsion and rejection?'

'Certainly.'

'Admitting this to be true of desire generally, let us suppose a particular class of desires, and out of these we will select hunger and thirst, as they are termed, which are the most obvious of them?'

'Let us take that class,' he said.

'The object of one is food, and of the other drink?'

'Yes.'

'And here comes the point: is not thirst the desire which the soul has of drink, and of drink only; not of drink qualified by anything else; for example warm or cold, or much or little, or, in a word, drink of any particular sort: but if the thirst be accompanied by heat, then the desire is of cold drink; or, if accompanied by cold, then of warm drink; or, if the thirst be excessive, then the drink which is desired will be excessive; or, if not great, the quantity of drink will also be small: but thirst pure and simple will desire drink pure and simple, which is the natural satisfaction of thirst, as food is of hunger?'

'Yes,' he said; 'the simple desire is, as you say, in every case of the simple object, and the qualified desire of the qualified object.'

'But here a confusion may arise; and I should wish to guard against an opponent starting up and saying that no man desires drink only, but good drink, or food only, but good food; for good is the universal object of desire, and thirst being a desire, will necessarily be thirst after good drink; and the same is true of every other desire.'

'Yes,' he replied, 'the opponent might have something to say.'

'Nevertheless I should still maintain that, of relatives, some have a quality attached to either term of the relation; others are simple and have their correlatives simple.'

'I do not know what you mean.'

'Well, you know of course that the greater is relative to the less?'

'Certainly.'

'And the much greater to the much less?'

'Yes.'

'And the sometime greater to the sometime less, and the greater that is to be to the less that is to be?'

'Certainly,' he said.

'And so of more and less, and of other correlative terms, such as the double and the half, or again, the heavier and the lighter, the swifter and the slower; and of hot and cold, and of any other relatives – is not this true of all of them?'

'Yes.'

'And does not the same principle hold in the sciences? The object of science is knowledge (assuming that to be the true definition), but the object of a particular science is a particular kind of knowledge; I mean, for example, that the science of house-building is a kind of knowledge which is defined and distinguished from other kinds and is therefore termed architecture.'

'Certainly.'

'Because it has a particular quality which no other has?'

'Yes.'

'And it has this particular quality because it has an object of a particular kind; and this is true of the other arts and sciences?'

'Yes.'

'Now, then, if I have made myself clear, you will understand my original meaning in what I said about relatives. My meaning was, that if one term of a relation is taken alone, the other is taken alone; if one term is qualified, the other is also qualified. I do not mean to say that relatives may not be disparate, or that the science of health is healthy, or of disease necessarily diseased, or that the sciences of good and evil are therefore good and evil; but only that, when the term science is no longer used absolutely, but has a qualified object which in this case is the nature of health and disease, it becomes defined, and is hence called not merely science, but the science of medicine.'

'I quite understand, and I think as you do.'

'Would you not say that thirst is one of these essentially relative terms, having clearly a relation –'

'Yes, thirst is relative to drink.'

'And a certain kind of thirst is relative to a certain kind of drink; but thirst taken alone is neither of much nor little, nor of good nor bad, nor of any particular kind of drink, but of drink only?'

'Certainly.'

'Then the soul of the thirsty one, in so far as he is thirsty, desires only drink; for this he yearns and tries to obtain it?'

'That is plain.'

'And if you suppose something which pulls a thirsty soul away from drink, that must be different from the thirsty principle which draws him like a beast to drink; for, as we were saying, the same thing cannot at the same time with the same part of itself act in contrary ways about the same.'

'Impossible.'

'No more than you can say that the hands of the archer push and pull the bow at the same time, but what you say is that one hand pushes and the other pulls.'

'Exactly so,' he replied.

'And might a man be thirsty, and yet unwilling to drink?'

'Yes,' he said, 'it constantly happens.'

'And in such a case what is one to say? Would you not say that there was something in the soul bidding a man to drink, and something else forbidding him, which is other and stronger than the principle which bids him?'

'I should say so.'

'And the forbidding principle is derived from reason, and that which bids and attracts proceeds from passion and disease?'

'Clearly.'

'Then we may fairly assume that they are two, and that they differ from one another; the one with which man reasons, we may call the rational principle of the soul, the other, with which he loves and hungers and thirsts and feels the flutterings of any other desire, may be termed the irrational or appetitive, the ally of sundry pleasures and satisfactions?'

'Yes,' he said, 'we may fairly assume them to be different.'

'Then let us finally determine that there are two principles existing in the soul. And what of passion, or spirit? Is it a third, or akin to one of the preceding?'

'I should be inclined to say – akin to desire.'

'Well,' I said, 'there is a story which I remember to have heard, and in which I put faith. The story is that Leontius, the son of Aglaion, coming up one day from the Piraeus, under the north wall on the outside, observed some dead bodies lying on the ground at the place of execution. He felt a desire to see them, and also a dread and abhorrence of them; for a time he struggled and covered his eyes, but at length the desire got the better of him; and forcing them open, he ran up to the dead bodies, saying, "Look, ye wretches, take your fill of the fair sight."'

'I have heard the story myself,' he said.

'The moral of the tale is that anger at times goes to war with desire, as though they were two distinct things.'

'Yes; that is the meaning,' he said.

'And are there not many other cases in which we observe that when a man's desires violently prevail over his reason, he reviles himself, and is angry at the violence within him, and that in this struggle, which is like the struggle of factions in a State, his spirit is on the side of his reason – but for the passionate or spirited element to take part with the desires when reason decides that she should not be opposed is a sort of thing which I believe that you never observed occurring in yourself, nor, as I should imagine, in anyone else?'

'Certainly not.'

'Suppose that a man thinks he has done a wrong to another, the nobler he is, the less able is he to feel indignant at any suffering, such as hunger, or cold, or any other pain which the injured person may inflict upon him – these he deems to be just, and, as I say, his anger refuses to be excited by them.'

'True,' he said.

'But when he thinks that he is the sufferer of the wrong, then he boils and chafes, and is on the side of what he believes to be justice; and because he suffers hunger or cold or other pain he is only the more determined to persevere and conquer. His noble spirit will not be quelled until he either slays or is slain; or until he hears the voice of the shepherd, that is, reason, bidding his dog bark no more.'

'The illustration is perfect,' he replied; 'and in our State, as we were saying, the auxiliaries were to be dogs, and to hear the voice of the rulers, who are their shepherds.'

'I perceive,' I said, 'that you quite understand me; there is, however, a further point which I wish you to consider.'

'What point?'

'You remember that passion or spirit appeared at first sight to be a kind of desire, but now we should say quite the contrary; for in the conflict of the soul spirit is arrayed on the side of the rational principle.'

'Most assuredly.'

'But a further question arises: is passion different from reason also, or only a kind of reason; in which latter case, instead of three principles in the soul, there will only be two, the rational and the concupiscent; or rather, as the State was composed of three classes, traders, auxiliaries, counsellors, so may there not be in the individual soul a third element which is passion or spirit, and when not corrupted by bad education is the natural auxiliary of reason?'

'Yes,' he said, 'there must be a third.'

'Yes,' I replied, 'if passion, which has already been shown to be different from desire, turns out also to be different from reason.'

'But that is easily proved: we may observe even in young children that they are full of spirit almost as soon as they are born, whereas some of them never seem to attain to the use of reason, and most of them late enough.'

'Excellent,' I said, 'and you may see passion equally in brute animals, which is a further proof of the truth of what you are saying. And we may once more appeal to the words of Homer, which have been already quoted by us,

"He smote his breast, and thus rebuked his soul,"

for in this verse Homer has clearly supposed the power which reasons about the better and worse to be different from the unreasoning anger which is rebuked by it.'

'Very true,' he said.

'And so, after much tossing, we have reached land, and are fairly agreed that the same principles which exist in the State exist also in the individual, and that they are three in number.'

'Exactly.'

'Must we not then infer that the individual is wise in the same way, and in virtue of the same quality which makes the State wise?'

'Certainly.'

'Also that the same quality which constitutes courage in the State constitutes courage in the individual, and that both the State and the individual bear the same relation to all the other virtues?'

'Assuredly.'

'And the individual will be acknowledged by us to be just in the same way in which the State is just?'

'That follows, of course.'

'We cannot but remember that the justice of the State consisted in each of the three classes doing the work of its own class?'

'We are not very likely to have forgotten,' he said.

'We must recollect that the individual in whom the several qualities of his nature do their own work will be just, and will do his own work?'

'Yes,' he said, 'we must remember that too.'

'And ought not the rational principle, which is wise, and has the care of the whole soul, to rule, and the passionate or spirited principle to be the subject and ally?'

'Certainly.'

'And, as we were saying, the united influence of music and gymnastics will bring them into accord, nerving and sustaining the reason with noble words and lessons, and moderating and soothing and civilising the wildness of passion by harmony and rhythm?'

'Quite true,' he said.

'And these two, thus nurtured and educated, and having learned truly to know their own functions, will rule over the concupiscent, which in each of us is the largest part of the soul and by nature most insatiable of gain; over this they will keep guard, lest, waxing great and strong with the fulness of bodily pleasures, as they are termed, the concupiscent soul, no longer confined to her own sphere, should attempt to enslave and rule those who are not her natural-born subjects, and overturn the whole life of man?'

'Very true,' he said.

'Both together will they not be the best defenders of the whole soul and the whole body against attacks from without; the one counselling, and the other fighting under his leader, and courageously executing his commands and counsels?'

'True.'

'And he is to be deemed courageous whose spirit retains in pleasure and in pain the commands of reason about what he ought or ought not to fear?'

'Right,' he replied.

'And him we call wise who has in him that little part which rules, and which proclaims these commands; that part too being supposed to have a knowledge of what is for the interest of each of the three parts and of the whole?'

'Assuredly.'

'And would you not say that he is temperate who has these same elements in friendly harmony, in whom the one ruling principle of reason, and the two subject ones of spirit and desire are equally agreed that reason ought to rule, and do not rebel?'

'Certainly,' he said, 'that is the true account of temperance, whether in the State or individual.'

'And surely,' I said, 'we have explained again and again how and by virtue of what quality a man will be just.'

'That is very certain.'

'And is justice dimmer in the individual, and is her form different, or is she the same which we found her to be in the State?'

'There is no difference in my opinion,' he said.

'Because, if any doubt is still lingering in our minds, a few commonplace instances will satisfy us of the truth of what I am saying.'

'What sort of instances do you mean?'

'If the case is put to us, must we not admit that the just State, or the man who is trained in the principles of such a State, will be less likely than the unjust to make away with a deposit of gold or silver? Would anyone deny this?'

'No one,' he replied.

'Will the just man or citizen ever be guilty of sacrilege or theft, or treachery either to his friends or to his country?'

'Never.'

'Neither will he ever break faith where there have been oaths or agreements?'

'Impossible.'

'No one will be less likely to commit adultery, or to dishonour his father and mother, or to fall in his religious duties?

'No one.'

'And the reason is that each part of him is doing its own business, whether in ruling or being ruled?'

'Exactly so.'

'Are you satisfied, then, that the quality which makes such men and such states is justice, or do you hope to discover some other?'

'Not I, indeed.'

'Then our dream has been realised; and the suspicion which we entertained at the beginning of our work of construction, that some divine power must have conducted us to a primary form of justice, has now been verified?'

'Yes, certainly.'

'And the division of labour which required the carpenter and the shoemaker and the rest of the citizens to be doing each his own business, and not another's, was a shadow of justice, and for that reason it was of use?'

'Clearly.'

'But in reality justice was such as we were describing, being concerned however, not with the outward man, but with the inward, which is the true self and concernment of man: for the just man does not permit the several elements within him to interfere with one another, or any of them to do the work of others

– he sets in order his own inner life, and is his own master and his own law, and at peace with himself; and when he has bound together the three principles within him, which may be compared to the higher, lower, and middle notes of the scale, and the intermediate intervals – when he has bound all these together, and is no longer many, but has become one entirely temperate and perfectly adjusted nature, then he proceeds to act, if he has to act, whether in a matter of property, or in the treatment of the body, or in some affair of politics or private business; always thinking and calling that which preserves and co-operates with this harmonious condition, just and good action, and the knowledge which presides over it, wisdom, and that which at any time impairs this condition, he will call unjust action, and the opinion which presides over it ignorance.'

'You have said the exact truth, Socrates.'

'Very good; and if we were to affirm that we had discovered the just man and the just State, and the nature of justice in each of them, we should not be telling a falsehood?'

'Most certainly not.'

'May we say so, then?'

'Let us say so.'

'And now,' I said, 'injustice has to be considered.'

'Clearly.'

'Must not injustice be a strife which arises among the three principles – a meddlesomeness, and interference, and rising up of a part of the soul against the whole, an assertion of unlawful authority, which is made by a rebellious subject against a true prince, of whom he is the natural vassal – what is all this confusion and delusion but injustice, and intemperance and cowardice and ignorance, and every form of vice?'

'Exactly so.'

'And if the nature of justice and injustice be known, then the meaning of acting unjustly and being unjust, or, again, of acting justly, will also be perfectly clear?'

'What do you mean?' he said.

'Why,' I said, 'they are like disease and health; being in the soul just what disease and health are in the body.'

'How so?' he said.

'Why,' I said, 'that which is healthy causes health, and that which is unhealthy causes disease.'

'Yes.'

'And just actions cause justice, and unjust actions cause injustice?'

'That is certain.'

'And the creation of health is the institution of a natural order and government of one by another in the parts of the body; and the creation of disease is the production of a state of things at variance with this natural order?'

'True.'

'And is not the creation of justice the institution of a natural order and government of one by another in the parts of the soul, and the creation of injustice the production of a state of things at variance with the natural order?'

'Exactly so,' he said.

'Then virtue is the health and beauty and wellbeing of the soul, and vice the disease and weakness and deformity of the same?'

'True.'

'And do not good practices lead to virtue, and evil practices to vice?'

'Assuredly.'

'Still our old question of the comparative advantage of justice and injustice has not been answered: which is the more profitable, to be just and act justly and practise virtue, whether seen or unseen of gods and men, or to be unjust and act unjustly, if only unpunished and unreformed?'

'In my judgment, Socrates, the question has now become ridiculous. We know that, when the bodily constitution is gone, life is no longer endurable, though pampered with all kinds of meats and drinks, and having all wealth and all power; and shall we be told that when the very essence of the vital principle is undermined and corrupted, life is still worth having to a man, if only he be allowed to do whatever he likes with the single exception that he is not to acquire justice and virtue, or to escape from injustice and vice; assuming them both to be such as we have described?'

'Yes,' I said, 'the question is, as you say, ridiculous. Still, as we are near the spot at which we may see the truth in the clearest manner with our own eyes, let us not faint by the way.'

'Certainly not,' he replied.

'Come up hither,' I said, 'and behold the various forms of vice, those of them, I mean, which are worth looking at.'

'I am following you,' he replied: 'proceed.'

I said, 'The argument seems to have reached a height from which, as from some tower of speculation, a man may look down and see that virtue is one, but that the forms of vice are innumerable; there being four special ones which are deserving of note.'

'What do you mean?' he said.

'I mean,' I replied, 'that there appear to be as many forms of the soul as there are distinct forms of the State.'

'How many?'

'There are five of the State, and five of the soul,' I said.

'What are they?

'The first', I said, 'is that which we have been describing, and which may be said to have two names, monarchy and aristocracy, accordingly as rule is exercised by one distinguished man or by many.'

'True,' he replied.

'But I regard the two names as describing one form only; for whether the government is in the hands of one or many, if the governors have been trained in the manner which we have supposed, the fundamental laws of the State will be maintained.'

'That is true,' he replied.

Book V

'Such is the good and true City or State, and the good and man is of the same pattern; and if this is right every other is wrong; and the evil is one which affects not only the ordering of the State, but also the regulation of the individual soul, and is exhibited in four forms.'

'What are they?' he said.

I was proceeding to tell the order in which the four evil forms appeared to me to succeed one another, when Polemarchus, who was sitting a little way off, just beyond Adeimantus, began to whisper to him: stretching forth his hand, he took hold of the upper part of his coat by the shoulder, and drew him towards him, leaning forward himself so as to be quite close and saying something in his ear, of which I only caught the words, 'Shall we let him off, or what shall we do?'

'Certainly not,' said Adeimantus, raising his voice.

'Who is it,' I said, 'whom you are refusing to let off?'

'You,' he said.

I repeated, 'Why am I especially not to be let off?'

'Why,' he said, 'we think that you are lazy, and mean to cheat us out of a whole chapter which is a very important part of the story; and you fancy that we shall not notice your airy way of proceeding; as if it were self-evident to everybody, that in the matter of women and children "friends have all things in common".'

'And was I not right, Adeimantus?'

'Yes,' he said; 'but what is right in this particular case, like everything else, requires to be explained; for community may be of many kinds. Please, therefore, to say what sort of community you mean. We have been long expecting that you would tell us something about the family life of your citizens – how they will bring children into the world, and rear them when they have arrived, and, in general, what is the nature of this community of women and children – for we are of opinion that the right or wrong management of such matters will have a great and paramount influence on the State for good or for evil. And now, since the question is still undetermined, and you are taking in hand another State, we have resolved, as you heard, not to let you go until you give an account of all this.'

'To that resolution', said Glaucon, 'you may regard me as saying Agreed.'

'And without more ado,' said Thrasymachus, 'you may consider us all to be equally agreed.'

I said, 'You know not what you are doing in thus assailing me. What an argument are you raising about the State! Just as I thought that I had finished, and was only too glad that I had laid this question to sleep, and was reflecting how fortunate I was in your acceptance of what I then said, you ask me to begin again at the very foundation, ignorant of what a hornet's nest of words you are stirring. Now I foresaw this gathering trouble, and avoided it.'

'For what purpose do you conceive that we have come here,' said Thrasymachus, '– to look for gold, or to hear discourse?'

'Yes, but discourse should have a limit.'

'Yes, Socrates,' said Glaucon, 'and the whole of life is the only limit which wise men assign to the hearing of such discourses. But never mind about us; take heart yourself and answer the question in your own way: what sort of community of women and children is this which is to prevail among our guardians? And how shall we manage the period between birth and education, which seems to require the greatest care? Tell us how these things will be.'

'Yes, my simple friend, but the answer is the reverse of easy; many more doubts arise about this than about our previous conclusions. For the practicability of what is said may be doubted; and looked at in another point of view, whether the scheme, if ever so practicable, would be for the best, is also doubtful. Hence I feel a reluctance to approach the subject, lest our aspiration, my dear friend, should turn out to be a dream only.'

'Fear not,' he replied, 'for your audience will not be hard upon you; they are not sceptical or hostile.'

I said: 'My good friend, I suppose that you mean to encourage me by these words.'

'Yes,' he said.

'Then let me tell you that you are doing just the reverse; the encouragement which you offer would have been all very well had I myself believed that I knew what I was talking about: to declare the truth about matters of high interest which a man honours and loves among wise men who love him need occasion no fear or faltering in his mind; but to carry on an argument when you are yourself only a hesitating enquirer, which is my condition, is a dangerous and slippery thing; and the danger is not that I shall be laughed at (of which the fear would be childish), but that I shall miss the truth where I have most need to be sure of my footing, and drag my friends after me in my fall. And I pray Nemesis not to visit upon me the words which I am going to utter. For I do indeed believe that to be an involuntary homicide is a less crime than to be a deceiver about beauty or goodness or justice in the matter of laws. And that is a risk which I would rather run among enemies than among friends, and therefore you do well to encourage me.'

Glaucon laughed and said: 'Well then, Socrates, in case you and your argument do us any serious injury you shall be acquitted beforehand of the homicide and shall not be held to be a deceiver; take courage then and speak.'

'Well,' I said, 'the law says that when a man is acquitted he is free from guilt, and what holds at law may hold in argument.'

'Then why should you mind?'

'Well,' I replied, 'I suppose that I must retrace my steps and say what I perhaps ought to have said before in the proper place. The part of the men has been played out, and now properly enough comes the turn of the women. Of them I will proceed to speak, and the more readily since I am invited by you.'

'For men born and educated like our citizens, the only way, in my opinion, of arriving at a right conclusion about the possession and use of women and children is to follow the path on which we originally started, when we said that the men were to be the guardians and watchdogs of the herd.'

'True.'

'Let us further suppose the birth and education of our women to be subject to similar or nearly similar regulations; then we shall see whether the result accords with our design.'

'What do you mean?'

'What I mean may be put into the form of a question,' I said: 'Are dogs divided into hes and shes, or do they both share equally in hunting and in keeping watch and in the other duties of dogs? Or do we entrust to the males the entire and exclusive care of the flocks, while we leave the females at home, under the idea that the bearing and suckling their puppies is labour enough for them?'

'No,' he said, 'they share alike; the only difference between them is that the males are stronger and the females weaker.'

'But can you use different animals for the same purpose, unless they are bred and fed in the same way?'

'You cannot.'

'Then, if women are to have the same duties as men, they must have the same nurture and education?'

'Yes.'

'The education which was assigned to the men was music and gymnastics.'

'Yes.'

'Then women must be taught music and gymnastics and also the art of war, which they must practise like the men?'

'That is the inference, I suppose.'

'I should rather expect,' I said, 'that several of our proposals, if they are carried out, being unusual, may appear ridiculous.'

'No doubt of it.'

'Yes, and the most ridiculous thing of all will be the sight of women naked in the palaestra, exercising with the men, especially when they are no longer young; they certainly will not be a vision of beauty, any more than the enthusiastic old men who, in spite of wrinkles and ugliness, continue to frequent the gymnasia.'

'Yes, indeed,' he said: 'according to present notions the proposal would be thought ridiculous.'

'But then,' I said, 'as we have determined to speak our minds, we must not fear the jests of the wits which will be directed against this sort of innovation; how they will talk of women's attainments both in music and gymnastics, and above all about their wearing armour and riding upon horseback!'

'Very true,' he replied.

'Yet having begun we must go forward to the rough places of the law; at the same time begging of these gentlemen for once in their life to be serious. Not long ago, as we shall remind them, the Hellenes were of the opinion, which is still generally received among the barbarians, that the sight of a naked man was ridiculous and improper; and when first the Cretans and then the Lacedaemonians introduced the custom, the wits of that day might equally have ridiculed the innovation.'

'No doubt.'

'But when experience showed that to let all things be uncovered was far better than to cover them up, and the ludicrous effect to the outward eye vanished before the better principle which reason asserted, then the man was perceived to be a fool who directs the shafts of his ridicule at any other sight but that of folly and vice, or seriously inclines to weigh the beautiful by any other standard but that of the good.'

'Very true,' he replied.

'First, then, whether the question is to be put in jest or in earnest, let us come to an understanding about the nature of woman: is she capable of sharing either wholly or partially in the actions of men, or not at all? And is the art of war one of those arts in which she can or can not share? That will be the best way of commencing the enquiry, and will probably lead to the fairest conclusion.'

'That will be much the best way.'

'Shall we take the other side first and begin by arguing against ourselves; in this manner the adversary's position will not be undefended.'

'Why not?' he said.

'Then let us put a speech into the mouths of our opponents. They will say: "Socrates and Glaucon, no adversary need convict you, for you yourselves, at the first foundation of the State, admitted the principle that everybody was to do the one work suited to his own nature." And certainly, if I am not mistaken, such an admission was made by us. "And do not the natures of men and women differ very much indeed?" And we shall reply: "Of course they do." Then we shall be asked whether the tasks assigned to men and to women should not be different, and such as are agreeable to their different natures. "Certainly they should." "But if so, have you not fallen into a serious inconsistency in saying that men and women, whose natures are so entirely different, ought to perform the same actions?" – What defence will you make for us, my good sir, against anyone who offers these objections?'

'That is not an easy question to answer when asked suddenly; and I shall and I do beg of you to draw out the case on our side.'

'These are the objections, Glaucon, and there are many others of a like kind, which I foresaw long ago; they made me afraid and reluctant to take in hand any law about the possession and nurture of women and children.'

'By Zeus,' he said, 'the problem to be solved is anything but easy.'

'Why yes,' I said, 'but the fact is that when a man is out of his depth, whether he has fallen into a little swimming bath or into mid-ocean, he has to swim all the same.'

'Very true.'

'And must not we swim and try to reach the shore: we will hope that Arion's dolphin or some other miraculous help may save us?'

'I suppose so,' he said.

'Well then, let us see if any way of escape can be found. We acknowledged – did we not? – that different natures ought to have different pursuits, and that men's and women's natures are different. And now what are we saying? That different natures ought to have the same pursuits – this is the inconsistency which is charged upon us.'

'Precisely.'

'Verily, Glaucon,' I said, 'glorious is the power of the art of contradiction!'

'Why do you say so?'

'Because I think that many a man falls into the practice against his will. When he thinks that he is reasoning he is really disputing, just because he cannot define and divide, and so know that of which he is speaking; and he will pursue a merely verbal opposition in the spirit of contention and not of fair discussion.'

'Yes,' he replied, 'such is very often the case; but what has that to do with us and our argument?'

'A great deal; for there is certainly a danger of our getting unintentionally into a verbal opposition.

'In what way?'

'Why, we valiantly and pugnaciously insist upon the verbal truth, that different natures ought to have different pursuits, but we never considered at all what was the meaning of sameness or difference of nature, or why we distinguished them when we assigned different pursuits to different natures and the same to the same natures.'

'Why, no,' he said, 'that was never considered by us.'

I said: 'Suppose that by way of illustration we were to ask the question whether there is not an opposition in nature between bald men and hairy men; and if this is admitted by us, then, if bald men are cobblers, we should forbid the hairy men to be cobblers, and conversely.'

'That would be a jest,' he said.

'Yes,' I said, 'a jest; and why? Because we never meant when we constructed the State, that the opposition of natures should extend to every difference, but only to those differences which affected the pursuit in which the individual is engaged; we should have argued, for example, that a physician and one who is in mind a physician may be said to have the same nature.'

'True.'

'Whereas the physician and the carpenter have different natures?'

'Certainly.'

'And if', I said, 'the male and female sex appear to differ in their fitness for any art or pursuit, we should say that such pursuit or art ought to be assigned to one or the other of them; but if the difference consists only in women bearing and men begetting children, this does not amount to a proof that a woman differs from a man in respect of the sort of education she should receive; and we shall therefore continue to maintain that our guardians and their wives ought to have the same pursuits.'

'Very true,' he said.

'Next, we shall ask our opponent how, in reference to any of the pursuits or arts of civic life, the nature of a woman differs from that of a man?'

'That will be quite fair.'

'And perhaps he, like yourself, will reply that to give a sufficient answer on the instant is not easy; but after a little reflection there is no difficulty.'

'Yes, perhaps. '

'Suppose then that we invite him to accompany us in the argument, and then we may hope to show him that there is nothing peculiar in the constitution of women which would affect them in the administration of the State.'

'By all means.'

'Let us say to him: "Come now, and we will ask you a question: when you spoke of a nature gifted or not gifted in any respect, did you mean to say that one man will acquire a thing easily, another with difficulty; a little learning will lead the one to discover a great deal; whereas the other, after much study and application, no sooner learns than he forgets; or again, did you mean that the one has a body which is a good servant to his mind, while the body of the other is a hindrance to him? Would not these be the sort of differences which distinguish the man gifted by nature from the one who is ungifted?"'

'No one will deny that.'

'And can you mention any pursuit of mankind in which the male sex has not all these gifts and qualities in a higher degree than the female? Need I waste time in speaking of the art of weaving, and the management of pancakes and preserves, in which womankind does really appear to be great, and in which for her to be beaten by a man is of all things the most absurd?'

'You are quite right', he replied, 'in maintaining the general inferiority of the female sex: although many women are in many things superior to many men, yet on the whole what you say is true.'

'And if so, my friend,' I said, 'there is no special faculty of administration in a state which a woman has because she is a woman, or which a man has by virtue of his sex, but the gifts of nature are alike diffused in both; all the pursuits of men are the pursuits of women also, but in all of them a woman is inferior to a man.'

'Very true.'

'Then are we to impose all our enactments on men and none of them on women?'

'That will never do.'

'One woman has a gift of healing, another not; one is a musician, and another has no music in her nature?'

'Very true.'

'And one woman has a turn for gymnastic and military exercises, and another is unwarlike and hates gymnastics?'

'Certainly.'

'And one woman is a philosopher, and another is an enemy of philosophy; one has spirit, and another is without spirit?'

'That is also true.'

'Then one woman will have the temper of a guardian, and another not. Was not the selection of the male guardians determined by differences of this sort?'

'Yes.'

'Men and women alike possess the qualities which make a guardian; they differ only in their comparative strength or weakness.'

'Obviously.'

'And those women who have such qualities are to be selected as the companions and colleagues of men who have similar qualities and whom they resemble in capacity and in character?'

'Very true.'

'And ought not the same natures to have the same pursuits?'

'They ought.'

'Then, as we were saying before, there is nothing unnatural in assigning music and gymnastics to the wives of the guardians – to that point we come round again.'

'Certainly not.'

'The law which we then enacted was agreeable to nature, and therefore not an impossibility or mere aspiration; and the contrary practice, which prevails at present, is in reality a violation of nature.'

'That appears to be true.'

'We had to consider, first, whether our proposals were possible, and secondly whether they were the most beneficial?'

'Yes.'

'And the possibility has been acknowledged?'

'Yes.'

'The very great benefit has next to be established?'

'Quite so.'

'You will admit that the same education which makes a man a good guardian will make a woman a good guardian; for their original nature is the same?'

'Yes.'

'I should like to ask you a question.'

'What is it?'

'Would you say that all men are equal in excellence, or is one man better than another?'

'The latter.'

'And in the commonwealth which we were founding do you conceive the guardians who have been brought up on our model system to be more perfect men, or the cobblers whose education has been cobbling?'

'What a ridiculous question!'

'You have answered me,' I replied. 'Well, and may we not further say that our guardians are the best of our citizens?'

'By far the best.'

'And will not their wives be the best women?'

'Yes, by far the best.'

'And can there be anything better for the interests of the State than that the men and women of a State should be as good as possible?'

'There can be nothing better.'

'And this is what the arts of music and gymnastic, when present in such manner as we have described, will accomplish?'

'Certainly.'

'Then we have made an enactment not only possible but in the highest degree beneficial to the State?'

'True.'

'Then let the wives of our guardians strip, for their virtue will be their robe, and let them share in the toils of war and the defence of their country; only in the distribution of labours the lighter are to be assigned to the women, who are the weaker natures, but in other respects their duties are to be the same. And as for the man who laughs at naked women exercising their bodies from the best of motives, in his laughter he is plucking

"A fruit of unripe wisdom,"

and he himself is ignorant of what he is laughing at, or what he is about – for that is, and ever will be, the best of sayings, that the useful is the noble and the hurtful is the base.'

'Very true.'

'Here, then, is one difficulty in our law about women, which we may say that we have now escaped; the wave has not swallowed us up alive for enacting that the guardians of either sex should have all their pursuits in common; to the utility and also to the possibility of this arrangement the consistency of the argument with itself bears witness.'

'Yes, that was a mighty wave which you have escaped.'

'Yes,' I said, 'but a greater is coming; you will of this when you see the next.'

'Go on; let me see.'

'The law,' I said, 'which is the sequel of this and of all that has preceded, is to the following effect – that the wives of our guardians are to be common, and their children are to be common, and no parent is to know his own child, nor any child his parent.'

'Yes,' he said, 'that is a much greater wave than the other; and the possibility as well as the utility of such a law is far more questionable.'

'I do not think', I said, 'that there can be any dispute about the very great utility of having wives and children in common; the possibility is quite another matter, and will be very much disputed.'

'I think that a good many doubts may be raised about both.'

'You imply that the two questions must be combined,' I replied. 'Now I meant that you should admit the utility; and in this way, as I thought, I should escape from one of them, and then there would remain only the possibility.'

'But that little attempt is detected, and therefore you will please to give a defence of both.'

'Well,' I said, 'I submit to my fate. Yet grant me a little favour: let me feast my mind with the dream as daydreamers are in the habit of feasting themselves when they are walking alone; for before they have discovered any means of effecting their wishes – that is a matter which never troubles them – they would rather not tire themselves by thinking about possibilities; but assuming that what they desire is already granted to them, they proceed with their plan, and delight in detailing what they mean to do when their wish has come true – that is a way which they have of not doing much good to a capacity which was never good for much. Now I myself am beginning to lose heart, and I should like, with your permission, to pass over the question of possibility at present. Assuming therefore the possibility of the proposal, I shall now proceed to enquire how the rulers will carry out these arrangements, and I shall demonstrate that our plan, if executed, will be of the greatest benefit to the State and to the guardians. First of all, then, if you have no objection, I will endeavour with your help to consider the advantages of the measure; and hereafter the question of possibility.'

'I have no objection; proceed.'

'First, I think that if our rulers and their auxiliaries are to be worthy of the name which they bear, there must be willingness to obey in the one and the power of command in the other; the guardians must themselves obey the laws, and they must also imitate the spirit of them in any details which are entrusted to their care.'

'That is right,' he said.

'You,' I said, 'who are their legislator, having selected the men, will now select the women and give them to them – they must be as far as possible of like natures with them; and they must live in common houses and meet at common meals. None of them will have anything specially his or her own; they will be together, and will be brought up together, and will associate at gymnastic exercises. And so they will be drawn by a necessity of their natures to have intercourse with each other – necessity is not too strong a word, I think?'

'Yes,' he said; 'necessity, not geometrical, but another sort of necessity which lovers know, and which is far more convincing and constraining to the mass of mankind.'

'True,' I said; 'and this, Glaucon, like all the rest, must proceed after an orderly fashion; in a city of the blessed, licentiousness is an unholy thing which the rulers will forbid.'

'Yes,' he said, 'and it ought not to be permitted.'

'Then clearly the next thing will be to make matrimony sacred in the highest degree, and what is most beneficial will be deemed sacred?'

'Exactly.'

'And how can marriages be made most beneficial? That is a question which I put to you, because I see in your house dogs for hunting, and of the nobler sort of birds not a few. Now, I beseech you, do tell me, have you ever attended to their pairing and breeding?'

'In what particulars?'

'Why, in the first place, although they are all of a good sort, are not some better than others?'

'True.'

'And do you breed from them all indifferently, or do you take care to breed from the best only?'

'From the best.'

'And do you take the oldest or the youngest, or only those of ripe age?'

'I choose only those of ripe age.'

'And if care was not taken in the breeding, your dogs and birds would greatly deteriorate?'

'Certainly.'

'And the same of horses and animals in general?'

'Undoubtedly.'

'Good heavens! My dear friend,' I said, 'what consummate skill will our rulers need if the same principle holds of the human species!'

'Certainly, the same principle holds; but why does this involve any particular skill?'

'Because', I said, 'our rulers will often have to practise upon the body corporate with medicines. Now you know that when patients do not require medicines, but have only to be put under a regimen, the inferior sort of practitioner is deemed to be good enough; but when medicine has to be given, then the doctor should be more of a man.'

'That is quite true,' he said; 'but to what are you alluding?'

'I mean', I replied, 'that our rulers will find a considerable dose of falsehood and deceit necessary for the good of their subjects: we were saying that the use of all these things regarded as medicines might be of advantage.'

'And we were very right.'

'And this lawful use of them seems likely to be often needed in the regulations of marriages and births.'

'How so?'

'Why,' I said, 'the principle has been already laid down that the best of either sex should be united with the best as often, and the inferior with the inferior, as seldom as possible; and that they should rear the offspring of the one sort of union, but not of the other, if the flock is to be maintained in first-rate condition. Now these goings on must be a secret which the rulers only know, or there will be a further danger of our herd, as the guardians may be termed, breaking out into rebellion.'

'Very true.'

'Had we not better appoint certain festivals at which we will bring together the brides and bridegrooms, and sacrifices will be offered and suitable hymeneal songs composed by our poets: the number of weddings is a matter which must be left to the discretion of the rulers, whose aim will be to preserve the average of population? There are many other things which they will have to consider, such as the effects of wars and diseases and any similar agencies, in order as far as this is possible to prevent the State from becoming either too large or too small.'

'Certainly,' he replied.

'We shall have to invent some ingenious kind of lots which the less worthy may draw on each occasion of our bringing them together, and then they will accuse their own ill-luck and not the rulers.'

'To be sure,' he said.

'And I think that our braver and better youth, besides their other honours and rewards, might have greater facilities of intercourse with women given them; their bravery will be a reason, and such fathers ought to have as many sons as possible.'

'True.'

'And the proper officers, whether male or female or both, for offices are to be held by women as well as by men –'

'Yes –'

'The proper officers will take the offspring of the good parents to the pen or fold, and there they will deposit them with certain nurses who dwell in a separate quarter; but the offspring of the inferior, or of the better when they chance to be deformed, will be put away in some mysterious, unknown place, as they should be.'

'Yes,' he said, 'that must be done if the breed of the guardians is to be kept pure.'

'They will provide for their nurture, and will bring the mothers to the fold when they are full of milk, taking the greatest possible care that no mother recognises her own child; and other wet-nurses may be engaged if more are required. Care will also be taken that the process of suckling shall not be protracted too long; and the mothers will have no getting up at night or other trouble, but will hand over all this sort of thing to the nurses and attendants.'

'You suppose the wives of our guardians to have a fine easy time of it when they are having children.'

'Why,' said I, 'and so they ought. Let us, however, proceed with our scheme. We were saying that the parents should be in the prime of life?'

'Very true.'

'And what is the prime of life? May it not be defined as a period of about twenty years in a woman's life, and thirty in a man's?'

'Which years do you mean to include?'

'A woman', I said, 'at twenty years of age may begin to bear children to the State, and continue to bear them until forty; a man may begin at five-and-twenty, when he has passed the point at which the pulse of life beats quickest, and continue to beget children until he be fifty-five.'

'Certainly,' he said, 'both in men and women those years are the prime of physical as well as of intellectual vigour.'

'Anyone above or below the prescribed ages who takes part in the public hymeneals shall be said to have done an unholy and unrighteous thing; the child of which he is the father, if it steals into life, will have been conceived under auspices very unlike the sacrifices and prayers, which at each hymeneal priestesses and priest and the whole city will offer, that the new generation may be better and more useful than their good and useful parents, whereas his child will be the offspring of darkness and strange lust.'

'Very true,' he replied.

'And the same law will apply to anyone of those within the prescribed age who forms a connection with any woman in the prime of life without the sanction of the rulers; for we shall say that he is raising up a bastard to the State, uncertified and unconsecrated.'

'Very true,' he replied.

'This applies, however, only to those who are within the specified age: after that we allow them to range at will, except that a man may not marry his daughter or his daughter's daughter, or his mother or his mother's mother; and women, on the other hand, are prohibited from marrying their sons or fathers, or son's son or father's father, and so on in either direction. And we grant all this, accompanying the permission with strict orders to prevent any embryo which may come into being from seeing the light; and if any force a way to the birth, the parents must understand that the offspring of such an union cannot be maintained, and arrange accordingly.'

'That also', he said, 'is a reasonable proposition. But how will they know who are fathers and daughters, and so on?'

'They will never know. The way will be this: dating from the day of the hymeneal, the bridegroom who was then married will call all the male children who are born in the seventh and tenth month afterwards his sons, and the female children his daughters, and they will call him father, and he will call their children his grandchildren, and they will call the elder generation grandfathers and grandmothers. All who were begotten at the time when their fathers and mothers came together will be called their brothers and sisters, and these, as I was saying, will be forbidden to inter-marry. This, however, is not to be understood as an absolute prohibition of the marriage of brothers and sisters; if the lot favours them, and they receive the sanction of the Pythian oracle, the law will allow them.'

'Quite right,' he replied.

'Such is the scheme, Glaucon, according to which the guardians of our State are to have their wives and families in common. And now you would have the argument show that this community is consistent with the rest of our polity, and also that nothing can be better – would you not?'

'Yes, certainly.'

'Shall we try to find a common basis by asking of ourselves what ought to be the chief aim of the legislator in making laws and in the organization of a State – what is the greatest good, and what is the greatest evil, and then consider whether our previous description has the stamp of the good or of the evil?'

'By all means.'

'Can there be any greater evil than discord and distraction and plurality where unity ought to reign? Or any greater good than the bond of unity?'

'There cannot.'

'And there is unity where there is community of pleasures and pains – where all the citizens are glad or grieved on the same occasions of joy and sorrow?'

'No doubt.'

'Yes; and where there is no common but only private feeling a State is disorganized – when you have one half of the world triumphing and the other plunged in grief at the same events happening to the city or the citizens?'

'Certainly.'

'Such differences commonly originate in a disagreement about the use of the terms "mine" and "not mine", "his" and "not his".'

'Exactly so.'

'And is not that the best-ordered State in which the greatest number of persons apply the terms "mine" and "not mine" in the same way to the same thing?'

'Quite true.'

'Or that again which most nearly approaches to the condition of the individual – as in the body, when but a finger of one of us is hurt, the whole frame, drawn towards the soul as a centre and forming one kingdom under the ruling power therein, feels the hurt and sympathises all together with the part affected, and we say that the man has a pain in his finger; and the same expression is used about any other part of the body, which has a sensation of pain at suffering or of pleasure at the alleviation of suffering.'

'Very true,' he replied; 'and I agree with you that in the best-ordered State there is the nearest approach to this common feeling which you describe.'

'Then when any one of the citizens experiences any good or evil, the whole State will make his case their own, and will either rejoice or sorrow with him?'

'Yes,' he said, 'that is what will happen in a well-ordered State.'

'It will now be time,' I said, 'for us to return to our State and see whether this or some other form is most in accordance with these fundamental principles.'

'Very good.'

'Our State like every other has rulers and subjects?'

'True.'

'All of whom will call one another citizens?'

'Of course.'

'But is there not another name which people give to their rulers in other States?'

'Generally they call them masters, but in democratic States they simply call them rulers.'

'And in our State what other name besides that of citizens do the people give the rulers?'

'They are called saviours and helpers,' he replied.

'And what do the rulers call the people?'

'Their maintainers and foster-fathers.'

'And what do they call them in other States?'

'Slaves.'

'And what do the rulers call one another in other States?'

'Fellow-rulers.'

'And what in ours?'

'Fellow-guardians.'

'Did you ever know an example in any other State of a ruler who would speak of one of his colleagues as his friend and of another as not being his friend?

'Yes, very often.'

'And the friend he regards and describes as one in whom he has an interest, and the other as a stranger in whom he has no interest?'

'Exactly.'

'But would any of your guardians think or speak of any other guardian as a stranger?'

'Certainly he would not; for everyone whom they meet will be regarded by them either as a brother or sister, or father or mother, or son or daughter, or as the child or parent of those who are thus connected with him.'

'Capital,' I said. 'But let me ask you once more: shall they be a family in name only; or shall they in all their actions be true to the name? For example, in the use of the word "father", would the care of a father be implied and the filial reverence and duty and obedience to him which the law commands; and is the violator of these duties to be regarded as an impious and unrighteous person who is not likely to receive much good either at the hands of God or of man? Are these to be or not to be the strains which the children will hear repeated in their ears by all the citizens about those who are intimated to them to be their parents and the rest of their kinsfolk?'

'These,' he said, 'and none other; for what can be more ridiculous than for them to utter the names of family ties with the lips only and not to act in the spirit of them?'

'Then in our city the language of harmony and concord will be more often heard than in any other. As I was describing before, when anyone is well or ill, the universal word will be with me "it is well" or "it is ill".'

'Most true.'

'And agreeably to this mode of thinking and speaking, were we not saying that they will have their pleasures and pains in common?'

'Yes, and so they will.'

'And they will have a common interest in the same thing which they will alike call "my own", and having this common interest they will have a common feeling of pleasure and pain?'

'Yes, far more so than in other States.'

'And the reason of this, over and above the general constitution of the State, will be that the guardians will have a community of women and children?'

'That will be the chief reason.'

'And this unity of feeling we admitted to be the greatest good, as was implied in our own comparison of a well-ordered State to the relation of the body and the members, when affected by pleasure or pain?'

'That we acknowledged, and very rightly.'

'Then the community of wives and children among our citizens is clearly the source of the greatest good to the State?'

'Certainly.'

'And this agrees with the other principle which we were affirming – that the guardians were not to have houses or lands or any other property; their pay was to be their food, which they were to receive from the other citizens, and they were to have no private expenses; for we intended them to preserve their true character of guardians.'

'Right,' he replied.

'Both the community of property and the community of families, as I am saying, tend to make them more truly guardians; they will not tear the city in pieces by differing about "mine" and "not mine"; each man dragging any acquisition which he has made into a separate house of his own, where he has a separate wife and children and private pleasures and pains; but all will be affected as far as may be by the same pleasures and pains because they are all of one opinion about what is near and dear to them, and therefore they all tend towards a common end.'

'Certainly,' he replied.

'And as they have nothing but their persons which they can call their own, suits and complaints will have no existence among them; they will be delivered from all those quarrels of which money or children or relations are the occasion.'

'Of course they will.'

'Neither will trials for assault or insult ever be likely to occur among them. For that equals should defend themselves against equals we shall maintain to be honourable and right; we shall make the protection of the person a matter of necessity.'

'That is good,' he said.

'Yes; and there is a further good in the law; *viz.* that if a man has a quarrel with another he will satisfy his resentment then and there, and not proceed to more dangerous lengths.'

'Certainly.'

'To the elder shall be assigned the duty of ruling and chastising the younger.'

'Clearly.'

'Nor can there be a doubt that the younger will not strike or do any other violence to an elder, unless the magistrates command him; nor will he slight him in any way. For there are two guardians, shame and fear, mighty to prevent him: shame, which makes men refrain from laying hands on those who are to them in the relation of parents; fear, that the injured one will be succoured by the others who are his brothers, sons, fathers.'

'That is true,' he replied.

'Then in every way the laws will help the citizens to keep the peace with one another?'

'Yes, there will be no want of peace.'

'And as the guardians will never quarrel among themselves there will be no danger of the rest of the city being divided either against them or against one another.'

'None whatever.'

'I hardly like even to mention the little meannesses of which they will be rid, for they are beneath notice: such, for example, as the flattery of the rich by the poor, and all the pains and pangs which men experience in bringing up a family, and in finding money to buy necessaries for their household, borrowing and then repudiating, getting how they can, and giving the money into the hands of women and slaves to keep – the many evils of so many kinds which people suffer in this way are mean enough and obvious enough, and not worth speaking of.'

'Yes,' he said, 'a man has no need of eyes in order to perceive that.'

'And from all these evils they will be delivered, and their life will be blessed as the life of Olympic victors and yet more blessed.'

'How so?'

'The Olympic victor', I said, 'is deemed happy in receiving a part only of the blessedness which is secured to our citizens, who have won a more glorious victory and have a more complete maintenance at the public cost. For the victory which they have won is the salvation of the whole State; and the crown with which they and their children are crowned is the fulness of all that life needs; they receive rewards from the hands of their country while living, and after death have an honourable burial.'

'Yes,' he said, 'and glorious rewards they are.'

'Do you remember', I said, 'how in the course of the previous discussion someone who shall be nameless accused us of making our guardians unhappy – they had nothing and might have possessed all things to whom we replied that, if an occasion offered, we might perhaps hereafter consider this question, but that, as at present advised, we would make our guardians truly guardians, and that we were fashioning the State with a view to the greatest happiness, not of any particular class, but of the whole?'

'Yes, I remember.'

'And what do you say, now that the life of our protectors is made out to be far better and nobler than that of Olympic victors – is the life of shoemakers, or any other artisans, or of husbandmen, to be compared with it?'

'Certainly not.'

'At the same time I ought here to repeat what I have said elsewhere, that if any of our guardians shall try to be happy in such a manner that he will cease to be a guardian, and is not content with this safe and harmonious life, which, in our judgment, is of all lives the best, but infatuated by some youthful conceit of happiness which gets up into his head shall seek to appropriate the whole State to himself, then he will have to learn how wisely Hesiod spoke, when he said, "Half is more than the whole."'

'If he were to consult me, I should say to him: "Stay where you are, when you have the offer of such a life."'

'You agree then', I said, 'that men and women are to have a common way of life such as we have described – common education, common children; and they are to watch over the citizens in common whether abiding in the city or going out to war; they are to keep watch together, and to hunt together like dogs; and always and in all things, as far as they are able, women are to share with the men? And in so doing they will do what is best, and will not violate, but preserve the natural relation of the sexes.'

'I agree with you,' he replied.

'The enquiry', I said, 'has yet to be made, whether such a community be found possible – as among other animals, so also among men – and if possible, in what way possible?'

'You have anticipated the question which I was about to suggest.'

'There is no difficulty', I said, 'in seeing how war will be carried on by them.'

'How?'

'Why, of course they will go on expeditions together; and will take with them any of their children who are strong enough, that, after the manner of the artisan's child, they may look on at the work which they will have to do when they are grown up; and besides looking on they will have to help and be of use in war, and to wait upon their fathers and mothers. Did you never observe in the arts how the potters' boys look on and help, long before they touch the wheel?'

'Yes, I have.'

'And shall potters be more careful in educating their children and in giving them the opportunity of seeing and practising their duties than our guardians will be?'

'The idea is ridiculous,' he said.

'There is also the effect on the parents, with whom, as with other animals, the presence of their young ones will be the greatest incentive to valour.'

'That is quite true, Socrates; and yet if they are defeated, which may often happen in war, how great the danger is! The children will be lost as well as their parents, and the State will never recover.'

'True,' I said; 'but would you never allow them to run any risk?'

'I am far from saying that.'

'Well, but if they are ever to run a risk should they not do so on some occasion when, if they escape disaster, they will be the better for it?'

'Clearly.'

'Whether the future soldiers do or do not see war in the days of their youth is a very important matter, for the sake of which some risk may fairly be incurred.'

'Yes, very important.'

'This then must be our first step – to make our children spectators of war; but we must also contrive that they shall be secured against danger; then all will be well.'

'True.'

'Their parents may be supposed not to be blind to the risks of war, but to know, as far as human foresight can, what expeditions are safe and what dangerous?'

'That may be assumed.'

'And they will take them on the safe expeditions and be cautious about the dangerous ones?'

'True.'

'And they will place them under the command of experienced veterans who will be their leaders and teachers?'

'Very properly.'

'Still, the dangers of war cannot be always foreseen; there is a good deal of chance about them?'

'True.'

'Then against such chances the children must be at once furnished with wings, in order that in the hour of need they may fly away and escape.'

'What do you mean?' he said.

'I mean that we must mount them on horses in their earliest youth, and when they have learnt to ride, take them on horseback to see war: the horses must be spirited and warlike, but the most tractable and yet the swiftest that can be had. In this way they will get an excellent view of what is hereafter to be their own business; and if there is danger they have only to follow their elder leaders and escape.'

'I believe that you are right,' he said.

'Next, as to war; what are to be the relations of your soldiers to one another and to their enemies? I should be inclined to propose that the soldier who leaves his rank or throws away his arms, or is guilty of any other act of cowardice, should be degraded into the rank of a husbandman or artisan. What do you think?'

'By all means, I should say.'

'And he who allows himself to be taken prisoner may as well be made a present of to his enemies; he is their lawful prey, and let them do what they like with him.'

'Certainly.'

'But the hero who has distinguished himself, what shall be done to him? In the first place, he shall receive honour in the army from his youthful comrades; every one of them in succession shall crown him. What do you say?'

'I approve.'

'And what do you say to his receiving the right hand of fellowship?'

'To that too, I agree.'

'But you will hardly agree to my next proposal.'

'What is your proposal?'

'That he should kiss and be kissed by them.'

'Most certainly, and I should be disposed to go further, and say: let no one whom he has a mind to kiss refuse to be kissed by him while the expedition lasts. So that if there be a lover in the army, whether his love be youth or maiden, he may be more eager to win the prize of valour.'

'Capital,' I said. 'That the brave man is to have more wives than others has been already determined: and he is to have first choices in such matters more than others, in order that he may have as many children as possible?'

'Agreed.'

'Again, there is another manner in which, according to Homer, brave youths should be honoured: for he tells how Ajax, after he had distinguished himself in battle, was rewarded with long chines, which seems to be a compliment appropriate to a hero in the flower of his age, being not only a tribute of honour but also a very strengthening thing.'

'Most true,' he said.

'Then in this,' I said, 'Homer shall be our teacher; and we too, at sacrifices and on the like occasions, will honour the brave according to the measure of their valour, whether men or women, with hymns and those other distinctions which we were mentioning; also with

"seats of precedence, and meats and full cups"

and in honouring them, we shall be at the same time training them.'

'That', he replied, 'is excellent.'

'Yes,' I said; 'and when a man dies gloriously in war shall we not say, in the first place, that he is of the golden race?'

'To be sure.'

'Nay, have we not the authority of Hesiod for affirming that when they are dead

"They are holy angels upon the earth, authors of good, averters of evil,
the guardians of speech-gifted men?"'

'Yes; and we accept his authority.'

'We must learn of the god how we are to order the sepulture of divine and heroic personages, and what is to be their special distinction and we must do as he bids?'

'By all means.'

'And in ages to come we will reverence them and kneel before their sepulchres as at the graves of heroes. And not only they but any who are deemed pre-eminently good, whether they die from age, or in any other way, shall be admitted to the same honours.'

'That is very right,' he said.

'Next, how shall our soldiers treat their enemies? What about this?'

'In what respect do you mean?'

'First of all, in regard to slavery? Do you think it right that Hellenes should enslave Hellenic States, or allow others to enslave them, if they can help? Should not their custom be to spare them, considering the danger which there is that the whole race may one day fall under the yoke of the barbarians?'

'To spare them is infinitely better.'

'Then no Hellene should be owned by them as a slave; that is a rule which they will observe and advise the other Hellenes to observe.'

'Certainly,' he said; 'they will in this way be united against the barbarians and will keep their hands off one another.'

'Next as to the slain: ought the conquerors', I said, 'to take anything but their armour? Does not the practice of despoiling an enemy afford an excuse for not facing the battle? Cowards skulk about the dead, pretending that they are fulfilling a duty, and many an army before now has been lost from this love of plunder.'

'Very true.'

'And is there not illiberality and avarice in robbing a corpse, and also a degree of meanness and womanishness in making an enemy of the dead body when the real enemy has flown away and left only his fighting gear behind him – is not this rather like a dog who cannot get at his assailant quarrelling with the stones which strike him instead?'

'Very like a dog,' he said.

'Then we must abstain from spoiling the dead or hindering their burial?'

'Yes,' he replied, 'we most certainly must.'

'Neither shall we offer up arms at the temples of the gods, least of all the arms of Hellenes, if we care to maintain good feeling with other Hellenes; and, indeed, we have reason to fear that the offering of spoils taken from kinsmen may be a pollution unless commanded by the god himself?'

'Very true.'

'Again, as to the devastation of Hellenic territory or the burning of houses, what is to be the practice?'

'May I have the pleasure', he said, 'of hearing your opinion?'

'Both should be forbidden, in my judgment; I would take the annual produce and no more. Shall I tell you why?'

'Pray do.'

'Why, you see, there is a difference in the names "discord" and "war", and I imagine that there is also a difference in their natures; the one is expressive of what is internal and domestic, the other of what is external and foreign; and the first of the two is termed discord, and only the second, war.'

'That is a very proper distinction,' he replied.

'And may I not observe with equal propriety that the Hellenic race is all united together by ties of blood and friendship, and alien and strange to the barbarians?'

'Very good,' he said.

'And therefore when Hellenes fight with barbarians and barbarians with Hellenes, they will be described by us as being at war when they fight, and by nature enemies, and this kind of antagonism should be called war; but when Hellenes fight with one another we shall say that Hellas is then in a state of disorder and discord, they being by nature friends and such enmity is to be called discord.'

'I agree.'

'Consider then,' I said, 'when that which we have acknowledged to be discord occurs, and a city is divided, if both parties destroy the lands and burn the houses of one another, how wicked does the strife appear! No true lover of his country would bring himself to tear in pieces his own nurse and mother: There might be reason in the conqueror depriving the conquered of their harvest, but still they would have the idea of peace in their hearts and would not mean to go on fighting for ever.'

'Yes,' he said, 'that is a better temper than the other.'

'And will not the city, which you are founding, be a Hellenic city?'

'It ought to be,' he replied.

'Then will not the citizens be good and civilised?'

'Yes, very civilised.'

'And will they not be lovers of Hellas, and think of Hellas as their own land, and share in the common temples?

'Most certainly.'

'And any difference which arises among them will be regarded by them as discord only – a quarrel among friends, which is not to be called a war?'

'Certainly not.'

'Then they will quarrel as those who intend some day to be reconciled?'

'Certainly.'

'They will use friendly correction, but will not enslave or destroy their opponents; they will be correctors, not enemies?'

'Just so.'

'And as they are Hellenes themselves they will not devastate Hellas, nor will they burn houses, not even suppose that the whole population of a city – men, women, and children – are equally their enemies, for they know that the guilt of war is always confined to a few persons and that the many are their friends. And for all these reasons they will be unwilling to waste their lands and raze their houses; their enmity to them will only last until the many innocent sufferers have compelled the guilty few to give satisfaction?'

'I agree, he said, that our citizens should thus deal with their Hellenic enemies; and with barbarians as the Hellenes now deal with one another.'

'Then let us enact this law also for our guardians: – that they are neither to devastate the lands of Hellenes nor to burn their houses.'

'Agreed; and we may agree also in thinking that these, all our previous enactments, are very good.'

'But still I must say, Socrates, that if you are allowed to go on in this way you will entirely forget the other question which at the commencement of this discussion you thrust aside: is such an order of things possible, and how, if at all? For I am quite ready to acknowledge that the plan which you propose, if only feasible, would do all sorts of good to the State. I will add, what you have omitted, that your citizens will be the bravest of warriors, and will never leave their ranks, for they will all know one another, and each will call the other father, brother, son; and if you suppose the women to join their armies, whether in the same rank or in the rear, either as a terror to the enemy, or as auxiliaries in case of need, I know that they will then be absolutely invincible; and there are many domestic advantages which might also be mentioned and which I also fully acknowledge: but, as I admit all these advantages and as many more as you please, if only this State of yours were to come into existence, we need say no more about them; assuming then the existence of the State, let us now turn to the question of possibility and ways and means – the rest may be left.'

'If I loiter for a moment, you instantly make a raid upon me, I said, and have no mercy; I have hardly escaped the first and second waves, and you seem not to be aware that you are now bringing upon me the third, which is the greatest and heaviest. When you have seen and heard the third wave, I think you will be more considerate and will acknowledge that some fear and hesitation was natural respecting a proposal so extraordinary as that which I have now to state and investigate.'

'The more appeals of this sort which you make,' he said, 'the more determined are we that you shall tell us how such a State is possible: speak out and at once.'

'Let me begin by reminding you that we found our way hither in the search after justice and injustice.'

'True,' he replied; 'but what of that?'

'I was only going to ask whether, if we have discovered them, we are to require that the just man should in nothing fail of absolute justice; or may we be satisfied with an approximation, and the attainment in him of a higher degree of justice than is to be found in other men?'

'The approximation will be enough.'

'We are enquiring into the nature of absolute justice and into the character of the perfectly just, and into injustice and the perfectly unjust, that we might have an ideal. We were to look at these in order that we might judge of our own happiness and unhappiness according to the standard which they exhibited and the degree in which we resembled them, but not with any view of showing that they could exist in fact.'

'True,' he said.

'Would a painter be any the worse because, after having delineated with consummate art an ideal of a perfectly beautiful man, he was unable to show that any such man could ever have existed?'

'He would be none the worse.'

'Well, and were we not creating an ideal of a perfect State?'

'To be sure.'

'And is our theory a worse theory because we are unable to prove the possibility of a city being ordered in the manner described?'

'Surely not,' he replied.

'That is the truth,' I said. 'But if, at your request, I am to try and show how and under what conditions the possibility is highest, I must ask you, having this in view, to repeat your former admissions.'

'What admissions?'

'I want to know whether ideals are ever fully realised in language? Does not the word express more than the fact, and must not the actual, whatever a man may think, always, in the nature of things, fall short of the truth? What do you say?'

'I agree.'

'Then you must not insist on my proving that the actual State will in every respect coincide with the ideal: if we are only able to discover how a city may be governed nearly as we proposed, you will admit that we have discovered the possibility which you demand; and will be contented. I am sure that I should be contented – will not you?'

'Yes, I will.'

'Let me next endeavour to show what is that fault in States which is the cause of their present maladministration, and what is the least change which will enable a State to pass into the truer form; and let the change, if possible, be of one thing only, or if not, of two; at any rate, let the changes be as few and slight as possible.'

'Certainly,' he replied.

'I think', I said, 'that there might be a reform of the State if only one change were made, which is not a slight or easy though still a possible one.'

'What is it?' he said.

'Now then,' I said, 'I go to meet that which I liken to the greatest of the waves; yet shall the word be spoken, even though the wave break and drown me in laughter and dishonour; and do you mark my words.'

'Proceed.'

I said: '"Until philosophers are kings, or the kings and princes of this world have the spirit and power of philosophy, and political greatness and wisdom meet in one, and those commoner natures who pursue either to the exclusion of the other are compelled to stand aside, cities will never have rest from their evils – nor the human race, as I believe – and then only will this our State have a possibility of life and behold the light of day." Such was the thought, my dear Glaucon, which I would fain have uttered if it had not seemed too extravagant; for to be convinced that in no other State can there be happiness private or public is indeed a hard thing.'

'Socrates, what do you mean? I would have you consider that the word which you have uttered is one at which numerous persons, and very respectable persons too, in a figure pulling off their coats all in a moment, and seizing any weapon that comes to hand, will run at you might and main, before you know where you are, intending to do heaven knows what; and if you don't prepare an answer, and put yourself in motion, you will be "pared by their fine wits", and no mistake.'

'You got me into the scrape,' I said.

'And I was quite right; however, I will do all I can to get you out of it; but I can only give you good-will and good advice, and, perhaps, I may be able to fit answers to your questions better than another – that is all. And now, having such an auxiliary, you must do your best to show the unbelievers that you are right.'

'I ought to try,' I said, 'since you offer me such invaluable assistance. And I think that, if there is to be a chance of our escaping, we must explain to them whom we mean when we say that philosophers are to rule in the State; then we shall be able to defend ourselves. There will be discovered to be some natures who ought to study philosophy and to be leaders in the State; and others who are not born to be philosophers, and are meant to be followers rather than leaders.'

'Then now for a definition,' he said.

'Follow me,' I said, 'and I hope that I may in some way or other be able to give you a satisfactory explanation.'

'Proceed.

'I dare say that you remember, and therefore I need not remind you, that a lover, if he is worthy of the name, ought to show his love, not to some one part of that which he loves, but to the whole.'

'I really do not understand, and therefore beg of you to assist my memory.'

'Another person', I said, 'might fairly reply as you do; but a man of pleasure like yourself ought to know that all who are in the flower of youth do somehow or other raise a pang or emotion in a lover's breast, and are thought by him to be worthy of his affectionate regards. Is not this a way which you have with the fair: one has a snub nose, and you praise his charming face; the hook-nose of another has, you say, a royal look; while he who is neither snub nor hooked has the grace of regularity: the dark visage is manly, the fair are children of the gods; and as to the sweet "honey pale", as they are called, what is the very name but the invention of a lover who talks in diminutives, and is not adverse to paleness if appearing on the cheek of youth? In a word, there is no excuse which you will not make, and nothing which you will not say, in order not to lose a single flower that blooms in the springtime of youth.'

'If you make me an authority in matters of love, for the sake of the argument, I assent.'

'And what do you say of lovers of wine? Do you not see them doing the same? They are glad of any pretext of drinking any wine.'

'Very good.'

'And the same is true of ambitious men; if they cannot command an army, they are willing to command a file; and if they cannot be honoured by really great and important persons, they are glad to be honoured by lesser and meaner people, but honour of some kind they must have.'

'Exactly.

'Once more let me ask: does he who desires any class of goods desire the whole class or a part only?'

'The whole.'

'And may we not say of the philosopher that he is a lover, not of a part of wisdom only, but of the whole?'

'Yes, of the whole.'

'And he who dislikes learnings, especially in youth, when he has no power of judging what is good and what is not, such an one we maintain not to be a philosopher or a lover of knowledge, just as he who refuses his food is not hungry, and may be said to have a bad appetite and not a good one?'

'Very true,' he said.

'Whereas he who has a taste for every sort of knowledge and who is curious to learn and is never satisfied, may be justly termed a philosopher? Am I not right?'

Glaucon said: 'If curiosity makes a philosopher, you will find many a strange being will have a title to the name. All the lovers of sights have a delight in learning, and must therefore be included. Musical amateurs, too, are a folk strangely out of place among philosophers, for they are the last persons in the world who would come to anything like a philosophical discussion, if they could help, while they run about at the Dionysiac festivals as if they had let out their ears to hear every chorus; whether the performance is in town or country – that makes no difference – they are there. Now are we to maintain that all these and any who have similar tastes, as well as the professors of quite minor arts, are philosophers?'

'Certainly not,' I replied; 'they are only an imitation.'

He said: 'Who then are the true philosophers?'

'Those', I said, 'who are lovers of the vision of truth.'

'That is also good,' he said; 'but I should like to know what you mean?'

'To another,' I replied, 'I might have a difficulty in explaining; but I am sure that you will admit a proposition which I am about to make.'

'What is the proposition?'

'That since beauty is the opposite of ugliness, they are two?'

'Certainly.'

'And inasmuch as they are two, each of them is one?'

'True again.'

'And of just and unjust, good and evil, and of every other class, the same remark holds: taken singly, each of them one; but from the various combinations of them with actions and things and with one another, they are seen in all sorts of lights and appear many? Very true.'

'And this is the distinction which I draw between the sight-loving, art-loving, practical class and those of whom I am speaking, and who are alone worthy of the name of philosophers.'

'How do you distinguish them?' he said.

'The lovers of sounds and sights', I replied, 'are, as I conceive, fond of fine tones and colours and forms and all the artificial products that are made out of them, but their mind is incapable of seeing or loving absolute beauty.'

'True,' he replied.

'Few are they who are able to attain to the sight of this.'

'Very true.'

'And he who, having a sense of beautiful things has no sense of absolute beauty, or who, if another lead him to a knowledge of that beauty is unable to follow – of such an one I ask, is he awake or in a dream only? Reflect: is not the dreamer, sleeping or waking, one who likens dissimilar things, who puts the copy in the place of the real object?'

'I should certainly say that such a one was dreaming.'

'But take the case of the other, who recognises the existence of absolute beauty and is able to distinguish the idea from the objects which participate in the idea, neither putting the objects in the place of the idea nor the idea in the place of the objects – is he a dreamer, or is he awake?'

'He is wide awake.'

'And may we not say that the mind of the one who knows has knowledge, and that the mind of the other, who opines only, has opinion?'

'Certainly.'

'But suppose that the latter should quarrel with us and dispute our statement, can we administer any soothing cordial or advice to him, without revealing to him that there is sad disorder in his wits?'

'We must certainly offer him some good advice,' he replied.

'Come, then, and let us think of something to say to him. Shall we begin by assuring him that he is welcome to any knowledge which he may have, and that we are rejoiced at his having it? But we should like to ask him a question: Does he who has knowledge know something or nothing? (You must answer for him.)'

'I answer that he knows something.'

'Something that is or is not?'

'Something that is; for how can that which is not ever be known?'

'And are we assured, after looking at the matter from many points of view, that absolute being is or may be absolutely known, but that the utterly non-existent is utterly unknown?'

'Nothing can be more certain.'

'Good. But if there be anything which is of such a nature as to be and not to be, that will have a place intermediate between pure being and the absolute negation of being?'

'Yes, between them.'

'And, as knowledge corresponded to being and ignorance of necessity to not-being, for that intermediate between being and not-being there has to be discovered a corresponding intermediate between ignorance and knowledge, if there be such?'

'Certainly.'

'Do we admit the existence of opinion?'

'Undoubtedly.'

'As being the same with knowledge, or another faculty?'

'Another faculty.'

'Then opinion and knowledge have to do with different kinds of matter corresponding to this difference of faculties?'

'Yes.'

'And knowledge is relative to being and knows being. But before I proceed further I will make a division.'

'What division?'

'I will begin by placing faculties in a class by themselves: they are powers in us, and in all other things, by which we do as we do. Sight and hearing, for example, I should call faculties. Have I clearly explained the class which I mean?'

'Yes, I quite understand.'

'Then let me tell you my view about them. I do not see them, and therefore the distinctions of fire, colour, and the like, which enable me to discern the differences of some things, do not apply to them. In speaking of a faculty I think only of its sphere and its result; and that which has the same sphere and the same result I call the same faculty, but that which has another sphere and another result I call different. Would that be your way of speaking?'

'Yes.'

'And will you be so very good as to answer one more question? Would you say that knowledge is a faculty, or in what class would you place it?'

'Certainly knowledge is a faculty, and the mightiest of all faculties.'

'And is opinion also a faculty?'

'Certainly,' he said; 'for opinion is that with which we are able to form an opinion.'

'And yet you were acknowledging a little while ago that knowledge is not the same as opinion?'

'Why, yes,' he said. 'How can any reasonable being ever identify that which is infallible with that which errs?'

'An excellent answer, proving', I said, 'that we are quite conscious of a distinction between them.'

'Yes.'

'Then knowledge and opinion having distinct powers have also distinct spheres or subject-matters?'

'That is certain.'

'Being is the sphere or subject-matter of knowledge, and knowledge is to know the nature of being?'

'Yes.'

'And opinion is to have an opinion?'

'Yes.'

'And do we know what we opine? Or is the subject-matter of opinion the same as the subject-matter of knowledge?'

'Nay,' he replied, 'that has been already disproven; if difference in faculty implies difference in the sphere or subject matter, and if, as we were saying, opinion and knowledge are distinct faculties, then the sphere of knowledge and of opinion cannot be the same.'

'Then if being is the subject-matter of knowledge, something else must be the subject-matter of opinion?'

'Yes, something else.'

'Well then, is not-being the subject-matter of opinion? Or, rather, how can there be an opinion at all about not-being? Reflect: when a man has an opinion, has he not an opinion about something? Can he have an opinion which is an opinion about nothing?'

'Impossible.'

'He who has an opinion has an opinion about some one thing?'

'Yes.'

'And not-being is not one thing but, properly speaking, nothing?'

'True.'

'Of not-being, ignorance was assumed to be the necessary correlative of being, knowledge?'

'True,' he said.

'Then opinion is not concerned either with being or with not-being?'

'Not with either.'

'And can therefore neither be ignorance nor knowledge?'

'That seems to be true.'

'But is opinion to be sought without and beyond either of them, in a greater clearness than knowledge, or in a greater darkness than ignorance?'

'In neither.'

'Then I suppose that opinion appears to you to be darker than knowledge, but lighter than ignorance?'

'Both; and in no small degree.'

'And also to be within and between them?'

'Yes.'

'Then you would infer that opinion is intermediate?'

'No question.'

'But were we not saying before that if anything appeared to be of a sort which is and is not at the same time, that sort of thing would appear also to lie in the interval between pure being and absolute not-being; and that the corresponding faculty is neither knowledge nor ignorance, but will be found in the interval between them?'

'True.'

'And in that interval there has now been discovered something which we call opinion?'

'There has.'

'Then what remains to be discovered is the object which partakes equally of the nature of being and not-being, and cannot rightly be termed either, pure and simple; this unknown term, when discovered, we may truly call the subject of opinion, and assign each to its proper faculty – the extremes to the faculties of the extremes and the mean to the faculty of the mean.'

'True.'

'This being premised, I would ask the gentleman who is of opinion that there is no absolute or unchangeable idea of beauty – in whose opinion the beautiful is the manifold – he, I say, your lover of beautiful sights, who cannot bear to be told that the beautiful is one, and the just is one, or that anything is one – to him I would appeal, saying, "Will you be so very kind, sir, as to tell us whether, of all these beautiful things, there is one which will not be found ugly; or of the just, which will not be found unjust; or of the holy, which will not also be unholy?"'

'No,' he replied; 'the beautiful will in some point of view be found ugly; and the same is true of the rest.'

'And may not the many which are doubles be also halves? – Doubles, that is, of one thing, and halves of another?'

'Quite true.'

'And things great and small, heavy and light, as they are termed, will not be denoted by these any more than by the opposite names?'

'True; both these and the opposite names will always attach to all of them.'

'And can any one of those many things which are called by particular names be said to be this rather than not to be this?'

He replied: 'They are like the punning riddles which are asked at feasts or the children's puzzle about the eunuch aiming at the bat, with what he hit him, as they say in the puzzle, and upon what the bat was sitting. The individual objects of which I am speaking are also a riddle, and have a double sense: nor can you fix them in your mind, either as being or not-being, or both, or neither.'

'Then what will you do with them?' I said. 'Can they have a better place than between being and not-being? For they are clearly not in greater darkness or negation than not-being, or more full of light and existence than being.'

'That is quite true,' he said.

'Thus, then, we seem to have discovered that the many ideas which the multitude entertain about the beautiful and about all other things are tossing about in some region which is halfway between pure being and pure not-being?'

'We have.'

'Yes; and we had before agreed that anything of this kind which we might find was to be described as matter of opinion, and not as matter of knowledge; being the intermediate flux which is caught and detained by the intermediate faculty.'

'Quite true.'

'Then those who see the many beautiful, and who yet neither see absolute beauty nor can follow any guide who points the way thither; who see the many just, and not absolute justice, and the like – such persons may be said to have opinion but not knowledge?'

'That is certain.'

'But those who see the absolute and eternal and immutable may be said to know, and not to have opinion only?'

'Neither can that be denied.'

'The one loves and embraces the subjects of knowledge, the other those of opinion? The latter are the same, as I dare say will remember, who listened to sweet sounds and gazed upon fair colours, but would not tolerate the existence of absolute beauty.'

'Yes, I remember.'

'Shall we then be guilty of any impropriety in calling them lovers of opinion rather than lovers of wisdom, and will they be very angry with us for thus describing them?'

'I shall tell them not to be angry; no man should be angry at what is true.'

'But those who love the truth in each thing are to be called lovers of wisdom and not lovers of opinion.'

'Assuredly.'

Book VI

'And thus, Glaucon, after the argument has gone a weary way, the true and the false philosophers have at length appeared in view.'

'I do not think', he said, 'that the way could have been shortened.'

'I suppose not,' I said; 'and yet I believe that we might have had a better view of both of them if the discussion could have been confined to this one subject and if there were not many other questions awaiting us, which he who desires to see in what respect the life of the just differs from that of the unjust must consider.'

'And what is the next question?' he asked.

'Surely,' I said, 'the one which follows next in order. Inasmuch as philosophers only are able to grasp the eternal and unchangeable, and those who wander in the region of the many and variable are not philosophers, I must ask you which of the two classes should be the rulers of our State?'

'And how can we rightly answer that question?'

'Whichever of the two are best able to guard the laws and institutions of our State – let them be our guardians.'

'Very good.'

'Neither', I said, 'can there be any question that the guardian who is to keep anything should have eyes rather than no eyes?'

'There can be no question of that.'

'And are not those who are verily and indeed wanting in the knowledge of the true being of each thing, and who have in their souls no clear pattern, and are unable as with a painter's eye to look at the absolute truth and to that original to repair, and having perfect vision of the other world to order the laws about beauty, goodness, justice in this, if not already ordered, and to guard and preserve the order of them – are not such persons, I ask, simply blind?'

'Truly,' he replied, 'they are much in that condition.'

'And shall they be our guardians when there are others who, besides being their equals in experience and falling short of them in no particular of virtue, also know the very truth of each thing?'

'There can be no reason', he said, 'for rejecting those who have this greatest of all great qualities; they must always have the first place unless they fail in some other respect.'

'Suppose, then,' I said, 'that we determine how far they can unite this and the other excellences.'

'By all means.'

'In the first place, as we began by observing, the nature of the philosopher has to be ascertained. We must come to an understanding about him, and, when we have done so, then, if I am not mistaken, we shall also acknowledge that such an union of qualities is possible, and that those in whom they are united, and those only, should be rulers in the State.'

'What do you mean?'

'Let us suppose that philosophical minds always love knowledge of a sort which shows them the eternal nature not varying from generation and corruption.'

'Agreed.'

'And further,' I said, 'let us agree that they are lovers of all true being; there is no part whether greater or less, or more or less honourable, which they are willing to renounce; as we said before of the lover and the man of ambition.'

'True.'

'And if they are to be what we were describing, is there not another quality which they should also possess?'

'What quality?'

'Truthfulness: they will never intentionally receive into their mind falsehood, which is their detestation, and they will love the truth.'

'Yes, that may be safely affirmed of them.'

'"May be", my friend,' I replied, 'is not the word; say rather "must be affirmed": for he whose nature is amorous of anything cannot help loving all that belongs or is akin to the object of his affections.'

'Right,' he said.

'And is there anything more akin to wisdom than truth?'

'How can there be?'

'Can the same nature be a lover of wisdom and a lover of falsehood?'

'Never.'

'The true lover of learning then must from his earliest youth, as far as in him lies, desire all truth?'

'Assuredly.'

'But then again, as we know by experience, he whose desires are strong in one direction will have them weaker in others; they will be like a stream which has been drawn off into another channel.'

'True.'

'He whose desires are drawn towards knowledge in every form will be absorbed in the pleasures of the soul, and will hardly feel bodily pleasure – I mean, if he be a true philosopher and not a sham one.'

'That is most certain.'

'Such a one is sure to be temperate and the reverse of covetous; for the motives which make another man desirous of having and spending, have no place in his character.'

'Very true.'

'Another criterion of the philosophical nature has also to be considered.'

'What is that?'

'There should be no secret corner of illiberality; nothing can more antagonistic than meanness to a soul which is ever longing after the whole of things both divine and human.'

'Most true,' he replied.

'Then how can he who has magnificence of mind and is the spectator of all time and all existence, think much of human life?'

'He cannot.'

'Or can such an one account death fearful?'

'No indeed.'

'Then the cowardly and mean nature has no part in true philosophy?'

'Certainly not.'

'Or again: can he who is harmoniously constituted, who is not covetous or mean, or a boaster, or a coward – can he, I say, ever be unjust or hard in his dealings?'

'Impossible.'

'Then you will soon observe whether a man is just and gentle, or rude and unsociable; these are the signs which distinguish even in youth the philosophical nature from the unphilosophical.'

'True.'

'There is another point which should be remarked.'

'What point?'

'Whether he has or has not a pleasure in learning; for no one will love that which gives him pain, and in which after much toil he makes little progress.'

'Certainly not.'

'And again, if he is forgetful and retains nothing of what he learns, will he not be an empty vessel?'

'That is certain.'

'Labouring in vain, he must end in hating himself and his fruitless occupation?'

'Yes.'

'Then a soul which forgets cannot be ranked among genuine philosophic natures; we must insist that the philosopher should have a good memory?'

'Certainly.'

'And once more, the inharmonious and unseemly nature can only tend to disproportion?'

'Undoubtedly.'

'And do you consider truth to be akin to proportion or to disproportion?'

'To proportion.'

'Then, besides other qualities, we must try to find a naturally well-proportioned and gracious mind, which will move spontaneously towards the true being of everything.'

'Certainly.'

'Well, and do not all these qualities, which we have been enumerating, go together, and are they not, in a manner, necessary to a soul which is to have a full and perfect participation of being?'

'They are absolutely necessary,' he replied.

'And must not that be a blameless study which he only can pursue who has the gift of a good memory, and is quick to learn – noble, gracious, the friend of truth, justice, courage, temperance – who are his kindred?'

'The god of jealousy himself', he said, 'could find no fault with such a study.'

'And to men like him,' I said, 'when perfected by years and education, and to these only you will entrust the State.'

Here Adeimantus interposed and said: 'To these statements, Socrates, no one can offer a reply; but when you talk in this way, a strange feeling passes over the minds of your hearers: they fancy that they are led astray a little at each step in the argument, owing to their own want of skill in asking and answering questions; these littles accumulate, and at the end of the discussion they are found to have sustained a mighty overthrow and all their former notions appear to be turned upside down. And as unskilful players of draughts are at last shut up by their more skilful adversaries and have no piece to move, so they too find themselves shut up at last; for they have nothing to say in this new game of which words are the counters; and yet all the time they are in the right. The observation is suggested to me by what is now occurring. For any one of us might say, that although in words he is not able to meet you at each step of the argument, he sees as a fact that the votaries of philosophy, when they carry on the study, not only in youth as a part of education, but as the pursuit of their maturer years, most of them become strange monsters, not to say utter rogues, and that those who may be considered the best of them are made useless to the world by the very study which you extol.'

'Well, and do you think that those who say so are wrong?'

'I cannot tell,' he replied; 'but I should like to know what is your opinion.'

'Hear my answer: I am of opinion that they are quite right.'

'Then how can you be justified in saying that cities will not cease from evil until philosophers rule in them, when philosophers are acknowledged by us to be of no use to them?'

'You ask a question', I said, 'to which a reply can only be given in a parable.'

'Yes, Socrates; and that is a way of speaking to which you are not at all accustomed, I suppose.'

'I perceive', I said, 'that you are vastly amused at having plunged me into such a hopeless discussion; but now hear the parable, and then you will be still more amused at the meagreness of my imagination: for the manner in which the best men are treated in their own States is so grievous that no single thing on earth is comparable to it; and therefore, if I am to plead their cause, I must have recourse to fiction, and put together a figure made up of many things, like the fabulous unions of goats and stags which are found in pictures. Imagine, then, a fleet or a ship in which there is a captain who is taller and stronger than any of the crew, but he is a little deaf and has a similar infirmity in sight, and his knowledge of navigation is not much better. The sailors are quarrelling with one another about the steering – everyone is of opinion that he has a right to steer, though he has never learned the art of navigation and cannot tell who taught him or when he learned, and will further assert that it cannot be taught, and they are ready to cut in pieces anyone who says the contrary. They throng about the captain, begging and praying him to commit the helm to them; and if at any time they do not prevail, but others are preferred to them, they kill the others or throw them overboard, and having first chained up the noble captain's senses with drink or some narcotic drug, they mutiny and take possession of the ship and make free with the stores; thus, eating and drinking, they proceed on their voyage in such a manner as might be expected of them. Him who is their partisan and cleverly aids them in their plot for getting the ship out of the captain's hands into their own, whether by force or persuasion, they compliment with the name of sailor, pilot, able seaman, and abuse the other sort of man, whom they call a good-for-nothing; but that the true pilot must pay attention to the year and seasons and sky and stars and winds, and whatever else belongs to his art, if he intends to be really qualified for the command of a ship, and that he must and will be the steerer, whether other people like or not – the possibility of this union of authority with the steerer's art has never seriously entered into their thoughts or been made part of their calling. Now in vessels which are in a state of mutiny and by sailors who are mutineers, how will the true pilot be regarded? Will he not be called by them a prater, a star-gazer, a good-for-nothing?'

'Of course,' said Adeimantus.'

'Then you will hardly need', I said, 'to hear the interpretation of the figure, which describes the true philosopher in his relation to the State; for you understand already.'

'Certainly.'

'Then suppose you now take this parable to the gentleman who is surprised at finding that philosophers have no honour in their cities; explain it to him and try to convince him that their having honour would be far more extraordinary.'

'I will.'

'Say to him, that, in deeming the best votaries of philosophy to be useless to the rest of the world, he is right; but also tell him to attribute their uselessness to the fault of those who will not use them, and not to themselves. The pilot should not humbly beg the sailors to be commanded by him – that is not the order of nature; neither are "the wise to go to the doors of the rich" – the ingenious author of this saying told a lie – but the truth is, that, when a man is ill, whether he be rich or poor, to the physician he must go, and he who wants to be governed, to him who is able to govern. The ruler who is good for anything ought not to beg his subjects to be ruled by him; although the present governors of mankind are of a different stamp; they may be justly compared to the mutinous sailors, and the true helmsmen to those who are called by them good-for-nothings and star-gazers.'

'Precisely so,' he said.

'For these reasons, and among men like these, philosophy, the noblest pursuit of all, is not likely to be much esteemed by those of the opposite faction; not that the greatest and most lasting injury is done to her by her opponents, but by her own professing followers, the same of whom you suppose the accuser to say, that the greater number of them are arrant rogues, and the best are useless; in which opinion I agreed.'

'Yes.'

'And the reason why the good are useless has now been explained?'

'True.'

'Then shall we proceed to show that the corruption of the majority is also unavoidable, and that this is not to be laid to the charge of philosophy any more than the other?'

'By all means.'

'And let us ask and answer in turn, first going back to the description of the gentle and noble nature. Truth, as you will remember, was his leader, whom he followed always and in all things; failing in this, he was an impostor, and had no part or lot in true philosophy.'

'Yes, that was said.'

'Well, and is not this one quality, to mention no others, greatly at variance with present notions of him?'

'Certainly,' he said.

'And have we not a right to say in his defence, that the true lover of knowledge is always striving after being – that is his nature; he will not rest in the multiplicity of individuals which is an appearance only, but will go on – the keen edge will not be blunted, nor the force of his desire abate until he have attained the knowledge of the true nature of every essence by a sympathetic and kindred power in the soul, and by that power drawing near and mingling and becoming incorporate with very being, having begotten mind and truth, he will have knowledge and will live and grow truly, and then, and not till then, will he cease from his travail.'

'Nothing', he said, 'can be more just than such a description of him.'

'And will the love of a lie be any part of a philosopher's nature? Will he not utterly hate a lie?'

'He will.'

'And when truth is the captain, we cannot suspect any evil of the band which he leads?'

'Impossible.'

'Justice and health of mind will be of the company, and temperance will follow after?'

'True,' he replied.

'Neither is there any reason why I should again set in array the philosopher's virtues, as you will doubtless remember that courage, magnificence, apprehension, memory, were his natural gifts. And you objected that, although no one could deny what I then said, still, if you leave words and look at facts, the persons who are thus described are some of them manifestly useless, and the greater number utterly depraved; we were then led to enquire into the grounds of these accusations, and have now arrived at the point of asking why are the majority bad, which question of necessity brought us back to the examination and definition of the true philosopher.'

'Exactly.'

'And we have next to consider the corruptions of the philosophic nature, why so many are spoiled and so few escape spoiling – I am speaking of those who were said to be useless but not wicked – and, when we have done with them, we will speak of the imitators of philosophy, what manner of men are they who aspire after a profession which is above them and of which they are unworthy, and then, by their manifold inconsistencies, bring upon philosophy, and upon all philosophers, that universal reprobation of which we speak.'

'What are these corruptions?' he said.

'I will see if I can explain them to you. Everyone will admit that a nature having in perfection all the qualities which we required in a philosopher is a rare plant which is seldom seen among men.'

'Rare indeed.'

'And what numberless and powerful causes tend to destroy these rare natures!'

'What causes?'

'In the first place there are their own virtues, their courage, temperance, and the rest of them, every one of which praiseworthy qualities (and this is a most singular circumstance) destroys and distracts from philosophy the soul which is the possessor of them.'

'That is very singular,' he replied.

'Then there are all the ordinary goods of life – beauty, wealth, strength, rank and great connections in the State – you understand the sort of things – these also have a corrupting and distracting effect.'

'I understand; but I should like to know more precisely what you mean about them.'

'Grasp the truth as a whole,' I said, 'and in the right way; you will then have no difficulty in apprehending the preceding remarks, and they will no longer appear strange to you.'

'And how am I to do so?' he asked.

'Why,' I said, 'we know that all germs or seeds, whether vegetable or animal, when they fail to meet with proper nutriment or climate or soil, in proportion to their vigour, are all the more sensitive to the want of a suitable environment, for evil is a greater enemy to what is good than what is not.'

'Very true.'

'There is reason in supposing that the finest natures, when under alien conditions, receive more injury than the inferior, because the contrast is greater.'

'Certainly.'

'And may we not say, Adeimantus, that the most gifted minds, when they are ill-educated, become pre-eminently bad? Do not great crimes and the spirit of pure evil spring out of a fulness of nature ruined by education rather than from any inferiority, whereas weak natures are scarcely capable of any very great good or very great evil?'

'There I think that you are right.'

'And our philosopher follows the same analogy – he is like a plant which, having proper nurture, must necessarily grow and mature into all virtue, but, if sown and planted in an alien soil, becomes the most noxious of all weeds, unless he be preserved by some divine power. Do you really think, as people so often say, that our youth are corrupted by Sophists, or that private teachers of the art corrupt them in any degree worth speaking of? Are not the public who say these things the greatest of all Sophists? And do they not educate to perfection young and old, men and women alike, and fashion them after their own hearts?'

'When is this accomplished?' he said.

'When they meet together, and the world sits down at an assembly, or in a court of law, or a theatre, or a camp, or in any other popular resort, and there is a great uproar, and they praise some things which are being said or done, and blame other things, equally exaggerating both, shouting and clapping their hands, and the echo of the rocks and the place in which they are assembled redoubles the sound of the praise or blame – at such a time will not a young man's heart, as they say, leap within him? Will any private training enable him to stand firm against the overwhelming flood of popular opinion? or will he be carried away by the stream? Will he not have the notions of good and evil which the public in general have – he will do as they do, and as they are, such will he be?'

'Yes, Socrates; necessity will compel him.'

'And yet,' I said, 'there is a still greater necessity, which has not been mentioned.'

'What is that?'

'The gentle force of attainder or confiscation or death which, as you are aware, these new Sophists and educators who are the public, apply when their words are powerless.'

'Indeed they do; and in right good earnest.'

'Now what opinion of any other Sophist, or of any private person, can be expected to overcome in such an unequal contest?'

'None,' he replied.

'No, indeed,' I said, 'even to make the attempt is a great piece of folly; there neither is, nor has been, nor is ever likely to be, any different type of character which has had no other training in virtue but that which is supplied by public opinion – I speak, my friend, of human virtue only; what is more than human, as the proverb says, is not included: for I would not have you ignorant that, in the present evil state of governments, whatever is saved and comes to good is saved by the power of God, as we may truly say.'

'I quite assent,' he replied.

'Then let me crave your assent also to a further observation.'

'What are you going to say?'

'Why, that all those mercenary individuals, whom the many call Sophists and whom they deem to be their adversaries, do, in fact, teach nothing but the opinion of the many, that is to say, the opinions of their assemblies; and this is their wisdom. I might compare them to a man who should study the tempers and desires of a mighty strong beast who is fed by him-he would learn how to approach and handle him, also at what times and from what causes he is dangerous or the reverse, and what is the meaning of his several cries, and by what sounds, when another utters them, he is soothed or infuriated; and you may suppose further, that when, by continually attending upon him, he has become perfect in all this, he calls his knowledge wisdom, and makes of it a system or art, which he proceeds to teach, although he has no real notion of what he means by the principles or passions of which he is speaking, but calls this honourable and that dishonourable, or good or evil, or just or unjust, all in accordance with the tastes and tempers of the great brute. Good he pronounces to be that in which the beast delights and evil to be that which he dislikes; and he can give no other account of them except that the just and noble are the necessary, having never himself seen, and having no power of explaining to others the nature of either, or the difference between them, which is immense. By heaven, would not such an one be a rare educator?'

'Indeed, he would.'

'And in what way does he who thinks that wisdom is the discernment of the tempers and tastes of the motley multitude, whether in painting or music, or, finally, in politics, differ from him whom I have been describing? For when a man consorts with the many, and exhibits to them his poem or other work of art or the service which he has done the State, making them his judges when he is not obliged, the so-called necessity of Diomede will oblige him to produce whatever they praise. And yet the reasons are utterly ludicrous which they give in confirmation of their own notions about the honourable and good. Did you ever hear any of them which were not?'

'No, nor am I likely to hear.'

'You recognise the truth of what I have been saying? Then let me ask you to consider further whether the world will ever be induced to believe in the existence of absolute beauty rather than of the many beautiful, or of the absolute in each kind rather than of the many in each kind?'

'Certainly not.'

'Then the world cannot possibly be a philosopher?'

'Impossible.'

'And therefore philosophers must inevitably fall under the censure of the world?'

'They must.'

'And of individuals who consort with the mob and seek to please them?'

'That is evident.'

'Then, do you see any way in which the philosopher can be preserved in his calling to the end? and remember what we were saying of him, that he was to have quickness and memory and courage and magnificence – these were admitted by us to be the true philosopher's gifts.'

'Yes.'

'Will not such an one from his early childhood be in all things first among all, especially if his bodily endowments are like his mental ones?'

'Certainly,' he said.

'And his friends and fellow-citizens will want to use him as he gets older for their own purposes?'

'No question.'

'Falling at his feet, they will make requests to him and do him honour and flatter him, because they want to get into their hands now, the power which he will one day possess.'

'That often happens,' he said.

'And what will a man such as he be likely to do under such circumstances, especially if he be a citizen of a great city, rich and noble, and a tall proper youth? Will he not be full of boundless aspirations, and fancy himself able to manage the affairs of Hellenes and of barbarians, and having got such notions into his head will he not dilate and elevate himself in the fulness of vain pomp and senseless pride?'

'To be sure he will.'

'Now, when he is in this state of mind, if someone gently comes to him and tells him that he is a fool and must get understanding, which can only be got by slaving for it, do you think that, under such adverse circumstances, he will be easily induced to listen?'

'Far otherwise.'

'And even if there be someone who through inherent goodness or natural reasonableness has had his eyes opened a little and is humbled and taken captive by philosophy, how will his friends behave when they think that they are likely to lose the advantage which they were hoping to reap from his companionship? Will they not do and say anything to prevent him from yielding to his better nature and to render his teacher powerless, using to this end private intrigues as well as public prosecutions?'

'There can be no doubt of it.'

'And how can one who is thus circumstanced ever become a philosopher?'

'Impossible.'

'Then were we not right in saying that even the very qualities which make a man a philosopher may, if he be ill-educated, divert him from philosophy, no less than riches and their accompaniments and the other so-called goods of life?'

'We were quite right.'

'Thus, my excellent friend, is brought about all that ruin and failure which I have been describing of the natures best adapted to the best of all pursuits; they are natures which we maintain to be rare at any time; this being the class out of which come the men who are the authors of the greatest evil to States and individuals; and also of the greatest good when the tide carries them in that direction; but a small man never was the doer of any great thing either to individuals or to States.'

'That is most true,' he said.

'And so philosophy is left desolate, with her marriage rite incomplete: for her own have fallen away and forsaken her, and while they are leading a false and unbecoming life, other unworthy persons, seeing that she has no kinsmen to be her protectors, enter in and dishonour her; and fasten upon her the reproaches which, as you say, her reprovers utter, who affirm of her votaries that some are good for nothing, and that the greater number deserve the severest punishment.'

'That is certainly what people say.'

'Yes; and what else would you expect,' I said, 'when you think of the puny creatures who, seeing this land open to them – a land well stocked with fair names and showy titles – like prisoners running out of prison into a sanctuary, take a leap out of their trades into philosophy; those who do so being probably the cleverest hands at their own miserable crafts? For, although philosophy be in this evil case, still there remains a dignity about her which is not to be found in the arts. And many are thus attracted by her whose natures are imperfect and whose souls are maimed and disfigured by their meannesses, as their bodies are by their trades and crafts. Is not this unavoidable?'

'Yes.'

'Are they not exactly like a bald little tinker who has just got out of durance and come into a fortune; he takes a bath and puts on a new coat, and is decked out as a bridegroom going to marry his master's daughter, who is left poor and desolate?'

'A most exact parallel.'

'What will be the issue of such marriages? Will they not be vile and bastard?'

'There can be no question of it.'

'And when persons who are unworthy of education approach philosophy and make an alliance with her who is a rank above them what sort of ideas and opinions are likely to be generated? Will they not be sophisms captivating to the ear, having nothing in them genuine, or worthy of or akin to true wisdom?'

'No doubt,' he said.

'Then, Adeimantus,' I said, 'the worthy disciples of philosophy will be but a small remnant: perchance some noble and well-educated person, detained by exile in her service, who in the absence of corrupting influences remains devoted to her; or some lofty soul born in a mean city, the politics of which he contemns and neglects; and there may be a gifted few who leave the arts, which they justly despise, and come to her – or peradventure there are some who are restrained by our friend Theages's bridle; for everything in the life of Theages conspired to divert him from philosophy; but ill-health kept him away from politics. My own case of the internal sign is hardly worth mentioning, for rarely, if ever, has such a monitor been given to any other man. Those who belong to this small class have tasted how sweet and blessed a possession philosophy is, and have also seen enough of the madness of the multitude; and they know that no politician is honest, nor is there any champion of justice at whose side they may fight and be saved. Such an one may be compared to a man who has fallen among wild beasts – he will not join in the wickedness of his fellows, but neither is he able singly to resist all their fierce natures, and therefore seeing that he would be of no use to the State or to his friends, and reflecting that he would have to throw away his life without doing any good either to himself or others, he holds his peace, and goes his own way. He is like one who, in the storm of dust and sleet which the driving wind hurries along, retires under the shelter of a wall; and seeing the rest of mankind full of wickedness, he is content, if only he can live his own life and be pure from evil or unrighteousness, and depart in peace and good-will, with bright hopes.'

'Yes,' he said, 'and he will have done a great work before he departs.'

'A great work – yes; but not the greatest, unless he find a State suitable to him; for in a State which is suitable to him, he will have a larger growth and be the saviour of his country, as well as of himself.'

'The causes why philosophy is in such an evil name have now been sufficiently explained: the injustice of the charges against her has been shown – is there anything more which you wish to say?'

'Nothing more on that subject,' he replied; 'but I should like to know which of the governments now existing is in your opinion the one adapted to her.'

'Not any of them,' I said; 'and that is precisely the accusation which I bring against them – not one of them is worthy of the philosophic nature, and hence that nature is warped and estranged, as the exotic seed which is sown in a foreign land becomes denaturalized, and is wont to be overpowered and to lose itself in the new soil, even so this growth of philosophy, instead of persisting, degenerates and receives another character. But if philosophy ever finds in the State that perfection which she herself is, then will be seen that she is in truth divine, and that all other things, whether natures of men or institutions, are but human. And now, I know that you are going to ask, what that State is.'

'No,' he said; 'there you are wrong, for I was going to ask another question – whether it is the State of which we are the founders and inventors, or some other?'

'Yes,' I replied, 'ours in most respects; but you may remember my saying before, that some living authority would always be required in the State having the same idea of the constitution which guided you when as legislator you were laying down the laws.'

'That was said,' he replied.

'Yes, but not in a satisfactory manner; you frightened us by interposing objections, which certainly showed that the discussion would be long and difficult; and what still remains is the reverse of easy.'

'What is there remaining?'

'The question how the study of philosophy may be so ordered as not to be the ruin of the State. All great attempts are attended with risk; "hard is the good," as men say.'

'Still,' he said, 'let the point be cleared up, and the enquiry will then be complete.'

'I shall not be hindered', I said, 'by any want of will, but, if at all, by a want of power: my zeal you may see for yourselves; and please to remark in what I am about to say how boldly and unhesitatingly I declare that States should pursue philosophy, not as they do now, but in a different spirit.'

'In what manner?'

'At present,' I said, 'the students of philosophy are quite young; beginning when they are hardly past childhood, they devote only the time saved from moneymaking and housekeeping to such pursuits; and even those of them who are reputed to have most of the philosophic spirit, when they come within sight of the great difficulty of the subject, I mean dialectic, take themselves off. In after life when invited by someone else, they may, perhaps, go and hear a lecture, and about this they make much ado, for philosophy is not considered by them to be their proper business: at last, when they grow old, in most cases they are extinguished more truly than Heracleitus's sun, inasmuch as they never light up again.'

'But what ought to be their course?'

'Just the opposite. In childhood and youth their study, and what philosophy they learn, should be suited to their tender years: during this period while they are growing up towards manhood, the chief and special care should be given to their bodies that they may have them to use in the service of philosophy; as life advances and the intellect begins to mature, let them increase the gymnastics of the soul; but when the strength of our citizens fails and is past civil and military duties, then let them range at will and engage in no serious labour, as we intend them to live happily here, and to crown this life with a similar happiness in another.'

'How truly in earnest you are, Socrates!' he said. 'I am sure of that; and yet most of your hearers, if I am not mistaken, are likely to be still more earnest in their opposition to you, and will never be convinced; Thrasymachus least of all.'

'Do not make a quarrel', I said, 'between Thrasymachus and me, who have recently become friends, although, indeed, we were never enemies; for I shall go on striving to the utmost until I either convert him and other men, or do something which may profit them against the day when they live again, and hold the like discourse in another state of existence.'

'You are speaking of a time which is not very near.'

'Rather', I replied, 'of a time which is as nothing in comparison with eternity. Nevertheless, I do not wonder that the many refuse to believe; for they have never seen that of which we are now speaking realised; they have seen only a conventional imitation of philosophy, consisting of words artificially brought together, not like these of ours having a natural unity. But a human being who in word and work is perfectly moulded, as far as he can be, into the proportion and likeness of virtue – such a man ruling in a city which bears the same image, they have never yet seen, neither one nor many of them – do you think that they ever did?'

'No indeed.'

'No, my friend, and they have seldom, if ever, heard free and noble sentiments; such as men utter when they are earnestly and by every means in their power seeking after truth for the sake of knowledge, while they look coldly on the subtleties of controversy, of which the end is opinion and strife, whether they meet with them in the courts of law or in society.'

'They are strangers', he said, 'to the words of which you speak.'

'And this was what we foresaw, and this was the reason why truth forced us to admit, not without fear and hesitation, that neither cities nor States nor individuals will ever attain perfection until the small class of philosophers whom we termed useless but not corrupt are providentially compelled, whether they will or not, to take care of the State, and until a like necessity be laid on the State to obey them; or until kings, or if not kings, the sons of kings or princes, are divinely inspired with a true love of true philosophy. That either or both of these alternatives are impossible, I see no reason to affirm: if they were so, we might indeed be justly ridiculed as dreamers and visionaries. Am I not right?'

'Quite right.'

'If then, in the countless ages of the past, or at the present hour in some foreign clime which is far away and beyond our ken, the perfected philosopher is or has been or hereafter shall be compelled by a superior power to have the charge of the State, we are ready to assert to the death, that this our constitution has been, and is – yea, and will be whenever the Muse of Philosophy is queen. There is no impossibility in all this; that there is a difficulty, we acknowledge ourselves.'

'My opinion agrees with yours,' he said.

'But do you mean to say that this is not the opinion of the multitude?'

'I should imagine not,' he replied.

'O my friend,' I said, 'do not attack the multitude: they will change their minds, if, not in an aggressive spirit, but gently and with the view of soothing them and removing their dislike of over-education, you show them your philosophers as they really are and describe as you were just now doing their character and profession, and then mankind will see that he of whom you are speaking is not such as they supposed – if they view him in this new light, they will surely change their notion of him, and answer in another strain. Who can be at enmity with one who loves them, who that is himself gentle and free from envy will be jealous of one in whom there is no jealousy? Nay, let me answer for you, that in a few this harsh temper may be found but not in the majority of mankind.'

'I quite agree with you,' he said.

'And do you not also think, as I do, that the harsh feeling which the many entertain towards philosophy originates in the pretenders, who rush in uninvited, and are always abusing them, and finding fault with them, who make persons instead of things the theme of their conversation? And nothing can be more unbecoming in philosophers than this.'

'It is most unbecoming.'

'For he, Adeimantus, whose mind is fixed upon true being, has surely no time to look down upon the affairs of earth, or to be filled with malice and envy, contending against men; his eye is ever directed towards things fixed and immutable, which he sees neither injuring nor injured by one another, but all in order moving according to reason; these he imitates, and to these he will, as far as he can, conform himself. Can a man help imitating that with which he holds reverential converse?'

'Impossible.'

'And the philosopher holding converse with the divine order, becomes orderly and divine, as far as the nature of man allows; but like everyone else, he will suffer from detraction.'

'Of course.'

'And if a necessity be laid upon him of fashioning, not only himself, but human nature generally, whether in States or individuals, into that which he beholds elsewhere, will he, think you, be an unskilful artificer of justice, temperance, and every civil virtue?'

'Anything but unskilful.'

'And if the world perceives that what we are saying about him is the truth, will they be angry with philosophy? Will they disbelieve us, when we tell them that no State can be happy which is not designed by artists who imitate the heavenly pattern?'

'They will not be angry if they understand,' he said. 'But how will they draw out the plan of which you are speaking?'

'They will begin by taking the State and the manners of men, from which, as from a tablet, they will rub out the picture, and leave a clean surface. This is no easy task. But whether easy or not, herein will lie the difference between them and every other legislator – they will have nothing to do either with individual or State, and will inscribe no laws, until they have either found, or themselves made, a clean surface.'

'They will be very right,' he said.

'Having effected this, they will proceed to trace an outline of the constitution?'

'No doubt.'

'And when they are filling in the work, as I conceive, they will often turn their eyes upwards and downwards: I mean that they will first look at absolute justice and beauty and temperance, and again at the human copy; and will mingle and temper the various elements of life into the image of a man; and thus they will conceive according to that other image, which, when existing among men, Homer calls the form and likeness of God.'

'Very true,' he said.

'And one feature they will erase, and another they will put in, until they have made the ways of men, as far as possible, agreeable to the ways of God?'

'Indeed,' he said, 'in no way could they make a fairer picture.'

'And now,' I said, 'are we beginning to persuade those whom you described as rushing at us with might and main, that the painter of constitutions is such an one as we are praising; at whom they were so very indignant because to his hands we committed the State; and are they growing a little calmer at what they have just heard?'

'Much calmer, if there is any sense in them.'

'Why, where can they still find any ground for objection? Will they doubt that the philosopher is a lover of truth and being?'

'They would not be so unreasonable.'

'Or that his nature, being such as we have delineated, is akin to the highest good?'

'Neither can they doubt this.'

'But again, will they tell us that such a nature, placed under favourable circumstances, will not be perfectly good and wise if any ever was? Or will they prefer those whom we have rejected?'

'Surely not.'

'Then will they still be angry at our saying, that, until philosophers bear rule, States and individuals will have no rest from evil, nor will this our imaginary State ever be realised?'

'I think that they will be less angry.'

'Shall we assume that they are not only less angry but quite gentle, and that they have been converted and for very shame, if for no other reason, cannot refuse to come to terms?'

'By all means,' he said.

'Then let us suppose that the reconciliation has been effected. Will anyone deny the other point, that there may be sons of kings or princes who are by nature philosophers?'

'Surely no man,' he said.

'And when they have come into being will anyone say that they must of necessity be destroyed; that they can hardly be saved is not denied even by us; but that in the whole course of ages no single one of them can escape – who will venture to affirm this?'

'Who indeed!'

'But', said I, 'one is enough; let there be one man who has a city obedient to his will, and he might bring into existence the ideal polity about which the world is so incredulous.'

'Yes, one is enough.'

'The ruler may impose the laws and institutions which we have been describing, and the citizens may possibly be willing to obey them?'

'Certainly.'

'And that others should approve of what we approve, is no miracle or impossibility?'

'I think not.'

'But we have sufficiently shown, in what has preceded, that all this, if only possible, is assuredly for the best.'

'We have.'

'And now we say not only that our laws, if they could be enacted, would be for the best, but also that the enactment of them, though difficult, is not impossible.'

'Very good.'

'And so with pain and toil we have reached the end of one subject, but more remains to be discussed: how and by what studies and pursuits will the saviours of the constitution be created, and at what ages are they to apply themselves to their several studies?'

'Certainly.'

'I omitted the troublesome business of the possession of women, and the procreation of children, and the appointment of the rulers, because I knew that the perfect State would be eyed with jealousy and was difficult of attainment; but that piece of cleverness was not of much service to me, for I had to discuss them all the same. The women and children are now disposed of, but the other question of the rulers must be investigated from the very beginning. We were saying, as you will remember, that they were to be lovers of their country, tried by the test of pleasures and pains, and neither in hardships, nor in dangers, nor at any other critical moment were to lose their patriotism – he was to be rejected who failed, but he who always came forth pure, like gold tried in the refiner's fire, was to be made a ruler, and to receive honours and rewards in life and after death. This was the sort of thing which was being said, and then the argument turned aside and veiled her face; not liking to stir the question which has now arisen.'

'I perfectly remember,' he said.

'Yes, my friend,' I said, 'and I then shrank from hazarding the bold word; but now let me dare to say – that the perfect guardian must be a philosopher.'

'Yes,' he said, 'let that be affirmed.'

'And do not suppose that there will be many of them; for the gifts which were deemed by us to be essential rarely grow together; they are mostly found in shreds and patches.'

'What do you mean?' he said.

'You are aware', I replied, 'that quick intelligence, memory, sagacity, cleverness and similar qualities do not often grow together, and that persons who possess them and are at the same time high-spirited and magnanimous are not so constituted by nature as to live orderly and in a peaceful and settled manner; they are driven any way by their impulses, and all solid principle goes out of them.'

'Very true,' he said.

'On the other hand, those steadfast natures which can better be depended upon, which in a battle are impregnable to fear and immovable, are equally immovable when there is anything to be learned; they are always in a torpid state, and are apt to yawn and go to sleep over any intellectual toil.'

'Quite true.'

'And yet we were saying that both qualities were necessary in those to whom the higher education is to be imparted, and who are to share in any office or command.'

'Certainly,' he said.

'And will they be a class which is rarely found?'

'Yes, indeed.'

'Then the aspirant must not only be tested in those labours and dangers and pleasures which we mentioned before, but there is another kind of probation which we did not mention – he must be exercised also in many kinds of knowledge, to see whether the soul will be able to endure the highest of all, will faint under them, as in any other studies and exercises.'

'Yes,' he said, 'you are quite right in testing him. But what do you mean by the highest of all knowledge?'

'You may remember', I said, 'that we divided the soul into three parts; and distinguished the several natures of justice, temperance, courage and wisdom?'

'Indeed,' he said, 'if I had forgotten, I should not deserve to hear more.'

'And do you remember the word of caution which preceded the discussion of them?'

'To what do you refer?'

'We were saying, if I am not mistaken, that he who wanted to see them in their perfect beauty must take a longer and more circuitous way, at the end of which they would appear; but that we could add on a popular exposition of them on a level with the discussion which had preceded. And you replied that such an exposition would be enough for you, and so the enquiry was continued in what to me seemed to be a very inaccurate manner; whether you were satisfied or not, it is for you to say.'

'Yes,' he said, 'I thought and the others thought that you gave us a fair measure of truth.'

'But, my friend,' I said, 'a measure of such things which in any degree falls short of the whole truth is not fair measure; for nothing imperfect is the measure of anything, although persons are too apt to be contented and think that they need search no further.'

'Not an uncommon case when people are indolent.'

'Yes,' I said; 'and there cannot be any worse fault in a guardian of the State and of the laws.'

'True.'

'The guardian then', I said, 'must be required to take the longer circuit, and toll at learning as well as at gymnastics, or he will never reach the highest knowledge of all which, as we were just now saying, is his proper calling.'

'What,' he said, 'is there a knowledge still higher than this – higher than justice and the other virtues?'

'Yes,' I said, 'there is. And of the virtues too we must behold not the outline merely, as at present – nothing short of the most finished picture should satisfy us. When little things are elaborated with an infinity of pains, in order that they may appear in their full beauty and utmost clearness, how ridiculous that we should not think the highest truths worthy of attaining the highest accuracy!'

'A right noble thought; but do you suppose that we shall refrain from asking you what is this highest knowledge?'

'Nay,' I said, 'ask if you will; but I am certain that you have heard the answer many times, and now you either do not understand me or, as I rather think, you are disposed to be troublesome; for you have been told that the idea of good is the highest knowledge, and that all other things become useful and advantageous only by their use of this. You can hardly be ignorant that of this I was about to speak, concerning which, as you have often heard me say, we know so little; and, without which, any other knowledge or possession of any kind will profit us nothing. Do you think that the possession of all other things is of any value if we do not possess the good? or the knowledge of all other things if we have no knowledge of beauty and goodness?'

'Assuredly not.'

'You are further aware that most people affirm pleasure to be the good, but the finer sort of wits say it is knowledge.'

'Yes.'

'And you are aware too that the latter cannot explain what they mean by knowledge, but are obliged after all to say knowledge of the good?'

'How ridiculous!'

'Yes,' I said, 'that they should begin by reproaching us with our ignorance of the good, and then presume our knowledge of it – for the good they define to be knowledge of the good, just as if we understood them when they use the term "good" – this is of course ridiculous.'

'Most true,' he said.

'And those who make pleasure their good are in equal perplexity; for they are compelled to admit that there are bad pleasures as well as good.'

'Certainly.'

'And therefore to acknowledge that bad and good are the same?'

'True.'

'There can be no doubt about the numerous difficulties in which this question is involved.'

'There can be none.'

'Further, do we not see that many are willing to do or to have or to seem to be what is just and honourable without the reality; but no one is satisfied with the appearance of good – the reality is what they seek; in the case of the good, appearance is despised by everyone.'

'Very true,' he said.

'Of this then, which every soul of man pursues and makes the end of all his actions, having a presentiment that there is such an end, and yet hesitating because neither knowing the nature nor having the same assurance of this as of other things, and therefore losing whatever good there is in other things – of a principle such and so great as this ought the best men in our State, to whom everything is entrusted, to be in the darkness of ignorance?'

'Certainly not,' he said.

'I am sure,' I said, 'that he who does not know now the beautiful and the just are likewise good will be but a sorry guardian of them; and I suspect that no one who is ignorant of the good will have a true knowledge of them.'

'That', he said, 'is a shrewd suspicion of yours.'

'And if we only have a guardian who has this knowledge our State will be perfectly ordered?'

'Of course,' he replied; 'but I wish that you would tell me whether you conceive this supreme principle of the good to be knowledge or pleasure, or different from either.'

'Aye,' I said, 'I knew all along that a fastidious gentleman like you would not be contented with the thoughts of other people about these matters.'

'True, Socrates; but I must say that one who like you has passed a lifetime in the study of philosophy should not be always repeating the opinions of others, and never telling his own.'

'Well, but has anyone a right to say positively what he does not know?'

'Not,' he said, 'with the assurance of positive certainty; he has no right to do that: but he may say what he thinks, as a matter of opinion.'

'And do you not know,' I said, 'that all mere opinions are bad, and the best of them blind? You would not deny that those who have any true notion without intelligence are only like blind men who feel their way along the road?'

'Very true.'

'And do you wish to behold what is blind and crooked and base, when others will tell you of brightness and beauty?'

'Still, I must implore you, Socrates,' said Glaucon, 'not to turn away just as you are reaching the goal; if you will only give such an explanation of the good as you have already given of justice and temperance and the other virtues, we shall be satisfied.'

'Yes, my friend, and I shall be at least equally satisfied, but I cannot help fearing that I shall fall, and that my indiscreet zeal will bring ridicule upon me. No, sweet sirs, let us not at present ask what is the actual nature of the good, for to reach what is now in my thoughts would be an effort too great for me. But of the child of the good who is likest him, I would fain speak, if I could be sure that you wished to hear – otherwise, not.'

'By all means,' he said, 'tell us about the child, and you shall remain in our debt for the account of the parent.'

'I do indeed wish', I replied, 'that I could pay, and you receive, the account of the parent, and not, as now, of the offspring only; take, however, this latter by way of interest, and at the same time have a care that I do not render a false account, although I have no intention of deceiving you.'

'Yes, we will take all the care that we can: proceed.'

'Yes,' I said, 'but I must first come to an understanding with you, and remind you of what I have mentioned in the course of this discussion, and at many other times.'

'What?'

'The old story, that there is a many beautiful and a many good, and so of other things which we describe and define; to all of them "many" is applied.'

'True,' he said.

'And there is an absolute beauty and an absolute good, and of other things to which the term "many" is applied there is an absolute; for they may be brought under a single idea, which is called the essence of each.'

'Very true.'

'The many, as we say, are seen but not known, and the ideas are known but not seen.'

'Exactly.'

'And what is the organ with which we see the visible things?'

'The sight,' he said.

'And with the hearing,' I said, 'we hear, and with the other senses perceive the other objects of sense?'

'True.'

'But have you remarked that sight is by far the most costly and complex piece of workmanship which the artificer of the senses ever contrived?'

'No, I never have,' he said.

'Then reflect: has the ear or voice need of any third or additional nature in order that the one may be able to hear and the other to be heard?'

'Nothing of the sort.'

'No, indeed,' I replied. 'And the same is true of most, if not all, the other senses – you would not say that any of them requires such an addition?'

'Certainly not.'

'But you see that without the addition of some other nature there is no seeing or being seen?'

'How do you mean?'

'Sight being, as I conceive, in the eyes, and he who has eyes wanting to see; colour being also present in them, still unless there be a third nature specially adapted to the purpose, the owner of the eyes will see nothing and the colours will be invisible.'

'Of what nature are you speaking?'

'Of that which you term light,' I replied.

'True,' he said.

'Noble, then, is the bond which links together sight and visibility, and great beyond other bonds by no small difference of nature; for light is their bond, and light is no ignoble thing?'

'Nay,' he said, 'the reverse of ignoble.'

'And which', I said, 'of the gods in heaven would you say was the lord of this element? Whose is that light which makes the eye to see perfectly and the visible to appear?'

'You mean the sun, as you and all mankind say.'

'May not the relation of sight to this deity be described as follows?'

'How?'

'Neither sight nor the eye in which sight resides is the sun?'

'No.'

'Yet of all the organs of sense the eye is the most like the sun?'

'By far the most like.'

'And the power which the eye possesses is a sort of effluence which is dispensed from the sun?'

'Exactly.'

'Then the sun is not sight, but the author of sight who is recognised by sight.'

'True,' he said.

'And this is he whom I call the child of the good, whom the good begat in his own likeness, to be in the visible world, in relation to sight and the things of sight, what the good is in the intellectual world in relation to mind and the things of mind.'

'Will you be a little more explicit?' he said.

'Why, you know', I said, 'that the eyes, when a person directs them towards objects on which the light of day is no longer shining, but the moon and stars only, see dimly, and are nearly blind; they seem to have no clearness of vision in them?'

'Very true.'

'But when they are directed towards objects on which the sun shines, they see clearly and there is sight in them?'

'Certainly.'

'And the soul is like the eye: when resting upon that on which truth and being shine, the soul perceives and understands and is radiant with intelligence; but when turned towards the twilight of becoming and perishing, then she has opinion only, and goes blinking about, and is first of one opinion and then of another, and seems to have no intelligence?'

'Just so.'

'Now, that which imparts truth to the known and the power of knowing to the knower is what I would have you term the idea of good, and this you will deem to be the cause of science, and of truth in so far as the latter becomes the subject of knowledge; beautiful too, as are both truth and knowledge, you will be right in esteeming this other nature as more beautiful than either; and, as in the previous instance, light and sight may be truly said to be like the sun, and yet not to be the sun, so in this other sphere, science and truth may be deemed to be like the good, but not the good; the good has a place of honour yet higher.'

'What a wonder of beauty that must be, he said, which is the author of science and truth, and yet surpasses them in beauty; for you surely cannot mean to say that pleasure is the good?'

'God forbid,' I replied. 'But may I ask you to consider the image in another point of view?'

'In what point of view?'

'You would say, would you not, that the sun is not only the author of visibility in all visible things, but of generation and nourishment and growth, though he himself is not generation?'

'Certainly.'

'In like manner the good may be said to be not only the author of knowledge to all things known, but of their being and essence, and yet the good is not essence, but far exceeds essence in dignity and power.'

Glaucon said, with a ludicrous earnestness: 'By the light of heaven, how amazing!'

'Yes,' I said, 'and the exaggeration may be set down to you; for you made me utter my fancies.'

'And pray continue to utter them; at any rate let us hear if there is anything more to be said about the similitude of the sun.'

'Yes,' I said, 'there is a great deal more.'

'Then omit nothing, however slight.'

'I will do my best,' I said; 'but I should think that a great deal will have to be omitted.'

'You have to imagine, then, that there are two ruling powers, and that one of them is set over the intellectual world, the other over the visible. I do not say heaven, lest you should fancy that I am playing upon the name (*ourhanoz*, *orhatoz*). May I suppose that you have this distinction of the visible and intelligible fixed in your mind?'

'I have.'

'Now take a line which has been cut into two unequal parts, and divide each of them again in thc same proportion, and suppose the two main divisions to answer, one to the visible and the other to the intelligible, and then compare the subdivisions in respect of their clearness and want of clearness, and you will find that the first section in the sphere of the visible consists of images. And by images I mean, in the first place, shadows, and in the second place, reflections in water and in solid, smooth and polished bodies and the like: Do you understand?'

'Yes, I understand.'

'Imagine, now, the other section, of which this is only the resemblance, to include the animals which we see, and everything that grows or is made.'

'Very good.'

'Would you not admit that both the sections of this division have different degrees of truth, and that the copy is to the original as the sphere of opinion is to the sphere of knowledge?'

'Most undoubtedly.'

'Next proceed to consider the manner in which the sphere of the intellectual is to be divided.'

'In what manner?'

'Thus: there are two subdivisions, in the lower of which the soul uses the figures given by the former division as images; the enquiry can only be hypothetical, and instead of going upwards to a principle descends to the other end; in the higher of the two, the soul passes out of hypotheses, and goes up to a principle which is above hypotheses, making no use of images as in the former case, but proceeding only in and through the ideas themselves.'

'I do not quite understand your meaning,' he said.

'Then I will try again; you will understand me better when I have made some preliminary remarks. You are aware that students of geometry, arithmetic, and the kindred sciences assume the odd and the even and the figures and three kinds of angles and the like in their several branches of science; these are their hypotheses, which they and everybody are supposed to know, and therefore they do not deign to give any account of them either to themselves or others; but they begin with them, and go on until they arrive at last, and in a consistent manner, at their conclusion?'

'Yes,' he said, 'I know.'

'And do you not know also that although they make use of the visible forms and reason about them, they are thinking not of these, but of the ideals which they resemble; not of the figures which they draw, but of the absolute square and the absolute diameter, and so on – the forms which they draw or make, and which have shadows and reflections in water of their own, are converted by them into images, but they are really seeking to behold the things themselves, which can only be seen with the eye of the mind?'

'That is true.'

'And of this kind I spoke as the intelligible, although in the search after it the soul is compelled to use hypotheses; not ascending to a first principle, because she is unable to rise above the region of hypothesis, but employing the objects of which the shadows below are resemblances in their turn as images, they having in relation to the shadows and reflections of them a greater distinctness, and therefore a higher value.'

'I understand', he said, 'that you are speaking of the province of geometry and the sister arts.'

'And when I speak of the other division of the intelligible, you will understand me to speak of that other sort of knowledge which reason herself attains by the power of dialectic, using the hypotheses not as first principles, but only as hypotheses – that is to say, as steps and points of departure into a world which is above hypotheses, in order that she may soar beyond them to the first principle of the whole; and clinging to this and then to that which depends on this, by successive steps she descends again without the aid of any sensible object, from ideas, through ideas, and in ideas she ends.'

'I understand you,' he replied; 'not perfectly, for you seem to me to be describing a task which is really tremendous; but, at any rate, I understand you to say that knowledge and being, which the science of dialectic contemplates, are clearer than the notions of the arts, as they are termed, which proceed from hypotheses only: these are also contemplated by the understanding, and not by the senses: yet, because they start from hypotheses and do not ascend to a principle, those who contemplate them appear to you not to exercise the higher reason upon them, although when a first principle is added to them they are cognizable by the higher reason. And the habit which is concerned with geometry and the cognate sciences I suppose that you would term understanding and not reason, as being intermediate between opinion and reason.'

'You have quite conceived my meaning,' I said. 'And now, corresponding to these four divisions, let there be four faculties in the soul – reason answering to the highest, understanding to the second, faith (or conviction) to the third, and perception of shadows to the last – and let there be a scale of them, and let us suppose that the several faculties have clearness in the same degree that their objects have truth.'

'I understand,' he replied, 'and give my assent, and accept your arrangement.'

Book VII

'And now,' I said, 'let me show in a figure how far our nature is enlightened or unenlightened. Behold! Human beings living in a underground den, which has a mouth open towards the light and reaching all along the den; here they have been from their childhood, and have their legs and necks chained so that they cannot move, and can only see before them, being prevented by the chains from turning round their heads. Above and behind them a fire is blazing at a distance, and between the fire and the prisoners there is a raised way; and you will see, if you look, a low wall built along the way, like the screen which marionette players have in front of them, over which they show the puppets.'

'I see.'

'And do you see', I said, 'men passing along the wall carrying all sorts of vessels, and statues and figures of animals made of wood and stone and various materials, which appear over the wall? Some of them are talking, others silent.'

'You have shown me a strange image, and they are strange prisoners.'

'Like ourselves,' I replied; 'and they see only their own shadows, or the shadows of one another, which the fire throws on the opposite wall of the cave?'

'True,' he said; 'how could they see anything but the shadows if they were never allowed to move their heads?'

'And of the objects which are being carried in like manner they would only see the shadows?'

'Yes,' he said.

'And if they were able to converse with one another, would they not suppose that they were naming what was actually before them?'

'Very true.'

'And suppose further that the prison had an echo which came from the other side, would they not be sure to fancy when one of the passers-by spoke that the voice which they heard came from the passing shadow?'

'No question,' he replied.

'To them', I said, 'the truth would be literally nothing but the shadows of the images.'

'That is certain.'

'And now look again, and see what will naturally follow if the prisoners are released and disabused of their error. At first, when any of them is liberated and compelled suddenly to stand up and turn his neck round and walk and look towards the light, he will suffer sharp pains; the glare will distress him, and he will be unable to see the realities of which in his former state he had seen the shadows; and then conceive someone saying to him, that what he saw before was an illusion, but that now, when he is approaching nearer to being and his eye is turned towards more real existence, he has a clearer vision – what will be his reply? And you may further imagine that his instructor is pointing to the objects as they pass and requiring him to name them – will he not be perplexed? Will he not fancy that the shadows which he formerly saw are truer than the objects which are now shown to him?'

'Far truer.'

'And if he is compelled to look straight at the light, will he not have a pain in his eyes which will make him turn away to take in the objects of vision which he can see, and which he will conceive to be in reality clearer than the things which are now being shown to him?'

'True,' he said.

'And suppose once more that he is reluctantly dragged up a steep and rugged ascent, and held fast until he is forced into the presence of the sun himself, is he not likely to be pained and irritated? When he approaches the light his eyes will be dazzled, and he will not be able to see anything at all of what are now called realities.'

'Not all in a moment,' he said.

'He will require to grow accustomed to the sight of the upper world. And first he will see the shadows best, next the reflections of men and other objects in the water, and then the objects themselves; then he will gaze upon the light of the moon and the stars and the spangled heaven; and he will see the sky and the stars by night better than the sun or the light of the sun by day?'

'Certainly.'

'Last of he will be able to see the sun, and not mere reflections of him in the water, but he will see him in his own proper place, and not in another; and he will contemplate him as he is.'

'Certainly.'

'He will then proceed to argue that this is he who gives the season and the years, and is the guardian of all that is in the visible world, and in a certain way the cause of all things which he and his fellows have been accustomed to behold?'

'Clearly,' he said, 'he would first see the sun and then reason about him.'

'And when he remembered his old habitation, and the wisdom of the den and his fellow-prisoners, do you not suppose that he would felicitate himself on the change, and pity them?'

'Certainly, he would.'

'And if they were in the habit of conferring honours among themselves on those who were quickest to observe the passing shadows and to remark which of them went before, and which followed after, and which were together; and who were therefore best able to draw conclusions as to the future, do you think that he would care for such honours and glories, or envy the possessors of them? Would he not say with Homer,

"Better to be the poor servant of a poor master,"

and to endure anything, rather than think as they do and live after their manner?'

'Yes,' he said, 'I think that he would rather suffer anything than entertain these false notions and live in this miserable manner.'

'Imagine once more', I said, 'such a one coming suddenly out of the sun to be replaced in his old situation; would he not be certain to have his eyes full of darkness?'

'To be sure,' he said.

'And if there were a contest, and he had to compete in measuring the shadows with the prisoners who had never moved out of the den, while his sight was still weak, and before his eyes had become steady (and the time which would be needed to acquire this new habit of sight might be very considerable) would he not be ridiculous? Men would say of him that up he went and down he came without his eyes; and that it was better not even to think of ascending; and if anyone tried to loose another and lead him up to the light, let them only catch the offender, and they would put him to death.'

'No question,' he said.

'This entire allegory', I said, 'you may now append, dear Glaucon, to the previous argument; the prison-house is the world of sight, the light of the fire is the sun, and you will not misapprehend me if you interpret the journey upwards to be the ascent of the soul into the intellectual world according to my poor belief, which, at your desire, I have expressed whether rightly or wrongly God knows. But, whether true or false, my opinion is that in the world of knowledge the idea of good appears last of all, and is seen only with an effort; and, when seen, is also inferred to be the universal author of all things beautiful and right, parent of light and of the lord of light in this visible world, and the immediate source of reason and truth in the intellectual; and that this is the power upon which he who would act rationally, either in public or private life, must have his eye fixed.'

'I agree,' he said, 'as far as I am able to understand you.'

'Moreover,' I said, 'you must not wonder that those who attain to this beatific vision are unwilling to descend to human affairs; for their souls are ever hastening into the upper world where they desire to dwell; which desire of theirs is very natural, if our allegory may be trusted.'

'Yes, very natural.'

'And is there anything surprising in one who passes from divine contemplations to the evil state of man, misbehaving himself in a ridiculous manner; if, while his eyes are blinking and before he has become accustomed to the surrounding darkness, he is compelled to fight in courts of law, or in other places, about the images or the shadows of images of justice, and is endeavouring to meet the conceptions of those who have never yet seen absolute justice?'

'Anything but surprising,' he replied.

'Anyone who has common sense will remember that the bewilderments of the eyes are of two kinds, and arise from two causes, either from coming out of the light or from going into the light, which is true of the mind's eye, quite as much as of the bodily eye; and he who remembers this when he sees anyone whose vision is perplexed and weak, will not be too ready to laugh; he will first ask whether that soul of man has come out of the brighter light, and is unable to see because unaccustomed to the dark, or having turned from darkness to the day is dazzled by excess of light. And he will count the one happy in his condition and state of being, and he will pity the other; or, if he have a mind to laugh at the soul which comes from below into the light, there will be more reason in this than in the laugh which greets him who returns from above out of the light into the den.'

'That', he said, 'is a very just distinction.'

'But then, if I am right, certain professors of education must be wrong when they say that they can put a knowledge into the soul which was not there before, like sight into blind eyes.'

'They undoubtedly say this,' he replied.

'Whereas, our argument shows that the power and capacity of learning exists in the soul already; and that just as the eye was unable to turn from darkness to light without the whole body, so too the instrument of knowledge can only by the movement of the whole soul be turned from the world of becoming into that of being, and learn by degrees to endure the sight of being, and of the brightest and best of being, or in other words, of the good.'

'Very true.'

'And must there not be some art which will effect conversion in the easiest and quickest manner; not implanting the faculty of sight, for that exists already but has been turned in the wrong direction, and is looking away from the truth?'

'Yes,' he said, 'such an art may be presumed.'

'And whereas the other so-called virtues of the soul seem to be akin to bodily qualities, for even when they are not originally innate they can be implanted later by habit and exercise, the virtue of wisdom more than anything else contains a divine element which always remains, and by this conversion is rendered useful and profitable; or, on the other hand, hurtful and useless. Did you never observe the narrow intelligence flashing from the keen eye of a clever rogue – how eager he is, how clearly his paltry soul sees the way to his end; he is the reverse of blind, but his keen eyesight is forced into the service of evil, and he is mischievous in proportion to his cleverness.'

'Very true,' he said.

'But what if there had been a circumcision of such natures in the days of their youth; and they had been severed from those sensual pleasures, such as eating and drinking, which, like leaden weights, were attached to them at their birth, and which drag them down and turn the vision of their souls upon the things that are below – if, I say, they had been released from these impediments and turned in the opposite direction, the very same faculty in them would have seen the truth as keenly as they see what their eyes are turned to now.'

'Very likely.'

'Yes,' I said; 'and there is another thing which is likely, or rather a necessary inference from what has preceded, that neither the uneducated and uninformed of the truth, nor yet those who never make an end of their education, will be able ministers of State; not the former, because they have no single aim of duty which is the rule of all their actions, private as well as public; nor the latter, because they will not act at all except upon compulsion, fancying that they are already dwelling apart in the islands of the blessed.'

'Very true,' he replied.

'Then', I said, 'the business of us who are the founders of the State will be to compel the best minds to attain that knowledge which we have already shown to be the greatest of all – they must continue to ascend until they arrive at the good; but when they have ascended and seen enough we must not allow them to do as they do now.'

'What do you mean?

'I mean that they remain in the upper world, but this must not be allowed; they must be made to descend again among the prisoners in the den, and partake of their labours and honours, whether they are worth having or not.'

'But is not this unjust?' he said. 'Ought we to give them a worse life, when they might have a better?'

'You have again forgotten, my friend,' I said, 'the intention of the legislator, who did not aim at making any one class in the State happy above the rest. The happiness was to be in the whole State, and he held the citizens together by persuasion and necessity, making them benefactors of the State, and therefore benefactors of one another; to this end he created them, not to please themselves, but to be his instruments in binding up the State.'

'True,' he said, 'I had forgotten.'

'Observe, Glaucon, that there will be no injustice in compelling our philosophers to have a care and providence of others; we shall explain to them that in other States, men of their class are not obliged to share in the toils of politics: and this is reasonable, for they grow up at their own sweet will, and the government would rather not have them. Being self-taught, they cannot be expected to show any gratitude for a culture which they have never received. But we have brought you into the world to be rulers of the hive, kings of yourselves and of the other citizens, and have educated you far better and more perfectly than they have been educated, and you are better able to share in the double duty. Wherefore each of you, when his turn comes, must go down to the general underground abode, and get the habit of seeing in the dark. When you have acquired the habit, you will see ten thousand times better than the inhabitants of the den, and you will know what the several images are, and what they represent, because you have seen the beautiful and just and good in their truth. And thus our State which is also yours will be a reality, and not a dream only, and will be administered in a spirit unlike that of other States, in which men fight with one another about shadows only and are distracted in the struggle for power, which in their eyes is a great good. Whereas the truth is that the State in which the rulers are most reluctant to govern is always the best and most quietly governed, and the State in which they are most eager, the worst.'

'Quite true,' he replied.

'And will our pupils, when they hear this, refuse to take their turn at the toils of State, when they are allowed to spend the greater part of their time with one another in the heavenly light?'

'Impossible,' he answered. 'For they are just men, and the commands which we impose upon them are just; there can be no doubt that every one of them will take office as a stern necessity, and not after the fashion of our present rulers of State.'

'Yes, my friend,' I said; 'and there lies the point. You must contrive for your future rulers another and a better life than that of a ruler, and then you may have a well-ordered State; for only in the State which offers this, will they rule who are truly rich, not in silver and gold, but in virtue and wisdom, which are the true blessings of life. Whereas if they go to the administration of public affairs, poor and hungering after their own private advantage, thinking that hence they are to snatch the chief good, order there can never be; for they will be fighting about office, and the civil and domestic broils which thus arise will be the ruin of the rulers themselves and of the whole State.'

'Most true,' he replied.

'And the only life which looks down upon the life of political ambition is that of true philosophy. Do you know of any other?'

'Indeed, I do not,' he said.

'And those who govern ought not to be lovers of the task? For, if they are, there will be rival lovers, and they will fight.'

'No question.'

'Who, then, are those whom we shall compel to be guardians? Surely they will be the men who are wisest about affairs of State, and by whom the State is best administered, and who at the same time have other honours and another and a better life than that of politics?'

'They are the men, and I will choose them,' he replied.

'And now shall we consider in what way such guardians will be produced, and how they are to be brought from darkness to light – as some are said to have ascended from the world below to the gods?'

'By all means,' he replied.

'The process', I said, 'is not the turning over of an oyster-shell, but the turning round of a soul passing from a day which is little better than night to the true day of being, that is, the ascent from below, which we affirm to be true philosophy?'

'Quite so.'

'And should we not enquire what sort of knowledge has the power of effecting such a change?'

'Certainly.'

'What sort of knowledge is there which would draw the soul from becoming to being? And another consideration has just occurred to me. You will remember that our young men are to be warrior athletes?'

'Yes, that was said.'

'Then this new kind of knowledge must have an additional quality?'

'What quality?'

'Usefulness in war.'

'Yes, if possible.'

'There were two parts in our former scheme of education, were there not?'

'Just so.'

'There was gymnastics which presided over the growth and decay of the body, and may therefore be regarded as having to do with generation and corruption?'

'True.'

'Then that is not the knowledge which we are seeking to discover?'

'No.'

'But what do you say of music, which also entered to a certain extent into our former scheme?'

'Music', he said, 'as you will remember, was the counterpart of gymnastics, and trained the guardians by the influences of habit, by harmony making them harmonious, by rhythm rhythmical, but not giving them science; and the words, whether fabulous or possibly true, had kindred elements of rhythm and harmony in them. But in music there was nothing which tended to that good which you are now seeking.'

'You are most accurate', I said, 'in your recollection; in music there certainly was nothing of the kind. But what branch of knowledge is there, my dear Glaucon, which is of the desired nature; since all the useful arts were reckoned mean by us?'

'Undoubtedly; and yet if music and gymnastics are excluded, and the arts are also excluded, what remains?'

'Well,' I said, 'there may be nothing left of our special subjects; and then we shall have to take something which is not special, but of universal application.'

'What may that be?'

'A something which all arts and sciences and intelligences use in common, and which everyone first has to learn among the elements of education.'

'What is that?'

'The little matter of distinguishing one, two and three – in a word, number and calculation: do not all arts and sciences necessarily partake of them?'

'Yes.'

'Then the art of war partakes of them?'

'To be sure.'

'Then Palamedes, whenever he appears in tragedy, proves Agamemnon ridiculously unfit to be a general. Did you never remark how he declares that he had invented number, and had numbered the ships and set in array the ranks of the army at Troy; which implies that they had never been numbered before, and Agamemnon must be supposed literally to have been incapable of counting his own feet – how could he if he was ignorant of number? And if that is true, what sort of general must he have been?'

'I should say a very strange one, if this was as you say.'

'Can we deny that a warrior should have a knowledge of arithmetic?'

'Certainly he should, if he is to have the smallest understanding of military tactics, or indeed, I should rather say, if he is to be a man at all.'

'I should like to know whether you have the same notion which I have of this study?'

'What is your notion?'

'It appears to me to be a study of the kind which we are seeking, and which leads naturally to reflection, but never to have been rightly used; for the true use of it is simply to draw the soul towards being.'

'Will you explain your meaning?' he said.

'I will try,' I said; 'and I wish you would share the enquiry with me, and say "yes" or "no" when I attempt to distinguish in my own mind what branches of knowledge have this attracting power, in order that we may have clearer proof that arithmetic is, as I suspect, one of them.'

'Explain,' he said.

'I mean to say that objects of sense are of two kinds: some of them do not invite thought because the sense is an adequate judge of them; while in the case of other objects sense is so untrustworthy that further enquiry is imperatively demanded.'

'You are clearly referring', he said, 'to the manner in which the senses are imposed upon by distance, and by painting in light and shade.'

'No,' I said, 'that is not at all my meaning.'

'Then what is your meaning?'

'When speaking of uninviting objects, I mean those which do not pass from one sensation to the opposite; inviting objects are those which do; in this latter case the sense coming upon the object, whether at a distance or near, gives no more vivid idea of anything in particular than of its opposite. An illustration will make my meaning clearer: here are three fingers – a little finger, a second finger and a middle finger.'

'Very good.'

'You may suppose that they are seen quite close. And here comes the point.'

'What is it?'

'Each of them equally appears a finger, whether seen in the middle or at the extremity, whether white or black, or thick or thin – it makes no difference: a finger is a finger all the same. In these cases a man is not compelled to ask of thought the question, what is a finger? For the sight never intimates to the mind that a finger is other than a finger.'

'True.'

'And therefore,' I said, 'as we might expect, there is nothing here which invites or excites intelligence.'

'There is not,' he said.

'But is this equally true of the greatness and smallness of the fingers? Can sight adequately perceive them? And is no difference made by the circumstance that one of the fingers is in the middle and another at the extremity? And in like manner does the touch adequately perceive the qualities of thickness or thinness, or softness or hardness? And so of the other senses: do they give perfect intimations of such matters? Is not their mode of operation on this wise – the sense which is concerned with the quality of hardness is necessarily concerned also with the quality of softness, and only intimates to the soul that the same thing is felt to be both hard and soft?'

'You are quite right,' he said.

'And must not the soul be perplexed at this intimation which the sense gives of a hard which is also soft? What, again, is the meaning of light and heavy, if that which is light is also heavy, and that which is heavy, light?'

'Yes,' he said, 'these intimations which the soul receives are very curious and require to be explained.'

'Yes,' I said, 'and in these perplexities the soul naturally summons to her aid calculation and intelligence, that she may see whether the several objects announced to her are one or two.'

'True.'

'And if they turn out to be two, is not each of them one and different?'

'Certainly.'

'And if each is one, and both are two, she will conceive the two as in a state of division, for if they were undivided they could only be conceived of as one?'

'True.'

'The eye certainly did see both small and great, but only in a confused manner; they were not distinguished.'

'Yes.'

'Whereas the thinking mind, intending to light up the chaos, was compelled to reverse the process, and look at small and great as separate and not confused.'

'Very true.'

'Was not this the beginning of the enquiry. "What is great?" and "What is small?"'

'Exactly so.'

'And thus arose the distinction of the visible and the intelligible.'

'Most true.'

'This was what I meant when I spoke of impressions which invited the intellect, or the reverse – those which are simultaneous with opposite impressions, invite thought; those which are not simultaneous do not.'

'I understand,' he said, 'and agree with you.'

'And to which class do unity and number belong?'

'I do not know,' he replied.

'Think a little and you will see that what has preceded will supply the answer; for if simple unity could be adequately perceived by the sight or by any other sense, then, as we were saying in the case of the finger, there would be nothing to attract towards being; but when there is some contradiction always present, and one is the reverse of one and involves the conception of plurality, then thought begins to be aroused within us, and the soul perplexed and wanting to arrive at a decision asks "What is absolute unity?" This is the way in which the study of the one has a power of drawing and converting the mind to the contemplation of true being.'

'And surely', he said, 'this occurs notably in the case of one; for we see the same thing to be both one and infinite in multitude?'

'Yes,' I said; 'and this being true of one must be equally true of all number?'

'Certainly.'

'And all arithmetic and calculation have to do with number?'

'Yes.'

'And they appear to lead the mind towards truth?'

'Yes, in a very remarkable manner.'

'Then this is knowledge of the kind for which we are seeking, having a double use, military and philosophical; for the man of war must learn the art of number or he will not know how to array his troops, and the philosopher also, because he has to rise out of the sea of change and lay hold of true being, and therefore he must be an arithmetician.'

'That is true.'

'And our guardian is both warrior and philosopher?'

'Certainly.'

'Then this is a kind of knowledge which legislation may fitly prescribe; and we must endeavour to persuade those who are prescribed to be the principal men of our State to go and learn arithmetic, not as amateurs, but they must carry on the study until they see the nature of numbers with the mind only; nor again, like merchants or retail-traders, with a view to buying or selling, but for the sake of their military use, and of the soul herself; and because this will be the easiest way for her to pass from becoming to truth and being.'

'That is excellent,' he said.

'Yes,' I said, 'and now having spoken of it, I must add how charming the science is! And in how many ways it conduces to our desired end, if pursued in the spirit of a philosopher, and not of a shopkeeper!'

'How do you mean?'

'I mean, as I was saying, that arithmetic has a very great and elevating effect, compelling the soul to reason about abstract number, and rebelling against the introduction of visible or tangible objects into the argument. You know how steadily the masters of the art repel and ridicule anyone who attempts to divide absolute unity when he is calculating, and if you divide, they multiply, taking care that one shall continue one and not become lost in fractions.'

'That is very true.'

'Now, suppose a person were to say to them: "O my friends, what are these wonderful numbers about which you are reasoning, in which, as you say, there is a unity such as you demand, and each unit is equal, invariable, indivisible?" – what would they answer?'

'They would answer, as I should conceive, that they were speaking of those numbers which can only be realised in thought.'

'Then you see that this knowledge may be truly called necessary, necessitating as it clearly does the use of the pure intelligence in the attainment of pure truth?'

'Yes; that is a marked characteristic of it.'

'And have you further observed that those who have a natural talent for calculation are generally quick at every other kind of knowledge; and even the dull if they have had an arithmetical training, although they may derive no other advantage from it, always become much quicker than they would otherwise have been?'

'Very true,' he said.

'And indeed, you will not easily find a more difficult study, and not many as difficult.'

'You will not.'

'And, for all these reasons, arithmetic is a kind of knowledge in which the best natures should be trained, and which must not be given up.'

'I agree.'

'Let this then be made one of our subjects of education. And next, shall we enquire whether the kindred science also concerns us?'

'You mean geometry?'

'Exactly so.'

'Clearly,' he said, 'we are concerned with that part of geometry which relates to war; for in pitching a camp, or taking up a position, or closing or extending the lines of an army, or any other military manoeuvre, whether in actual battle or on a march, it will make all the difference whether a general is or is not a geometrician.'

'Yes,' I said, 'but for that purpose a very little of either geometry or calculation will be enough; the question relates rather to the greater and more advanced part of geometry – whether that tends in any degree to make more easy the vision of the idea of good; and thither, as I was saying, all things tend which compel the soul to turn her gaze towards that place, where is the full perfection of being, which she ought, by all means, to behold.'

'True,' he said.

'Then if geometry compels us to view being, it concerns us; if becoming only, it does not concern us?'

'Yes, that is what we assert.'

'Yet anybody who has the least acquaintance with geometry will not deny that such a conception of the science is in flat contradiction to the ordinary language of geometricians.'

'How so?'

'They have in view practice only, and are always speaking in a narrow and ridiculous manner, of squaring and extending and applying and the like – they confuse the necessities of geometry with those of daily life; whereas knowledge is the real object of the whole science.'

'Certainly,' he said.

'Then must not a further admission be made?'

'What admission?'

'That the knowledge at which geometry aims is knowledge of the eternal, and not of aught perishing and transient.'

'That', he replied, 'may be readily allowed, and is true.'

'Then, my noble friend, geometry will draw the soul towards truth, and create the spirit of philosophy, and raise up that which is now unhappily allowed to fall down.'

'Nothing will be more likely to have such an effect.'

'Then nothing should be more sternly laid down than that the inhabitants of your fair city should by all means learn geometry. Moreover the science has indirect effects, which are not small.'

'Of what kind?' he said.

'There are the military advantages of which you spoke,' I said. 'And in all departments of knowledge, as experience proves, anyone who has studied geometry is infinitely quicker of apprehension than one who has not.'

'Yes indeed,' he said, 'there is an infinite difference between them.'

'Then shall we propose this as a second branch of knowledge which our youth will study?'

'Let us do so,' he replied.

'And suppose we make astronomy the third – what do you say?'

'I am strongly inclined to it,' he said; 'the observation of the seasons and of months and years is as essential to the general as it is to the farmer or sailor.'

'I am amused', I said, 'at your fear of the world, which makes you guard against the appearance of insisting upon useless studies; and I quite admit the difficulty of believing that in every man there is an eye of the soul which, when by other pursuits lost and dimmed, is by these purified and re-illumined; and is more precious far than ten thousand bodily eyes, for by it alone is truth seen. Now there are two classes of persons: one class of those who will agree with you and will take your words as a revelation; another class to whom they will be utterly unmeaning, and who will naturally deem them to be idle tales, for they see no sort of profit which is to be obtained from them. And therefore you had better decide at once with which of the two you are proposing to argue. You will very likely say with neither, and that your chief aim in carrying on the argument is your own improvement; at the same time you do not grudge to others any benefit which they may receive.'

'I think that I should prefer to carry on the argument mainly on my own behalf.'

'Then take a step backward, for we have gone wrong in the order of the sciences.'

'What was the mistake?' he said.

'After plane geometry,' I said, 'we proceeded at once to solids in revolution, instead of taking solids in themselves; whereas after the second dimension the third, which is concerned with cubes and dimensions of depth, ought to have followed.'

'That is true, Socrates; but so little seems to be known as yet about these subjects.'

'Why, yes,' I said, 'and for two reasons:– in the first place, no government patronises them; this leads to a want of energy in the pursuit of them, and they are difficult; in the second place, students cannot learn them unless they have a director. But then a director can hardly be found, and even if he could, as matters now stand, the students, who are very conceited, would not attend to him. That, however, would be otherwise if the whole State became the director of these studies and gave honour to them; then disciples would want to come, and there would be continuous and earnest search, and discoveries would be made; since even now, disregarded as they are by the world, and maimed of their fair proportions, and although none of their votaries can tell the use of them, still these studies force their way by their natural charm, and very likely, if they had the help of the State, they would some day emerge into light.'

'Yes,' he said, 'there is a remarkable charm in them. But I do not clearly understand the change in the order. First you began with a geometry of plane surfaces?'

'Yes', I said.

'And you placed astronomy next, and then you made a step backward?'

'Yes, and I have delayed you by my hurry; the ludicrous state of solid geometry, which, in natural order, should have followed, made me pass over this branch and go on to astronomy, or motion of solids.'

'True,' he said.

'Then assuming that the science now omitted would come into existence if encouraged by the State, let us go on to astronomy, which will be fourth.'

'The right order,' he replied. 'And now, Socrates, as you rebuked the vulgar manner in which I praised astronomy before, my praise shall be given in your own spirit. For everyone, as I think, must see that astronomy compels the soul to look upwards and leads us from this world to another.'

'Everyone but myself,' I said. 'To everyone else this may be clear, but not to me.'

'And what then would you say?'

'I should rather say that those who elevate astronomy into philosophy appear to me to make us look downwards and not upwards.'

'What do you mean?' he asked.

'You', I replied, 'have in your mind a truly sublime conception of our knowledge of the things above. And I dare say that if a person were to throw his head back and study the fretted ceiling, you would still think that his mind was the percipient, and not his eyes. And you are very likely right, and I may be a simpleton, but, in my opinion, that knowledge only which is of being and of the unseen can make the soul look upwards, and whether a man gapes at the heavens or blinks on the ground, seeking to learn some particular of sense,

I would deny that he can learn, for nothing of that sort is a matter of science; his soul is looking downwards, not upwards, whether his way to knowledge is by water or by land, whether he floats, or only lies on his back.'

'I acknowledge', he said, 'the justice of your rebuke. Still, I should like to ascertain how astronomy can be learned in any manner more conducive to that knowledge of which we are speaking?'

'I will tell you,' I said. 'The starry heaven which we behold is wrought upon a visible ground, and therefore, although the fairest and most perfect of visible things, must necessarily be deemed inferior far to the true motions of absolute swiftness and absolute slowness, which are relative to each other, and carry with them that which is contained in them, in the true number and in every true figure. Now, these are to be apprehended by reason and intelligence, but not by sight.'

'True,' he replied.

'The spangled heavens should be used as a pattern and with a view to that higher knowledge; their beauty is like the beauty of figures or pictures excellently wrought by the hand of Daedalus, or some other great artist, which we may chance to behold; any geometrician who saw them would appreciate the exquisiteness of their workmanship, but he would never dream of thinking that in them he could find the true equal or the true double, or the truth of any other proportion.'

'No,' he replied, 'such an idea would be ridiculous.'

'And will not a true astronomer have the same feeling when he looks at the movements of the stars? Will he not think that heaven and the things in heaven are framed by the Creator of them in the most perfect manner? But he will never imagine that the proportions of night and day, or of both to the month, or of the month to the year, or of the stars to these and to one another, and any other things that are material and visible can also be eternal and subject to no deviation – that would be absurd; and it is equally absurd to take so much pains in investigating their exact truth.'

'I quite agree, though I never thought of this before.'

'Then', I said, 'in astronomy, as in geometry, we should employ problems, and let the heavens alone if we would approach the subject in the right way and so make the natural gift of reason to be of any real use.'

'That', he said, 'is a work infinitely beyond our present astronomers.'

'Yes,' I said, 'and there are many other things which must also have a similar extension given to them, if our legislation is to be of any value. But can you tell me of any other suitable study?'

'No,' he said, 'not without thinking.'

'Motion', I said, 'has many forms, and not one only; two of them are obvious enough even to wits no better than ours; and there are others, as I imagine, which may be left to wiser persons.'

'But where are the two?'

'There is a second,' I said, 'which is the counterpart of the one already named.'

'And what may that be?'

'The second', I said, 'would seem relatively to the ears to be what the first is to the eyes; for I conceive that as the eyes are designed to look up at the stars, so are the ears to hear harmonious motions; and these are sister sciences – as the Pythagoreans say, and we, Glaucon, agree with them?'

'Yes,' he replied.

'But this', I said, 'is a laborious study, and therefore we had better go and learn of them; and they will tell us whether there are any other applications of these sciences. At the same time, we must not lose sight of our own higher object.'

'What is that?'

'There is a perfection which all knowledge ought to reach, and which our pupils ought also to attain, and not to fall short of, as I was saying that they did in astronomy. For in the science of harmony, as you probably know, the same thing happens. The teachers of harmony compare the sounds and consonances which are heard only, and their labour, like that of the astronomers, is in vain.'

'Yes, by heaven!' he said. 'And 'tis as good as a play to hear them talking about their condensed notes, as they call them; they put their ears close alongside of the strings like persons catching a sound from their neighbour's wall – one set of them declaring that they distinguish an intermediate note and have found the least interval which should be the unit of measurement; the others insisting that the two sounds have passed into the same – either party setting their ears before their understanding.'

'You mean', I said, 'those gentlemen who tease and torture the strings and rack them on the pegs of the instrument: might carry on the metaphor and speak after their manner of the blows which the plectrum gives, and make accusations against the strings, both of backwardness and forwardness to sound; but this would be tedious, and therefore I will only say that these are not the men, and that I am referring to the Pythagoreans, of whom I was just now proposing to enquire about harmony. For they too are in error, like the astronomers; they investigate the numbers of the harmonies which are heard, but they never attain to problems – that is to say, they never reach the natural harmonies of number, or reflect why some numbers are harmonious and others not.'

'That,' he said, 'is a thing of more than mortal knowledge.'

'A thing', I replied, 'which I would rather call useful; that is, if sought after with a view to the beautiful and good; but if pursued in any other spirit, useless.'

'Very true,' he said.

'Now, when all these studies reach the point of inter-communion and connection with one another, and come to be considered in their mutual affinities, then, I think, but not till then, will the pursuit of them have a value for our objects; otherwise there is no profit in them.'

'I suspect so; but you are speaking, Socrates, of a vast work.'

'What do you mean?' I said. 'The prelude or what? Do you not know that all this is but the prelude to the actual strain which we have to learn? For you surely would not regard the skilled mathematician as a dialectician?'

'Assuredly not,' he said. 'I have hardly ever known a mathematician who was capable of reasoning.'

'But do you imagine that men who are unable to give and take a reason will have the knowledge which we require of them?'

'Neither can this be supposed.'

'And so, Glaucon,' I said, 'we have at last arrived at the hymn of dialectic. This is that strain which is of the intellect only, but which the faculty of sight will nevertheless be found to imitate; for sight, as you may remember, was imagined by us after a while to behold the real animals and stars, and last of all the sun himself. And so with dialectic; when a person starts on the discovery of the absolute by the light of reason only, and without any assistance of sense, and perseveres until by pure intelligence he arrives at the perception of the absolute good, he at last finds himself at the end of the intellectual world, as in the case of sight at the end of the visible.'

'Exactly,' he said.

'Then this is the progress which you call dialectic?'

'True.'

'But the release of the prisoners from chains, and their translation from the shadows to the images and to the light, and the ascent from the underground den to the sun, while in his presence they are vainly trying to look on animals and plants and the light of the sun, but are able to perceive even with their weak eyes the images in the water (which are divine), and are the shadows of true existence (not shadows of images cast by a light of fire, which compared with the sun is only an image) – this power of elevating the highest principle in the soul to the contemplation of that which is best in existence, with which we may compare the raising of that faculty which is the very light of the body to the sight of that which is brightest in the material and visible world – this power is given, as I was saying, by all that study and pursuit of the arts which has been described.'

'I agree with what you are saying,' he replied, 'which may be hard to believe, yet, from another point of view, is harder still to deny. This, however, is not a theme to be treated of in passing only, but will have to be discussed again and again. And so, whether our conclusion be true or false, let us assume all this, and proceed at once from the prelude or preamble to the chief strain, and describe that in like manner. Say, then, what is the nature and what are the divisions of dialectic, and what are the paths which lead thither; for these paths will also lead to our final rest?'

'Dear Glaucon,' I said, 'you will not be able to follow me here, though I would do my best, and you should behold not an image only but the absolute truth, according to my notion. Whether what I told you would or would not have been a reality I cannot venture to say; but you would have seen something like reality, of that I am confident.'

'Doubtless,' he replied.

'But I must also remind you that the power of dialectic alone can reveal this, and only to one who is a disciple of the previous sciences.'

'Of that assertion you may be as confident as of the last.'

'And assuredly no one will argue that there is any other method of comprehending by any regular process all true existence or of ascertaining what each thing is in its own nature; for the arts in general are concerned with the desires or opinions of men, or are cultivated with a view to production and construction, or for the preservation of such productions and constructions; and as to the mathematical sciences which, as we were saying, have some apprehension of true being – geometry and the like – they only dream about being, but never can they behold the waking reality so long as they leave the hypotheses which they use unexamined, and are unable to give an account of them. For when a man knows not his own first principle, and when the conclusion and intermediate steps are also constructed out of he knows not what, how can he imagine that such a fabric of convention can ever become science?'

'Impossible,' he said.

'Then dialectic, and dialectic alone, goes directly to the first principle and is the only science which does away with hypotheses in order to make her ground secure; the eye of the soul, which is literally buried in an outlandish slough, is by her gentle aid lifted upwards; and she uses as handmaids and helpers in the work of conversion the sciences which we have been discussing. Custom terms them sciences, but they ought to have some other name, implying greater clearness than opinion and less clearness than science; and this, in our previous sketch, was called understanding. But why should we dispute about names when we have realities of such importance to consider?'

'Why indeed,' he said, 'when any name will do which expresses the thought of the mind with clearness?'

'At any rate, we are satisfied, as before, to have four divisions – two for intellect and two for opinion – and to call the first division science, the second understanding, the third belief and the fourth perception of shadows; opinion being concerned with becoming, and intellect with being, and so to make a proportion:

> "As being is to becoming, so is pure intellect to opinion.
> And as intellect is to opinion, so is science to belief, and understanding to the perception of shadows."

But let us defer the further correlation and subdivision of the subjects of opinion and of intellect, for it will be a long enquiry, many times longer than this has been.'

'As far as I understand,' he said, 'I agree.'

'And do you also agree', I said, 'in describing the dialectician as one who attains a conception of the essence of each thing? And he who does not possess and is therefore unable to impart this conception, in whatever degree he fails, may in that degree also be said to fail in intelligence? Will you admit so much?'

'Yes,' he said; 'how can I deny it?'

'And you would say the same of the conception of the good?'

'Until the person is able to abstract and define rationally the idea of good, and unless he can run the gauntlet of all objections, and is ready to disprove them, not by appeals to opinion, but to absolute truth, never faltering at any step of the argument – unless he can do all this, you would say that he knows neither the idea of good nor any other good: he apprehends only a shadow, if anything at all, which is given by opinion and not by science. Dreaming and slumbering in this life, before he is well awake here, he arrives at the world below, and has his final quietus.'

'In all that I should most certainly agree with you.'

'And surely you would not have the children of your ideal State, whom you are nurturing and educating – if the ideal ever becomes a reality – you would not allow the future rulers to be like posts, having no reason in them, and yet to be set in authority over the highest matters?'

'Certainly not.'

'Then you will make a law that they shall have such an education as will enable them to attain the greatest skill in asking and answering questions?'

'Yes,' he said, 'you and I together will make it.'

'Dialectic, then, as you will agree, is the coping-stone of the sciences, and is set over them: no other science can be placed higher – the nature of knowledge can no further go?'

'I agree,' he said.

'But to whom we are to assign these studies, and in what way they are to be assigned, are questions which remain to be considered?'

'Yes, clearly.'

'You remember', I said, 'how the rulers were chosen before?

'Certainly,' he said.

'The same natures must still be chosen, and the preference again given to the surest and the bravest, and, if possible, to the fairest; and, having noble and generous tempers, they should also have the natural gifts which will facilitate their education.'

'And what are these?'

'Such gifts as keenness and ready powers of acquisition; for the mind more often faints from the severity of study than from the severity of gymnastics: the toil is more entirely the mind's own, and is not shared with the body.'

'Very true,' he replied.

'Further, he of whom we are in search should have a good memory, and be an unwearied solid man who is a lover of labour in any line; or he will never be able to endure the great amount of bodily exercise and to go through all the intellectual discipline and study which we require of him.'

'Certainly,' he said; 'he must have natural gifts.'

'The mistake at present is that those who study philosophy have no vocation, and this, as I was before saying, is the reason why she has fallen into disrepute: her true sons should take her by the hand and not bastards.'

'What do you mean?'

'In the first place, her votary should not have a lame or halting industry – I mean, that he should not be half industrious and half idle: as, for example, when a man is a lover of gymnastics and hunting, and all other bodily exercises, but a hater rather than a lover of the labour of learning or listening or enquiring. Or the occupation to which he devotes himself may be of an opposite kind, and he may have the other sort of lameness.'

'Certainly,' he said.

'And as to truth,' I said, 'is not a soul equally to be deemed halt and lame which hates voluntary falsehood and is extremely indignant at herself and others when they tell lies, but is patient of involuntary falsehood, and does not mind wallowing like a swinish beast in the mire of ignorance, and has no shame at being detected?'

'To be sure.'

'And, again, in respect of temperance, courage, magnificence and every other virtue, should we not carefully distinguish between the true son and the bastard? For where there is no discernment of such qualities States and individuals unconsciously err and the State makes a ruler, and the individual a friend, of one who, being defective in some part of virtue, is in a figure lame or a bastard.'

'That is very true,' he said.

'All these things, then, will have to be carefully considered by us; and if only those whom we introduce to this vast system of education and training are sound in body and mind, justice herself will have nothing to say against us, and we shall be the saviours of the constitution and of the State; but, if our pupils are men of another stamp, the reverse will happen, and we shall pour a still greater flood of ridicule on philosophy than she has to endure at present.'

'That would not be creditable.'

'Certainly not,' I said. 'And yet perhaps, in thus turning jest into earnest I am equally ridiculous.'

'In what respect?'

'I had forgotten', I said, 'that we were not serious, and spoke with too much excitement. For when I saw philosophy so undeservedly trampled under foot of men I could not help feeling a sort of indignation at the authors of her disgrace; and my anger made me too vehement.'

'Indeed! I was listening, and did not think so.'

'But I, who am the speaker, felt that I was. And now let me remind you that, although in our former selection we chose old men, we must not do so in this. Solon was under a delusion when he said that a man when he grows old may learn many things – for he can no more learn much than he can run much; youth is the time for any extraordinary toil.'

'Of course.'

'And, therefore, calculation and geometry and all the other elements of instruction, which are a preparation for dialectic, should be presented to the mind in childhood; not, however, under any notion of forcing our system of education.'

'Why not?'

'Because a freeman ought not to be a slave in the acquisition of knowledge of any kind. Bodily exercise, when compulsory, does no harm to the body; but knowledge which is acquired under compulsion obtains no hold on the mind.'

'Very true.'

'Then, my good friend,' I said, 'do not use compulsion, but let early education be a sort of amusement; you will then be better able to find out the natural bent.'

'That is a very rational notion,' he said.

'Do you remember that the children, too, were to be taken to see the battle on horseback; and that if there were no danger they were to be brought close up and, like young hounds, have a taste of blood given them?'

'Yes, I remember.'

'The same practice may be followed', I said, 'in all these things – labours, lessons, dangers – and he who is most at home in all of them ought to be enrolled in a select number.'

'At what age?'

'At the age when the necessary gymnastics are over: the period, whether of two or three years, which passes in this sort of training is useless for any other purpose; for sleep and exercise are unpropitious to learning; and the trial of who is first in gymnastic exercises is one of the most important tests to which our youth are subjected.'

'Certainly,' he replied.

'After that time those who are selected from the class of twenty years old will be promoted to higher honour, and the sciences which they learned without any order in their early education will now be brought together, and they will be able to see the natural relationship of them to one another and to true being.'

'Yes,' he said, 'that is the only kind of knowledge which takes lasting root.'

'Yes,' I said; 'and the capacity for such knowledge is the great criterion of dialectical talent: the comprehensive mind is always the dialectical.'

'I agree with you,' he said.

'These', I said, 'are the points which you must consider; and those who have most of this comprehension, and who are more steadfast in their learning, and in their military and other appointed duties, when they have arrived at the age of thirty have to be chosen by you out of the select class, and elevated to higher honour; and you will have to prove them by the help of dialectic, in order to learn which of them is able to give up the use of sight and the other senses, and in company with truth to attain absolute being. And here, my friend, great caution is required.'

'Why great caution?'

'Do you not remark', I said, 'how great is the evil which dialectic has introduced?'

'What evil?' he said.

'The students of the art are filled with lawlessness.'

'Quite true,' he said.

'Do you think that there is anything so very unnatural or inexcusable in their case? Or will you make allowance for them?'

'In what way make allowance?'

'I want you', I said, 'by way of parallel, to imagine a supposititious son who is brought up in great wealth; he is one of a great and numerous family, and has many flatterers. When he grows up to manhood, he learns that his alleged are not his real parents; but who the real are he is unable to discover. Can you guess how he will be likely to behave towards his flatterers and his supposed parents, first of all during the period when he is ignorant of the false relation, and then again when he knows? Or shall I guess for you?'

'If you please.'

'Then I should say that while he is ignorant of the truth he will be likely to honour his father and his mother and his supposed relations more than the flatterers; he will be less inclined to neglect them when in need, or to do or say anything against them; and he will be less willing to disobey them in any important matter.'

'He will.'

'But when he has made the discovery, I should imagine that he would diminish his honour and regard for them, and would become more devoted to the flatterers; their influence over him would greatly increase; he would now live after their ways, and openly associate with them, and, unless he were of an unusually good disposition, he would trouble himself no more about his supposed parents or other relations.'

'Well, all that is very probable. But how is the image applicable to the disciples of philosophy?'

'In this way: you know that there are certain principles about justice and honour, which were taught us in childhood, and under their parental authority we have been brought up, obeying and honouring them.'

'That is true.'

'There are also opposite maxims and habits of pleasure which flatter and attract the soul, but do not influence those of us who have any sense of right, and they continue to obey and honour the maxims of their fathers.'

'True.'

'Now, when a man is in this state, and the questioning spirit asks what is fair or honourable, and he answers as the legislator has taught him, and then arguments many and diverse refute his words, until he is driven into believing that nothing is honourable any more than dishonourable, or just and good any more than the reverse, and so of all the notions which he most valued, do you think that he will still honour and obey them as before?'

'Impossible.'

'And when he ceases to think them honourable and natural as heretofore, and he fails to discover the true, can he be expected to pursue any life other than that which flatters his desires?'

'He cannot.'

'And from being a keeper of the law he is converted into a breaker of it?'

'Unquestionably.'

'Now all this is very natural in students of philosophy such as I have described, and also, as I was just now saying, most excusable.'

'Yes,' he said; 'and, I may add, pitiable.'

'Therefore, that your feelings may not be moved to pity about our citizens who are now thirty years of age, every care must be taken in introducing them to dialectic.'

'Certainly.'

'There is a danger lest they should taste the dear delight too early; for youngsters, as you may have observed, when they first get the taste in their mouths, argue for amusement, and are always contradicting and refuting others in imitation of those who refute them; like puppy-dogs, they rejoice in pulling and tearing at all who come near them.'

'Yes,' he said, 'there is nothing which they like better.'

'And when they have made many conquests and received defeats at the hands of many, they violently and speedily get into a way of not believing anything which they believed before, and hence, not only they, but philosophy and all that relates to it is apt to have a bad name with the rest of the world.'

'Too true,' he said.

'But when a man begins to get older, he will no longer be guilty of such insanity; he will imitate the dialectician who is seeking for truth, and not the eristic, who is contradicting for the sake of amusement; and the greater moderation of his character will increase instead of diminishing the honour of the pursuit.'

'Very true,' he said.

'And did we not make special provision for this, when we said that the disciples of philosophy were to be orderly and steadfast, not, as now, any chance aspirant or intruder?'

'Very true.'

'Suppose', I said, 'the study of philosophy to take the place of gymnastics and to be continued diligently and earnestly and exclusively for twice the number of years which were passed in bodily exercise – will that be enough?'

'Would you say six or four years?' he asked.

'Say five years,' I replied; 'at the end of the time they must be sent down again into the den and compelled to hold any military or other office which young men are qualified to hold: in this way they will get their experience of life, and there will be an opportunity of trying whether, when they are drawn all manner of ways by temptation, they will stand firm or flinch.'

'And how long is this stage of their lives to last?'

'Fifteen years, I answered; and when they have reached fifty years of age, then let those who still survive and have distinguished themselves in every action of their lives and in every branch of knowledge come at last to their consummation; the time has now arrived at which they must raise the eye of the soul to the universal light which lightens all things, and behold the absolute good; for that is the pattern according to which they are to order the State and the lives of individuals, and the remainder of their own lives also; making philosophy their chief pursuit, but, when their turn comes, toiling also at politics and ruling for the public good, not as though they were performing some heroic action, but simply as a matter of duty; and when they have brought up in each generation others like themselves and left them in their place to be governors of the State, then they will depart to the Islands of the Blessed and dwell there; and the city will give them public memorials and sacrifices and honour them, if the Pythian oracle consent, as demi-gods, but if not, as in any case blessed and divine.'

'You are a sculptor, Socrates, and have made statues of our governors faultless in beauty.'

'Yes,' I said, 'Glaucon, and of our governesses too; for you must not suppose that what I have been saying applies to men only and not to women as far as their natures can go.'

'There you are right,' he said, 'since we have made them to share in all things like the men.'

'Well,' I said, 'and you would agree (would you not?) that what has been said about the State and the government is not a mere dream, and although difficult not impossible, but only possible in the way which has been supposed; that is to say, when the true philosopher kings are born in a State, one or more of them, despising the honours of this present world which they deem mean and worthless, esteeming above all things right and the honour that springs from right, and regarding justice as the greatest and most necessary of all things, whose ministers they are, and whose principles will be exalted by them when they set in order their own city?'

'How will they proceed?'

'They will begin by sending out into the country all the inhabitants of the city who are more than ten years old, and will take possession of their children, who will be unaffected by the habits of their parents; these they will train in their own habits and laws, I mean in the laws which we have given them. And in this way the State and constitution of which we were speaking will soonest and most easily attain happiness, and the nation which has such a constitution will gain most.'

'Yes, that will be the best way. And I think, Socrates, that you have very well described how, if ever, such a constitution might come into being.'

'Enough, then, of the perfect State, and of the man who bears its image – there is no difficulty in seeing how we shall describe him.'

'There is no difficulty,' he replied; 'and I agree with you in thinking that nothing more need be said.'

Book VIII

'And so, Glaucon, we have arrived at the conclusion that in the perfect State wives and children are to be in common; and that all education and the pursuits of war and peace are also to be common, and the best philosophers and the bravest warriors are to be their kings?'

'That', replied Glaucon, 'has been acknowledged.'

'Yes,' I said; 'and we have further acknowledged that the governors, when appointed themselves, will take their soldiers and place them in houses such as we were describing, which are common to all, and contain nothing private, or individual; and about their property, you remember what we agreed?'

'Yes, I remember that no one was to have any of the ordinary possessions of mankind; they were to be warrior athletes and guardians, receiving from the other citizens, in lieu of annual payment, only their maintenance, and they were to take care of themselves and of the whole State.'

'True,' I said; 'and now that this division of our task is concluded, let us find the point at which we digressed, that we may return into the old path.'

'There is no difficulty in returning; you implied, then as now, that you had finished the description of the State: you said that such a State was good, and that the man was good who answered to it, although, as now appears, you had more excellent things to relate both of State and man. And you said further, that if this was the true form, then the others were false; and of the false forms, you said, as I remember, that there were four principal ones, and that their defects, and the defects of the individuals corresponding to them, were worth examining. When we had seen all the individuals, and finally agreed as to who was the best and who was the worst of them, we were to consider whether the best was not also the happiest, and the worst the most miserable. I asked you what were the four forms of government of which you spoke, and then Polemarchus and Adeimantus put in their word; and you began again, and have found your way to the point at which we have now arrived.'

'Your recollection', I said, 'is most exact.'

'Then, like a wrestler,' he replied, 'you must put yourself again in the same position; and let me ask the same questions, and do you give me the same answer which you were about to give me then.'

'Yes, if I can, I will,' I said.

'I shall particularly wish to hear what were the four constitutions of which you were speaking.'

'That question', I said, 'is easily answered: the four governments of which I spoke, so far as they have distinct names, are, first, those of Crete and Sparta, which are generally applauded; what is termed oligarchy comes next – this is not equally approved, and is a form of government which teems with evils; thirdly, democracy, which naturally follows oligarchy, although very different; and lastly comes tyranny, great and famous, which differs from them all, and is the fourth and worst disorder of a State. I do not know, do you, of any other constitution which can be said to have a distinct character? There are lordships and principalities which are bought and sold, and some other intermediate forms of government. But these are nondescripts and may be found equally among Hellenes and among barbarians.'

'Yes,' he replied, 'we certainly hear of many curious forms of government which exist among them.'

'Do you know', I said, 'that governments vary as the dispositions of men vary, and that there must be as many of the one as there are of the other? For we cannot suppose that States are made of "oak and rock", and not out of the human natures which are in them, and which in a figure turn the scale and draw other things after them?'

'Yes,' he said, 'the States are as the men are; they grow out of human characters.'

'Then if the constitutions of States are five, the dispositions of individual minds will also be five?'

'Certainly.'

'Him who answers to aristocracy, and whom we rightly call just and good, we have already described.'

'We have.'

'Then let us now proceed to describe the inferior sort of natures, being the contentious and ambitious, who answer to the Spartan polity; also the oligarchical, democratical, and tyrannical. Let us place the most just by the side of the most unjust, and when we see them we shall be able to compare the relative happiness or unhappiness of him who leads a life of pure justice or pure injustice. The enquiry will then be completed. And we shall know whether we ought to pursue injustice, as Thrasymachus advises, or in accordance with the conclusions of the argument to prefer justice.'

'Certainly,' he replied, 'we must do as you say.'

'Shall we follow our old plan, which we adopted with a view to clearness, of taking the State first and then proceeding to the individual, and begin with the government of honour? I know of no name for such a government other than timocracy, or perhaps timarchy. We will compare with this the like character in the individual; and, after that, consider oligarchical man; and then again we will turn our attention to democracy and the democratical man; and lastly, we will go and view the city of tyranny, and once more take a look into the tyrant's soul, and try to arrive at a satisfactory decision.'

'That way of viewing and judging of the matter will be very suitable.'

'First, then,' I said, 'let us enquire how timocracy (the government of honour) arises out of aristocracy (the government of the best). Clearly, all political changes originate in divisions of the actual governing power; a government which is united, however small, cannot be moved.'

'Very true,' he said.

'In what way, then, will our city be moved, and in what manner the two classes of auxiliaries and rulers disagree among themselves or with one another? Shall we, after the manner of Homer, pray the Muses to tell us "how discord first arose"? Shall we imagine them in solemn mockery, to play and jest with us as if we were children, and to address us in a lofty tragic vein, making believe to be in earnest?'

'How would they address us?'

'After this manner: a city which is thus constituted can hardly be shaken; but, seeing that everything which has a beginning has also an end, even a constitution such as yours will not last for ever, but will in time be dissolved. And this is the dissolution: in plants that grow in the earth, as well as in animals that move on the earth's surface, fertility and sterility of soul and body occur when the circumferences of the circles of each are completed, which in short-lived existences pass over a short space, and in long-lived ones over a long space. But to the knowledge of human fecundity and sterility all the wisdom and education of your rulers will not attain; the laws which regulate them will not be discovered by an intelligence which is alloyed with sense, but will escape them, and they will bring children into the world when they ought not. Now that which is of divine birth has a period which is contained in a perfect number, but the period of human birth is comprehended in a number in which first increments by involution and evolution (or squared and cubed) obtaining three intervals and four terms of like and unlike, waxing and waning numbers, make all the terms commensurable and agreeable to one another. The base of these (3) with a third added (4) when combined with five (20) and raised to the third power furnishes two harmonies: the first a square which is a hundred times as great (400 = 4 × 100), and the other a figure having one side equal to the former, but oblong, consisting of a hundred numbers squared upon rational diameters of a square (i. e. omitting fractions), the side of which is five (7 × 7 = 49 × 100 = 4900), each of them being less by one (than the perfect square which includes the fractions, sc. 50) or less by two perfect squares of irrational diameters (of a square the side of which is five = 50 + 50 = 100); and a hundred cubes of three (27 × 100 = 2700 + 4900 + 400 = 8000). Now this number represents a geometrical figure which has control over the good and evil of births. For when your guardians are ignorant of the law of births, and unite bride and bridegroom out of season, the children will not be goodly or fortunate. And though only the best of them will be appointed by their predecessors, still they will be unworthy to hold their fathers' places, and when they come into power as guardians, they will soon be found to fail in taking care of us, the Muses, first by under-valuing music; which neglect will soon extend to gymnastics; and hence the young men of your State will be less cultivated. In the succeeding generation rulers will be appointed who have lost the guardian power of testing the metal of your different races, which, like Hesiod's, are of gold and silver and brass and iron. And so iron will be mingled with silver, and brass with gold, and hence there will arise dissimilarity and inequality and irregularity, which always and in all places are causes of hatred and war. This the Muses affirm to be the stock from which discord has sprung, wherever arising; and this is their answer to us.'

'Yes, and we may assume that they answer truly.'

'Why, yes,' I said, 'of course they answer truly; how can the Muses speak falsely?'

'And what do the Muses say next?'

'When discord arose, then the two races were drawn different ways: the iron and brass fell to acquiring money and land and houses and gold and silver; but the gold and silver races, not wanting money but having the true riches in their own nature, inclined towards virtue and the ancient order of things. There was a battle between them, and at last they agreed to distribute their land and houses among individual owners; and they enslaved their friends and maintainers, whom they had formerly protected in the condition of freemen, and made of them subjects and servants; and they themselves were engaged in war and in keeping a watch against them.'

'I believe that you have rightly conceived the origin of the change.'

'And the new government which thus arises will be of a form intermediate between oligarchy and aristocracy?'

'Very true.'

'Such will be the change, and after the change has been made, how will they proceed? Clearly, the new State, being in a mean between oligarchy and the perfect State, will partly follow one and partly the other, and will also have some peculiarities.'

'True,' he said.

'In the honour given to rulers, in the abstinence of the warrior class from agriculture, handicrafts, and trade in general, in the institution of common meals, and in the attention paid to gymnastics and military training – in all these respects this State will resemble the former.'

'True.'

'But in the fear of admitting philosophers to power, because they are no longer to be had simple and earnest, but are made up of mixed elements; and in turning from them to passionate and less complex characters, who are by nature fitted for war rather than peace; and in the value set by them upon military stratagems and contrivances, and in the waging of everlasting wars – this State will be for the most part peculiar.'

'Yes.'

'Yes,' I said; 'and men of this stamp will be covetous of money, like those who live in oligarchies; they will have a fierce secret longing after gold and silver, which they will hoard in dark places, having magazines and treasuries of their own for the deposit and concealment of them; also castles which are just nests for their eggs, and in which they will spend large sums on their wives, or on any others whom they please.'

'That is most true,' he said.

'And they are miserly because they have no means of openly acquiring the money which they prize; they will spend that which is another man's on the gratification of their desires, stealing their pleasures and running away like children from the law, their father: they have been schooled not by gentle influences but by force, for they have neglected her who is the true Muse, the companion of reason and philosophy, and have honoured gymnastic more than music.'

'Undoubtedly,' he said, 'the form of government which you describe is a mixture of good and evil.'

'Why, there is a mixture,' I said, 'but one thing, and one thing only, is predominantly seen – the spirit of contention and ambition; and these are due to the prevalence of the passionate or spirited element.'

'Assuredly,' he said.

'Such is the origin and such the character of this State, which has been described in outline only; the more perfect execution was not required, for a sketch is enough to show the type of the most perfectly just and most perfectly unjust; and to go through all the States and all the characters of men, omitting none of them, would be an interminable labour.'

'Very true,' he replied.

'Now what man answers to this form of government – how did he come into being, and what is he like?'

'I think', said Adeimantus, 'that in the spirit of contention which characterises him, he is not unlike our friend Glaucon.'

'Perhaps', I said, 'he may be like him in that one point; but there are other respects in which he is very different.'

'In what respects?'

'He should have more of self-assertion and be less cultivated, and yet a friend of culture; and he should be a good listener, but no speaker. Such a person is apt to be rough with slaves, unlike the educated man, who is too proud for that; and he will also be courteous to freemen, and remarkably obedient to authority; he is a lover of power and a lover of honour; claiming to be a ruler, not because he is eloquent, or on any ground of that sort, but because he is a soldier and has performed feats of arms; he is also a lover of gymnastic exercises and of the chase.'

'Yes, that is the type of character which answers to timocracy.'

'Such a one will despise riches only when he is young; but as he gets older he will be more and more attracted to them, because he has a piece of the avaricious nature in him, and is not singleminded towards virtue, having lost his best guardian.'

'Who was that?' said Adeimantus.

'Philosophy,' I said, 'tempered with music, who comes and takes her abode in a man, and is the only saviour of his virtue throughout life.'

'Good,' he said.

'Such', I said, 'is the timocratical youth, and he is like the timocratical State.'

'Exactly.'

'His origin is as follows: he is often the young son of a grave father, who dwells in an ill-governed city, of which he declines the honours and offices, and will not go to law, or exert himself in any way, but is ready to waive his rights in order that he may escape trouble.'

'And how does the son come into being?'

'The character of the son begins to develop when he hears his mother complaining that her husband has no place in the government, of which the consequence is that she has no precedence among other women. Further, when she sees her husband not very eager about money, and instead of battling and railing in the law courts or assembly, taking whatever happens to him quietly; and when she observes that his thoughts always centre in himself, while he treats her with very considerable indifference, she is annoyed, and says to her son that his father is only half a man and far too easy-going, adding all the other complaints about her own ill-treatment which women are so fond of rehearsing.'

'Yes,' said Adeimantus, 'they give us plenty of them, and their complaints are so like themselves.'

'And you know,' I said, 'that the old servants also, who are supposed to be attached to the family, from time to time talk privately in the same strain to the son; and if they see anyone who owes money to his father, or is wronging him in any way, and he falls to prosecute them, they tell the youth that when he grows up he must retaliate upon people of this sort, and be more of a man than his father. He has only to walk abroad and he hears and sees the same sort of thing: those who do their own business in the city are called simpletons, and held in no esteem, while the busy-bodies are honoured and applauded. The result is that the young man, hearing and seeing all these thing – hearing too, the words of his father, and having a nearer view of his way of life, and making comparisons of him and others – is drawn opposite ways: while his father is watering and nourishing the rational principle in his soul, the others are encouraging the passionate and appetitive; and he being not originally of a bad nature, but having kept bad company, is at last brought by their joint influence to a middle point, and gives up the kingdom which is within him to the middle principle of contentiousness and passion, and becomes arrogant and ambitious.

'You seem to me to have described his origin perfectly.'

'Then we have now', I said, 'the second form of government and the second type of character?'

'We have.'

'Next, let us look at another man who, as Aeschylus says,

"Is set over against another State"

or rather, as our plan requires, begin with the State.'

'By all means.'

'I believe that oligarchy follows next in order.'

'And what manner of government do you term oligarchy?'

'A government resting on a valuation of property, in which the rich have power and the poor man is deprived of it.'

'I understand,' he replied.

'Ought I not to begin by describing how the change from timocracy to oligarchy arises?'

'Yes.'

'Well,' I said, 'no eyes are required in order to see how the one passes into the other.'

'How?'

'The accumulation of gold in the treasury of private individuals is the ruin of timocracy; they invent illegal modes of expenditure; for what do they or their wives care about the law?'

'Yes, indeed.'

'And then one, seeing another grow rich, seeks to rival him, and thus the great mass of the citizens become lovers of money.'

'Likely enough.'

'And so they grow richer and richer, and the more they think of making a fortune the less they think of virtue; for when riches and virtue are placed together in the scales of the balance, the one always rises as the other falls.'

'True.'

'And in proportion as riches and rich men are honoured in the State, virtue and the virtuous are dishonoured.'

'Clearly.'

'And what is honoured is cultivated, and that which has no honour is neglected.'

'That is obvious.'

'And so at last, instead of loving contention and glory, men become lovers of trade and money; they honour and look up to the rich man, and make a ruler of him, and dishonour the poor man.'

'They do so.'

'They next proceed to make a law which fixes a sum of money as the qualification of citizenship; the sum is higher in one place and lower in another, as the oligarchy is more or less exclusive; and they allow no one whose property falls below the amount fixed to have any share in the government. These changes in the constitution they effect by force of arms, if intimidation has not already done their work.'

'Very true.'

'And this, speaking generally, is the way in which oligarchy is established.'

'Yes,' he said, 'but what are the characteristics of this form of government, and what are the defects of which we were speaking?'

'First of all,' I said, 'consider the nature of the qualification. Just think what would happen if pilots were to be chosen according to their property, and a poor man were refused permission to steer, even though he were a better pilot?'

'You mean that they would shipwreck?'

'Yes; and is not this true of the government of anything?'

'I should imagine so.'

'Except a city? Or would you include a city?'

'Nay,' he said, 'the case of a city is the strongest of all, inasmuch as the rule of a city is the greatest and most difficult of all.'

'This, then, will be the first great defect of oligarchy?'

'Clearly.'

'And here is another defect which is quite as bad.'

'What defect?'

'The inevitable division: such a State is not one, but two States, the one of poor, the other of rich men; and they are living on the same spot and always conspiring against one another.'

'That, surely, is at least as bad.'

'Another discreditable feature is, that, for a like reason, they are incapable of carrying on any war. Either they arm the multitude, and then they are more afraid of them than of the enemy; or, if they do not call them out in the hour of battle, they are oligarchs indeed, few to fight as they are few to rule. And at the same time their fondness for money makes them unwilling to pay taxes.'

'How discreditable!'

'And, as we said before, under such a constitution the same persons have too many callings – they are husbandmen, tradesmen, warriors, all in one. Does that look well?'

'Anything but well.'

'There is another evil which is, perhaps, the greatest of all, and to which this State first begins to be liable.'

'What evil?'

'A man may sell all that he has, and another may acquire his property; yet after the sale he may dwell in the city of which he is no longer a part, being neither trader, nor artisan, nor horseman, nor hoplite, but only a poor, helpless creature.'

'Yes, that is an evil which also first begins in this State.'

'The evil is certainly not prevented there; for oligarchies have both the extremes of great wealth and utter poverty.'

'True.'

'But think again: in his wealthy days, while he was spending his money, was a man of this sort a whit more good to the State for the purposes of citizenship? Or did he only seem to be a member of the ruling body, although in truth he was neither ruler nor subject, but just a spendthrift?'

'As you say, he seemed to be a ruler, but was only a spendthrift.'

'May we not say that this is the drone in the house who is like the drone in the honeycomb, and that the one is the plague of the city as the other is of the hive?'

'Just so, Socrates.'

'And God has made the flying drones, Adeimantus, all without stings, whereas of the walking drones he has made some without stings but others have dreadful stings; of the stingless class are those who in their old age end as paupers; of the stingers come all the criminal class, as they are termed.'

'Most true,' he said.

'Clearly then, whenever you see paupers in a State, somewhere in that neighborhood there are hidden away thieves, and cutpurses and robbers of temples, and all sorts of malefactors.'

'Clearly.'

'Well,' I said, 'and in oligarchical States do you not find paupers?'

'Yes,' he said; 'nearly everybody is a pauper who is not a ruler.'

'And may we be so bold as to affirm that there are also many criminals to be found in them, rogues who have stings, and whom the authorities are careful to restrain by force?'

'Certainly, we may be so bold.'

'The existence of such persons is to be attributed to want of education, ill-training, and an evil constitution of the State?'

'True.'

'Such, then, is the form and such are the evils of oligarchy; and there may be many other evils.'

'Very likely.'

'Then oligarchy, or the form of government in which the rulers are elected for their wealth, may now be dismissed. Let us next proceed to consider the nature and origin of the individual who answers to this State.'

'By all means.'

'Does not the timocratical man change into the oligarchical on this wise?'

'How?'

'A time arrives when the representative of timocracy has a son: at first he begins by emulating his father and walking in his footsteps, but presently he sees him of a sudden foundering against the State as upon a sunken reef, and he and all that he has is lost; he may have been a general or some other high officer who is brought to trial under a prejudice raised by informers, and either put to death, or exiled, or deprived of the privileges of a citizen, and all his property taken from him.'

'Nothing more likely.'

'And the son has seen and known all this – he is a ruined man, and his fear has taught him to knock ambition and passion head-foremost from his bosom's throne; humbled by poverty, he takes to money-making and by mean and miserly savings and hard work gets a fortune together. Is not such an one likely to seat the concupiscent and covetous element on the vacant throne and to suffer it to play the great king within him, girt with tiara and chain and scimitar?'

'Most true,' he replied.

'And when he has made reason and spirit sit down on the ground obediently on either side of their sovereign, and taught them to know their place, he compels the one to think only of how lesser sums may be turned into larger ones, and will not allow the other to worship and admire anything but riches and rich men, or to be ambitious of anything so much as the acquisition of wealth and the means of acquiring it.'

'Of all changes,' he said, 'there is none so speedy or so sure as the conversion of the ambitious youth into the avaricious one.'

'And the avaricious,' I said, 'is the oligarchical youth?'

'Yes,' he said; 'at any rate the individual out of whom he came is like the State out of which oligarchy came.'

'Let us then consider whether there is any likeness between them.'

'Very good.'

'First, then, they resemble one another in the value which they set upon wealth?'

'Certainly.'

'Also in their penurious, laborious character; the individual only satisfies his necessary appetites, and confines his expenditure to them; his other desires he subdues, under the idea that they are unprofitable.'

'True.'

'He is a shabby fellow, who saves something out of everything and makes a purse for himself; and this is the sort of man whom the vulgar applaud. Is he not a true image of the State which he represents?'

'He appears to me to be so; at any rate money is highly valued by him as well as by the State.'

'You see that he is not a man of cultivation,' I said.

'I imagine not,' he said. 'Had he been educated he would never have made a blind god director of his chorus, or given him chief honour.'

'Excellent!' I said. 'Yet consider: must we not further admit that owing to this want of cultivation there will be found in him dronelike desires as of pauper and rogue, which are forcibly kept down by his general habit of life?'

'True.'

'Do you know where you will have to look if you want to discover his rogueries?'

'Where must I look?'

'You should see him where he has some great opportunity of acting dishonestly, as in the guardianship of an orphan.'

'Aye.'

'It will be clear enough then that in his ordinary dealings which give him a reputation for honesty he coerces his bad passions by an enforced virtue; not making them see that they are wrong, or taming them by reason, but by necessity and fear constraining them, and because he trembles for his possessions.'

'To be sure.'

'Yes, indeed, my dear friend, but you will find that the natural desires of the drone commonly exist in him all the same whenever he has to spend what is not his own.'

'Yes, and they will be strong in him too.'

'The man, then, will be at war with himself; he will be two men, and not one; but, in general, his better desires will be found to prevail over his inferior ones.'

'True.'

'For these reasons such an one will be more respectable than most people; yet the true virtue of a unanimous and harmonious soul will flee far away and never come near him.'

'I should expect so.'

'And surely, the miser individually will be an ignoble competitor in a State for any prize of victory, or other object of honourable ambition; he will not spend his money in the contest for glory; so afraid is he of awakening his expensive appetites and inviting them to help and join in the struggle; in true oligarchical fashion he fights with a small part only of his resources, and the result commonly is that he loses the prize and saves his money.'

'Very true.'

'Can we any longer doubt, then, that the miser and money-maker answers to the oligarchical State?'

'There can be no doubt.'

'Next comes democracy; of this the origin and nature have still to be considered by us; and then we will enquire into the ways of the democratic man, and bring him up for judgement.'

'That', he said, 'is our method.'

'Well,' I said, 'and how does the change from oligarchy into democracy arise? Is it not on this wise? – The good at which such a State aims is to become as rich as possible, a desire which is insatiable?'

'What then?'

'The rulers, being aware that their power rests upon their wealth, refuse to curtail by law the extravagance of the spendthrift youth because they gain by their ruin; they take interest from them and buy up their estates and thus increase their own wealth and importance?'

'To be sure.'

'There can be no doubt that the love of wealth and the spirit of moderation cannot exist together in citizens of the same State to any considerable extent; one or the other will be disregarded.'

'That is tolerably clear.'

'And in oligarchical States, from the general spread of carelessness and extravagance, men of good family have often been reduced to beggary?'

'Yes, often.'

'And still they remain in the city; there they are, ready to sting and fully armed, and some of them owe money, some have forfeited their citizenship; a third class are in both predicaments; and they hate and conspire against those who have got their property, and against everybody else, and are eager for revolution.'

'That is true.'

'On the other hand, the men of business, stooping as they walk, and pretending not even to see those whom they have already ruined, insert their sting – that is, their money – into someone else who is not on his guard against them, and recover the parent sum many times over multiplied into a family of children: and so they make drone and pauper to abound in the State.'

'Yes,' he said, 'there are plenty of them – that is certain.'

'The evil blazes up like a fire; and they will not extinguish it, either by restricting a man's use of his own property, or by another remedy:'

'What other?'

'One which is the next best, and has the advantage of compelling the citizens to look to their characters: let there be a general rule that everyone shall enter into voluntary contracts at his own risk, and there will be less of this scandalous money-making, and the evils of which we were speaking will be greatly lessened in the State.'

'Yes, they will be greatly lessened.'

'At present the governors, induced by the motives which I have named, treat their subjects badly; while they and their adherents, especially the young men of the governing class, are habituated to lead a life of luxury and idleness both of body and mind; they do nothing, and are incapable of resisting either pleasure or pain.'

'Very true.'

'They themselves care only for making money, and are as indifferent as the pauper to the cultivation of virtue.'

'Yes, quite as indifferent.'

'Such is the state of affairs which prevails among them. And often rulers and their subjects may come in one another's way, whether on a pilgrimage or a march, as fellow-soldiers or fellow-sailors; aye, and they may observe the behaviour of each other in the very moment of danger – for where danger is, there is no fear that the poor will be despised by the rich – and very likely the wiry sunburnt poor man may be placed in battle at the side of a wealthy one who has never spoilt his complexion and has plenty of superfluous flesh, and when he sees such an one puffing and at his wit's end, how can he avoid drawing the conclusion that men like him are only rich because no one has the courage to despoil them? And when they meet in private will not people be saying to one another, "Our warriors are not good for much"?'

'Yes,' he said, 'I am quite aware that this is their way of talking.'

'And, as in a body which is diseased the addition of a touch from without may bring on illness, and sometimes even when there is no external provocation a commotion may arise within – in the same way wherever there is weakness in the State there is also likely to be illness, of which the occasions may be very slight, the one party introducing from without their oligarchical, the other their democratical allies, and then the State falls sick, and is at war with herself; and may be at times distracted, even when there is no external cause.'

'Yes, surely.'

'And then democracy comes into being after the poor have conquered their opponents, slaughtering some and banishing some, while to the remainder they give an equal share of freedom and power; and this is the form of government in which the magistrates are commonly elected by lot.'

'Yes,' he said, 'that is the nature of democracy, whether the revolution has been effected by arms, or whether fear has caused the opposite party to withdraw.'

'And now what is their manner of life, and what sort of a government have they? For as the government is, such will be the man.'

'Clearly,' he said.

'In the first place, are they not free; and is not the city full of freedom and frankness – a man may say and do what he likes?'

''Tis said so,' he replied.

'And where freedom is, the individual is clearly able to order for himself his own life as he pleases?'

'Clearly.'

'Then in this kind of State there will be the greatest variety of human natures?'

'There will.'

'This, then, seems likely to be the fairest of States, being an embroidered robe which is spangled with every sort of flower. And just as women and children think a variety of colours to be of all things most charming, so there are many men to whom this State, which is spangled with the manners and characters of mankind, will appear to be the fairest of States.'

'Yes.'

'Yes, my good Sir, and there will be no better in which to look for a government.'

'Why?'

'Because of the liberty which reigns there – they have a complete assortment of constitutions; and he who has a mind to establish a State, as we have been doing, must go to a democracy as he would to a bazaar at which they sell them, and pick out the one that suits him; then, when he has made his choice, he may found his State.'

'He will be sure to have patterns enough.'

'And there being no necessity', I said, 'for you to govern in this State, even if you have the capacity, or to be governed, unless you like, or go to war when the rest go to war, or to be at peace when others are at peace, unless you are so disposed – there being no necessity also, because some law forbids you to hold office or be a dicast, that you should not hold office or be a dicast, if you have a fancy – is not this a way of life which for the moment is supremely delightful?'

'For the moment, yes.'

'And is not their humanity to the condemned in some cases quite charming? Have you not observed how, in a democracy, many persons, although they have been sentenced to death or exile, just stay where they are and walk about the world – the gentleman parades like a hero, and nobody sees or cares?'

'Yes,' he replied, 'many and many a one.'

'See too,' I said, 'the forgiving spirit of democracy, and the "don't care" about trifles, and the disregard which she shows of all the fine principles which we solemnly laid down at the foundation of the city – as when we said that, except in the case of some rarely gifted nature, there never will be a good man who has not from his childhood been used to play amid things of beauty and make of them a joy and a study – how grandly does she trample all these fine notions of ours under her feet, never giving a thought to the pursuits which make a statesman, and promoting to honour anyone who professes to be the people's friend.'

'Yes, she is of a noble spirit.'

'These and other kindred characteristics are proper to democracy, which is a charming form of government, full of variety and disorder, and dispensing a sort of equality to equals and unequals alike.'

'We know her well.'

'Consider now', I said, 'what manner of man the individual is, or rather consider, as in the case of the State, how he comes into being.'

'Very good,' he said.

'Is not this the way – he is the son of the miserly and oligarchical father who has trained him in his own habits?'

'Exactly.'

'And, like his father, he keeps under by force the pleasures which are of the spending and not of the getting sort, being those which are called unnecessary?'

'Obviously.'

'Would you like, for the sake of clearness, to distinguish which are the necessary and which are the unnecessary pleasures?'

'I should.'

'Are not necessary pleasures those of which we cannot get rid, and of which the satisfaction is a benefit to us? And they are rightly so, because we are framed by nature to desire both what is beneficial and what is necessary, and cannot help it.'

'True.'

'We are not wrong therefore in calling them necessary?'

'We are not.'

'And the desires of which a man may get rid, if he takes pains from his youth upwards – of which the presence, moreover, does no good, and in some cases the reverse of good – shall we not be right in saying that all these are unnecessary?'

'Yes, certainly.'

'Suppose we select an example of either kind, in order that we may have a general notion of them?'

'Very good.'

'Will not the desire of eating, that is, of simple food and condiments, in so far as they are required for health and strength, be of the necessary class?'

'That is what I should suppose.'

'The pleasure of eating is necessary in two ways: it does us good and it is essential to the continuance of life?'

'Yes.'

'But the condiments are only necessary in so far as they are good for health?'

'Certainly.'

'And the desire which goes beyond this, or more delicate food, or other luxuries, which might generally be got rid of, if controlled and trained in youth, and is hurtful to the body, and hurtful to the soul in the pursuit of wisdom and virtue, may be rightly called unnecessary?'

'Very true'.

'May we not say that these desires spend, and that the others make money because they conduce to production?'

'Certainly.'

'And of the pleasures of love, and all other pleasures, the same holds good?'

'True.'

'And the drone of whom we spoke was he who was surfeited in pleasures and desires of this sort, and was the slave of the unnecessary desires, whereas he who was subject o the necessary only was miserly and oligarchical?'

'Very true.'

'Again, let us see how the democratical man grows out of the oligarchical: the following, as I suspect, is commonly the process.'

'What is the process?'

'When a young man who has been brought up as we were just now describing, in a vulgar and miserly way, has tasted drones' honey and has come to associate with fierce and crafty natures who are able to provide for him all sorts of refinements and varieties of pleasure – then, as you may imagine, the change will begin of the oligarchical principle within him into the democratical?'

'Inevitably.'

'And as in the city like was helping like, and the change was effected by an alliance from without assisting one division of the citizens, so too the young man is changed by a class of desires coming from without to assist the desires within him, that which is and alike again helping that which is akin and alike?

'Certainly.'

'And if there be any ally which aids the oligarchical principle within him, whether the influence of a father or of kindred, advising or rebuking him, then there arises in his soul a faction and an opposite faction, and he goes to war with himself.'

'It must be so.'

'And there are times when the democratical principle gives way to the oligarchical, and some of his desires die, and others are banished; a spirit of reverence enters into the young man's soul and order is restored.'

'Yes,' he said, 'that sometimes happens.'

'And then, again, after the old desires have been driven out, fresh ones spring up, which are akin to them, and because he, their father, does not know how to educate them, wax fierce and numerous.'

'Yes,' he said, 'that is apt to be the way.'

'They draw him to his old associates, and holding secret intercourse with them, breed and multiply in him.'

'Very true.'

'At length they seize upon the citadel of the young man's soul, which they perceive to be void of all accomplishments and fair pursuits and true words, which make their abode in the minds of men who are dear to the gods, and are their best guardians and sentinels.'

'None better.'

'False and boastful conceits and phrases mount upwards and take their place.'

'They are certain to do so.'

'And so the young man returns into the country of the lotus-eaters, and takes up his dwelling there in the face of all men; and if any help be sent by his friends to the oligarchical part of him, the aforesaid vain conceits shut the gate of the king's fastness; and they will neither allow the embassy itself to enter, nor if private advisers offer the fatherly counsel of the aged will they listen to them or receive them. There is a battle and they gain the day, and then modesty, which they call silliness, is ignominiously thrust into exile by them, and temperance, which they nickname unmanliness, is trampled in the mire and cast forth; they persuade men that moderation and orderly expenditure are vulgarity and meanness, and so, by the help of a rabble of evil appetites, they drive them beyond the border.'

'Yes, with a will.'

'And when they have emptied and swept clean the soul of him who is now in their power and who is being initiated by them in great mysteries, the next thing is to bring back to their house insolence and anarchy and waste and impudence in bright array having garlands on their heads, and a great company with them, hymning their praises and calling them by sweet names; insolence they term breeding, and anarchy liberty, and waste magnificence, and impudence courage. And so the young man passes out of his original nature, which was trained in the school of necessity, into the freedom and libertinism of useless and unnecessary pleasures.'

'Yes,' he said, 'the change in him is visible enough.'

'After this he lives on, spending his money and labour and time on unnecessary pleasures quite as much as on necessary ones; but if he be fortunate, and is not too much disordered in his wits, when years have elapsed, and the heyday of passion is over – supposing that he then re-admits into the city some part of the exiled virtues, and does not wholly give himself up to their successors – in that case he balances his pleasures and lives in a sort of equilibrium, putting the government of himself into the hands of the one which comes first and wins the turn; and when he has had enough of that, then into the hands of another; he despises none of them but encourages them all equally.'

'Very true,' he said.

'Neither does he receive or let pass into the fortress any true word of advice; if anyone says to him that some pleasures are the satisfactions of good and noble desires, and others of evil desires, and that he ought to use and honour some and chastise and master the others – whenever this is repeated to him he shakes his head and says that they are all alike, and that one is as good as another.'

'Yes,' he said; 'that is the way with him.'

'Yes,' I said, 'he lives from day to day indulging the appetite of the hour; and sometimes he is lapped in drink and strains of the flute; then he becomes a water-drinker, and tries to get thin; then he takes a turn at gymnastics; sometimes idling and neglecting everything, then once more living the life of a philosopher; often he is busy with politics, and starts to his feet and says and does whatever comes into his head; and, if he is emulous of anyone who is a warrior, off he is in that direction, or of men of business, once more in that. His life has neither law nor order; and this distracted existence he terms joy and bliss and freedom; and so he goes on.'

'Yes,' he replied, 'he is all liberty and equality.'

'Yes,' I said; 'his life is motley and manifold and an epitome of the lives of many; he answers to the State which we described as fair and spangled. And many a man and many a woman will take him for their pattern, and many a constitution and many an example of manners is contained in him.'

'Just so.'

'Let him then be set over against democracy; he may truly be called the democratic man.'

'Let that be his place,' he said.

'Last of all comes the most beautiful of all, man and State alike, tyranny and the tyrant; these we have now to consider.'

'Quite true,' he said.

'Say then, my friend, in what manner does tyranny arise? – that it has a democratic origin is evident.'

'Clearly.'

'And does not tyranny spring from democracy in the same manner as democracy from oligarchy – I mean, after a sort?'

'How?'

'The good which oligarchy proposed to itself and the means by which it was maintained was excess of wealth – am I not right?'

'Yes.'

'And the insatiable desire of wealth and the neglect of all other things for the sake of money-getting was also the ruin of oligarchy?'

'True.'

'And democracy has her own good, of which the insatiable desire brings her to dissolution?'

'What good?'

'Freedom,' I replied. 'Which, as they tell you in a democracy, is the glory of the State – and that therefore in a democracy alone will the freeman of nature deign to dwell.'

'Yes; the saying is in everybody's mouth.'

'I was going to observe that the insatiable desire of this and the neglect of other things introduces the change in democracy, which occasions a demand for tyranny.'

'How so?'

'When a democracy which is thirsting for freedom has evil cupbearers presiding over the feast, and has drunk too deeply of the strong wine of freedom, then, unless her rulers are very amenable and give a plentiful draught, she calls them to account and punishes them, and says that they are cursed oligarchs.'

'Yes,' he replied, 'a very common occurrence.'

'Yes,' I said. 'And loyal citizens are insultingly termed by her slaves who hug their chains and men of naught; she would have subjects who are like rulers, and rulers who are like subjects: these are men after her own heart, whom she praises and honours both in private and public. Now, in such a State, can liberty have any limit?'

'Certainly not.'

'By degrees the anarchy finds a way into private houses, and ends by getting among the animals and infecting them.'

'How do you mean?'

'I mean that the father grows accustomed to descend to the level of his sons and to fear them, and the son is on a level with his father, he having no respect or reverence for either of his parents; and this is his freedom, and metic is equal with the citizen and the citizen with the metic, and the stranger is quite as good as either.'

'Yes,' he said, 'that is the way.'

'And these are not the only evils,' I said. 'There are several lesser ones: in such a state of society the master fears and flatters his scholars, and the scholars despise their masters and tutors; young and old are all alike; and the young man is on a level with the old, and is ready to compete with him in word or deed; and old men condescend to the young and are full of pleasantry and gaiety; they are loth to be thought morose and authoritative, and therefore they adopt the manners of the young.'

'Quite true,' he said.

'The last extreme of popular liberty is when the slave bought with money, whether male or female, is just as free as his or her purchaser; nor must I forget to tell of the liberty and equality of the two sexes in relation to each other.'

'Why not, as Aeschylus says, utter the word which rises to our lips?'

'That is what I am doing,' I replied. 'And I must add that no one who does not know would believe how much greater is the liberty which the animals who are under the dominion of man have in a democracy than in any other State: for truly, the she-dogs, as the proverb says, are as good as their she-mistresses, and the horses and asses have a way of marching along with all the rights and dignities of freemen; and they will run at anybody who comes in their way if he does not leave the road clear for them; and all things are just ready to burst with liberty.'

'When I take a country walk,' he said, 'I often experience what you describe. You and I have dreamed the same thing.'

'And above all,' I said, 'and as the result of all, see how sensitive the citizens become: they chafe impatiently at the least touch of authority and at length, as you know, they cease to care even for the laws, written or unwritten; they will have no one over them.'

'Yes,' he said, 'I know it too well.'

'Such, my friend,' I said, 'is the fair and glorious beginning out of which springs tyranny.'

'Glorious indeed,' he said. 'But what is the next step?'

'The ruin of oligarchy is the ruin of democracy; the same disease magnified and intensified by liberty overmasters democracy – the truth being that the excessive increase of anything often causes a reaction in the opposite direction; and this is the case not only in the seasons and in vegetable and animal life, but above all in forms of government.'

'True.'

'The excess of liberty, whether in States or individuals, seems only to pass into excess of slavery.'

'Yes, the natural order.'

'And so tyranny naturally arises out of democracy, and the most aggravated form of tyranny and slavery out of the most extreme form of liberty?'

'As we might expect.'

'That, however, was not, as I believe, your question – you rather desired to know what is that disorder which is generated alike in oligarchy and democracy, and is the ruin of both?'

'Just so,' he replied.

'Well,' I said, 'I meant to refer to the class of idle spendthrifts, of whom the more courageous are the leaders and the more timid the followers, the same whom we were comparing to drones, some stingless, and others having stings.'

'A very just comparison.'

'These two classes are the plagues of every city in which they are generated, being what phlegm and bile are to the body. And the good physician and lawgiver of the State ought, like the wise bee-master, to keep them at a distance and prevent, if possible, their ever coming in; and if they have anyhow found a way in, then he should have them and their cells cut out as speedily as possible.'

'Yes, by all means,' he said.

'Then, in order that we may see clearly what we are doing, let us imagine democracy to be divided, as indeed it is, into three classes; for in the first place freedom creates rather more drones in the democratic than there were in the oligarchical State.'

'That is true.'

'And in the democracy they are certainly more intensified.'

'How so?'

'Because in the oligarchical State they are disqualified and driven from office, and therefore they cannot train or gather strength; whereas in a democracy they are almost the entire ruling power, and while the keener sort speak and act, the rest keep buzzing about the bema and do not suffer a word to be said on the other side; hence in democracies almost everything is managed by the drones.'

'Very true,' he said.

'Then there is another class which is always being severed from the mass.'

'What is that?'

'They are the orderly class, which in a nation of traders is sure to be the richest.'

'Naturally so.'

'They are the most squeezable persons and yield the largest amount of honey to the drones.'

'Why,' he said, 'there is little to be squeezed out of people who have little.'

'And this is called the wealthy class, and the drones feed upon them.'

'That is pretty much the case,' he said.

'The people are a third class, consisting of those who work with their own hands; they are not politicians, and have not much to live upon. This, when assembled, is the largest and most powerful class in a democracy.'

'True,' he said; 'but then the multitude is seldom willing to congregate unless they get a little honey.'

'And do they not share?' I said. 'Do not their leaders deprive the rich of their estates and distribute them among the people – at the same time taking care to reserve the larger part for themselves?'

'Why, yes,' he said, 'to that extent the people do share.'

'And the persons whose property is taken from them are compelled to defend themselves before the people as they best can?'

'What else can they do?'

'And then, although they may have no desire of change, the others charge them with plotting against the people and being friends of oligarchy?'

'True.'

'And the end is that when they see the people, not of their own accord, but through ignorance, and because they are deceived by informers, seeking to do them wrong, then at last they are forced to become oligarchs in reality; they do not wish to be, but the sting of the drones torments them and breeds revolution in them.'

'That is exactly the truth.'

'Then come impeachments and judgments and trials of one another.'

'True.'

'The people have always some champion whom they set over them and nurse into greatness.'

'Yes, that is their way.'

'This and no other is the root from which a tyrant springs; when he first appears above ground he is a protector.'

'Yes, that is quite clear.'

'How then does a protector begin to change into a tyrant? Clearly when he does what the man is said to do in the tale of the Arcadian temple of Lycaean Zeus.'

'What tale?'

'The tale is that he who has tasted the entrails of a single human victim minced up with the entrails of other victims is destined to become a wolf. Did you never hear it?'

'Oh, yes.'

'And the protector of the people is like him; having a mob entirely at his disposal, he is not restrained from shedding the blood of kinsmen; by the favourite method of false accusation he brings them into court and murders them, making the life of man to disappear, and with unholy tongue and lips tasting the blood of his fellow citizen; some he kills and others he banishes, at the same time hinting at the abolition of debts and partition of lands; and after this, what will be his destiny? Must he not either perish at the hands of his enemies, or from being a man become a wolf – that is, a tyrant?'

'Inevitably.'

'This,' I said, 'is he who begins to make a party against the rich?'

'The same.'

'After a while he is driven out, but comes back, in spite of his enemies, a tyrant full grown.'

'That is clear.'

'And if they are unable to expel him, or to get him condemned to death by a public accusation, they conspire to assassinate him.'

'Yes,' he said, 'that is their usual way.'

'Then comes the famous request for a bodyguard, which is the device of all those who have got thus far in their tyrannical career – "Let not the people's friend", as they say, "be lost to them."'

'Exactly.'

'The people readily assent; all their fears are for him – they have none for themselves.'

'Very true.'

'And when a man who is wealthy and is also accused of being an enemy of the people sees this, then, my friend, as the oracle said to Croesus,

> "By pebbly Hermus's shore he flees and rests not and is not ashamed to be a coward."'

'And quite right too,' said he, 'for if he were, he would never be ashamed again.'

'But if he is caught he dies.'

'Of course.'

'And he, the protector of whom we spoke, is to be seen, not "larding the plain" with his bulk, but himself the overthrower of many, standing up in the chariot of State with the reins in his hand, no longer protector, but tyrant absolute.'

'No doubt,' he said.

'And now let us consider the happiness of the man, and also of the State in which a creature like him is generated.'

'Yes,' he said, 'let us consider that.'

'At first, in the early days of his power, he is full of smiles, and he salutes everyone whom he meets – he to be called a tyrant, who is making promises in public and also in private! Liberating debtors, and distributing land to the people and his followers, and wanting to be so kind and good to everyone!'

'Of course,' he said.

'But when he has disposed of foreign enemies by conquest or treaty, and there is nothing to fear from them, then he is always stirring up some war or other, in order that the people may require a leader.'

'To be sure.'

'Has he not also another object, which is that they may be impoverished by payment of taxes, and thus compelled to devote themselves to their daily wants and therefore less likely to conspire against him? Clearly.'

'And if any of them are suspected by him of having notions of freedom, and of resistance to his authority, he will have a good pretext for destroying them by placing them at the mercy of the enemy; and for all these reasons the tyrant must be always getting up a war.'

'He must.'

'Now he begins to grow unpopular.'

'A necessary result.'

'Then some of those who joined in setting him up, and who are in power, speak their minds to him and to one another, and the more courageous of them cast in his teeth what is being done.'

'Yes, that may be expected.'

'And the tyrant, if he means to rule, must get rid of them; he cannot stop while he has a friend or an enemy who is good for anything.'

'He cannot.'

'And therefore he must look about him and see who is valiant, who is high-minded, who is wise, who is wealthy; happy man, he is the enemy of them all, and must seek occasion against them whether he will or no, until he has made a purgation of the State.'

'Yes,' he said, 'and a rare purgation.'

'Yes,' I said, 'not the sort of purgation which the physicians make of the body; for they take away the worse and leave the better part, but he does the reverse.'

'If he is to rule, I suppose that he cannot help himself.'

'What a blessed alternative,' I said: 'to be compelled to dwell only with the many bad, and to be by them hated, or not to live at all!'

'Yes, that is the alternative.'

'And the more detestable his actions are to the citizens, the more satellites and the greater devotion in them will he require?'

'Certainly.'

'And who are the devoted band, and where will he procure them?'

'They will flock to him', he said, 'of their own accord, if he pays them.'

'By the dog!' I said. 'Here are more drones, of every sort and from every land.'

'Yes,' he said, 'there are.'

'But will he not desire to get them on the spot?'

'How do you mean?'

'He will rob the citizens of their slaves; he will then set them free and enrol them in his bodyguard.'

'To be sure,' he said; 'and he will be able to trust them best of all.'

'What a blessed creature', I said, 'must this tyrant be: he has put to death the others and has these for his trusted friends.'

'Yes,' he said; 'they are quite of his sort.'

'Yes,' I said, 'and these are the new citizens whom he has called into existence, who admire him and are his companions, while the good hate and avoid him.'

'Of course.'

'Verily, then, tragedy is a wise thing and Euripides a great tragedian.'

'Why so?'

'Why, because he is the author of the pregnant saying,

"Tyrants are wise by living with the wise;"

and he clearly meant to say that they are the wise whom the tyrant makes his companions.'

'Yes,' he said, 'and he also praises tyranny as godlike; and many other things of the same kind are said by him and by the other poets.'

'And therefore,' I said, 'the tragic poets, being wise men, will forgive us and any others who live after our manner if we do not receive them into our State, because they are the eulogists of tyranny.'

'Yes,' he said, 'those who have the wit will doubtless forgive us.'

'But they will continue to go to other cities and attract mobs, and hire voices fair and loud and persuasive, and draw the cities over to tyrannies and democracies.'

'Very true.'

'Moreover, they are paid for this and receive honour – the greatest honour, as might be expected, from tyrants, and the next greatest from democracies; but the higher they ascend our constitution hill, the more their reputation fails, and seems unable from shortness of breath to proceed further.'

'True.'

'But we are wandering from the subject. Let us therefore return and enquire how the tyrant will maintain that fair and numerous and various and ever-changing army of his.'

'If', he said, 'there are sacred treasures in the city, he will confiscate and spend them; and in so far as the fortunes of attainted persons may suffice, he will be able to diminish the taxes which he would otherwise have to impose upon the people.'

'And when these fail?'

'Why, clearly,' he said, 'then he and his boon companions, whether male or female, will be maintained out of his father's estate.'

'You mean to say that the people, from whom he has derived his being, will maintain him and his companions?'

'Yes,' he said; 'they cannot help themselves.'

'But what if the people fly into a passion, and aver that a grown-up son ought not to be supported by his father, but that the father should be supported by the son? The father did not bring him into being, or settle him in life, in order that when his son became a man he should himself be the servant of his own servants and should support him and his rabble of slaves and companions; but that his son should protect him, and that by his help he might be emancipated from the government of the rich and aristocratic, as they are termed. And so he bids him and his companions depart, just as any other father might drive out of the house a riotous son and his undesirable associates.'

'By heaven,' he said, 'then the parent will discover what a monster he has been fostering in his bosom; and, when he wants to drive him out, he will find that he is weak and his son strong.'

'Why, you do not mean to say that the tyrant will use violence? What! Beat his father if he opposes him?'

'Yes, he will, having first disarmed him.'

'Then he is a parricide, and a cruel guardian of an aged parent; and this is real tyranny, about which there can be no longer a mistake: as the saying is, the people who would escape the smoke which is the slavery of freemen have fallen into the fire which is the tyranny of slaves. Thus liberty, getting out of all order and reason, passes into the harshest and bitterest form of slavery.'

'True,' he said.

'Very well; and may we not rightly say that we have sufficiently discussed the nature of tyranny, and the manner of the transition from democracy to tyranny?'

'Yes, quite enough,' he said.

Book IX

'Last of all comes the tyrannical man; about whom we have once more to ask, how is he formed out of the democratical? And how does he live, in happiness or in misery?'

'Yes,' he said, 'he is the only one remaining.'

'There is, however,' I said, 'a previous question which remains unanswered.'

'What question? '

'I do not think that we have adequately determined the nature and number of the appetites, and until this is accomplished the enquiry will always be confused.'

'Well,' he said, 'it is not too late to supply the omission.'

'Very true,' I said; 'and observe the point which I want to understand: certain of the unnecessary pleasures and appetites I conceive to be unlawful; everyone appears to have them, but in some persons they are controlled by the laws and by reason, and the better desires prevail over them – either they are wholly banished or they become few and weak; while in the case of others they are stronger, and there are more of them.'

'Which appetites do you mean?'

'I mean those which are awake when the reasoning and human and ruling power is asleep; then the wild beast within us, gorged with meat or drink, starts up and having shaken off sleep, goes forth to satisfy his desires; and there is no conceivable folly or crime – not excepting incest or any other unnatural union, or parricide, or the eating of forbidden food – which at such a time, when he has parted company with all shame and sense, a man may not be ready to commit.'

'Most true,' he said.

'But when a man's pulse is healthy and temperate, and when before going to sleep he has awakened his rational powers, and fed them on noble thoughts and enquiries, collecting himself in meditation; after having first indulged his appetites neither too much nor too little, but just enough to lay them to sleep, and prevent them and their enjoyments and pains from interfering with the higher principle – which he leaves in the solitude of pure abstraction, free to contemplate and aspire to the knowledge of the unknown, whether in past, present, or future: when again he has allayed the passionate element, if he has a quarrel against anyone – I say, when, after pacifying the two irrational principles, he rouses up the third, which is reason, before he takes his rest, then, as you know, he attains truth most nearly, and is least likely to be the sport of fantastic and lawless visions.'

'I quite agree.'

'In saying this I have been running into a digression; but the point which I desire to note is that in all of us, even in good men, there is a lawless wild-beast nature, which peers out in sleep. Pray, consider whether I am right, and you agree with me.'

'Yes, I agree.'

'And now remember the character which we attributed to the democratic man. He was supposed from his youth upwards to have been trained under a miserly parent, who encouraged the saving appetites in him, but discountenanced the unnecessary, which aim only at amusement and ornament?'

'True.'

'And then he got into the company of a more refined, licentious sort of people, and taking to all their wanton ways rushed into the opposite extreme from an abhorrence of his father's meanness. At last, being a better man than his corruptors, he was drawn in both directions until he halted midway and led a life, not of vulgar and slavish passion, but of what he deemed moderate indulgence in various pleasures. After this manner the democrat was generated out of the oligarch?'

'Yes,' he said; 'that was our view of him, and is so still.'

'And now,' I said, 'years will have passed away, and you must conceive this man, such as he is, to have a son, who is brought up in his father's principles.

'I can imagine him.'

'Then you must further imagine the same thing to happen to the son which has already happened to the father: he is drawn into a perfectly lawless life, which by his seducers is termed perfect liberty; and his father and friends take part with his moderate desires, and the opposite party assist the opposite ones. As soon as these dire magicians and tyrant-makers find that they are losing their hold on him, they contrive to implant in him a master passion, to be lord over his idle and spendthrift lusts – a sort of monstrous winged drone – that is the only image which will adequately describe him.'

'Yes,' he said, 'that is the only adequate image of him.'

'And when his other lusts, amid clouds of incense and perfumes and garlands and wines, and all the pleasures of a dissolute life, now let loose, come buzzing around him, nourishing to the utmost the sting of desire which they implant in his drone-like nature, then at last this lord of the soul, having Madness for the captain of his guard, breaks out into a frenzy; and if he finds in himself any good opinions or appetites in process of formation, and there is in him any sense of shame remaining, to these better principles he puts an end, and casts them forth until he has purged away temperance and brought in madness to the full.'

'Yes,' he said, 'that is the way in which the tyrannical man is generated.'

'And is not this the reason why of old love has been called a tyrant?'

'I should not wonder.'

'Further,' I said, 'has not a drunken man also the spirit of a tyrant?'

'He has.'

'And you know that a man who is deranged and not right in his mind will fancy that he is able to rule, not only over men, but also over the gods?'

'That he will.'

'And the tyrannical man in the true sense of the word comes into being when, either under the influence of nature, or habit, or both, he becomes drunken, lustful, passionate? O my friend, is not that so?'

'Assuredly.'

'Such is the man and such is his origin. And next, how does he live?'

'Suppose, as people facetiously say, you were to tell me.'

'I imagine', I said, 'at the next step in his progress, that there will be feasts and carousals and revellings and courtesans, and all that sort of thing; love is the lord of the house within him, and orders all the concerns of his soul.'

'That is certain.'

'Yes; and every day and every night desires grow up many and formidable, and their demands are many.'

'They are indeed,' he said.

'His revenues, if he has any, are soon spent.'

'True.'

'Then comes debt and the cutting down of his property.'

'Of course.'

'When he has nothing left, must not his desires, crowding in the nest like young ravens, be crying aloud for food; and he, goaded on by them, and especially by love himself, who is in a manner the captain of them, is in a frenzy, and would fain discover whom he can defraud or despoil of his property, in order that he may gratify them?'

'Yes, that is sure to be the case.'

'He must have money, no matter how, if he is to escape horrid pains and pangs.'

'He must.'

'And as in himself there was a succession of pleasures, and the new got the better of the old and took away their rights, so he being younger will claim to have more than his father and his mother, and if he has spent his own share of the property, he will take a slice of theirs.'

'No doubt he will.'

'And if his parents will not give way, then he will try first of all to cheat and deceive them.'

'Very true.'

'And if he fails, then he will use force and plunder them.'

'Yes, probably.'

'And if the old man and woman fight for their own, what then, my friend? Will the creature feel any compunction at tyrannizing over them?'

'Nay,' he said, 'I should not feel at all comfortable about his parents.'

'But, O heavens! Adeimantus, on account of some newfangled love of a harlot, who is anything but a necessary connection, can you believe that he would strike the mother who is his ancient friend and necessary to his very existence, and would place her under the authority of the other, when she is brought under the same roof with her; or that, under like circumstances, he would do the same to his withered old father, first and most indispensable of friends, for the sake of some newly found blooming youth who is the reverse of indispensable?'

'Yes, indeed,' he said; 'I believe that he would.'

'Truly, then,' I said, 'a tyrannical son is a blessing to his father and mother.'

'He is indeed,' he replied.

'He first takes their property, and when that falls, and pleasures are beginning to swarm in the hive of his soul, then he breaks into a house, or steals the garments of some nightly wayfarer; next he proceeds to clear a temple. Meanwhile the old opinions which he had when a child, and which gave judgment about good and evil, are overthrown by those others which have just been emancipated, and are now the bodyguard of love and share his empire. These in his democratic days, when he was still subject to the laws and to his father, were only let loose in the dreams of sleep. But now that he is under the dominion of love, he becomes always and in waking reality what he was then very rarely and in a dream only; he will commit the foulest murder, or eat forbidden food, or be guilty of any other horrid act. Love is his tyrant, and lives lordly in him and lawlessly, and being himself a king, leads him on, as a tyrant leads a State, to the performance of any reckless deed by which he can maintain himself and the rabble of his associates, whether those whom evil communications have brought in from without, or those whom he himself has allowed to break loose within him by reason of a similar evil nature in himself. Have we not here a picture of his way of life?'

'Yes, indeed,' he said.

'And if there are only a few of them in the State, the rest of the people are well disposed, they go away and become the bodyguard or mercenary soldiers of some other tyrant who may probably want them for a war; and if there is no war, they stay at home and do many little pieces of mischief in the city.'

'What sort of mischief?'

'For example, they are the thieves, burglars, cutpurses, footpads, robbers of temples, man-stealers of the community; or if they are able to speak they turn informers, and bear false witness, and take bribes.'

'A small catalogue of evils, even if the perpetrators of them are few in number.'

'Yes,' I said; 'but small and great are comparative terms, and all these things, in the misery and evil which they inflict upon a State, do not come within a thousand miles of the tyrant; when this noxious class and their followers grow numerous and become conscious of their strength, assisted by the infatuation of the people, they choose from among themselves the one who has most of the tyrant in his own soul, and him they create their tyrant.'

'Yes, he said, and he will be the most fit to be a tyrant.'

'If the people yield, well and good; but if they resist him, as he began by beating his own father and mother, so now, if he has the power, he beats them, and will keep his dear old fatherland or motherland, as the Cretans say, in subjection to his young retainers whom he has introduced to be their rulers and masters. This is the end of his passions and desires.'

'Exactly.'

'When such men are only private individuals and before they get power, this is their character; they associate entirely with their own flatterers or ready tools; or if they want anything from anybody, they in their turn are equally ready to bow down before them: they profess every sort of affection for them; but when they have gained their point they know them no more.'

'Yes, truly.'

'They are always either the masters or servants and never the friends of anybody; the tyrant never tastes of true freedom or friendship.'

'Certainly not.'

'And may we not rightly call such men treacherous?'

'No question.'

'Also they are utterly unjust, if we were right in our notion of justice?'

'Yes,' he said, 'and we were perfectly right.'

'Let us then sum up in a word', I said, 'the character of the worst man: he is the waking reality of what we dreamed.'

'Most true.'

'And this is he who, being by nature most of a tyrant, bears rule, and the longer he lives the more of a tyrant he becomes.'

'That is certain,' said Glaucon, taking his turn to answer.

'And will not he who has been shown to be the wickedest, be also the most miserable? And he who has tyrannized longest and most, most continually and truly miserable; although this may not be the opinion of men in general?'

'Yes,' he said, 'inevitably.'

'And must not the tyrannical man be like the tyrannical State, and the democratical man like the democratical State; and the same of the others?'

'Certainly.'

'And as State is to State in virtue and happiness, so is man in relation to man?'

'To be sure.'

'Then comparing our original city, which was under a king, and the city which is under a tyrant, how do they stand as to virtue?'

'They are the opposite extremes,' he said, 'for one is the very best and the other is the very worst.'

'There can be no mistake,' I said, 'as to which is which, and therefore I will at once enquire whether you would arrive at a similar decision about their relative happiness and misery. And here we must not allow ourselves to be panic-stricken at the apparition of the tyrant, who is only a unit and may perhaps have a few retainers about him; but let us go as we ought into every corner of the city and look all about, and then we will give our opinion.'

'A fair invitation,' he replied. 'And I see, as everyone must, that a tyranny is the wretchedest form of government, and the rule of a king the happiest.'

'And in estimating the men too, may I not fairly make a like request, that I should have a judge whose mind can enter into and see through human nature? He must not be like a child who looks at the outside and is dazzled at the pompous aspect which the tyrannical nature assumes to the beholder, but let him be one who has a clear insight. May I suppose that the judgment is given in the hearing of us all by one who is able to judge, and has dwelt in the same place with him, and been present at his daily life and known him in his family relations, where he may be seen stripped of his tragedy attire, and again in the hour of public danger – he shall tell us about the happiness and misery of the tyrant when compared with other men?'

'That again', he said, 'is a very fair proposal.'

'Shall I assume that we ourselves are able and experienced judges and have before now met with such a person? We shall then have someone who will answer our enquiries.'

'By all means.'

'Let me ask you not to forget the parallel of the individual and the State; bearing this in mind, and glancing in turn from one to the other of them, will you tell me their respective conditions?'

'What do you mean?' he asked.

'Beginning with the State,' I replied, 'would you say that a city which is governed by a tyrant is free or enslaved?'

'No city', he said, 'can be more completely enslaved.'

'And yet, as you see, there are freemen as well as masters in such a State?'

'Yes,' he said, 'I see that there are – a few; but the people, speaking generally, and the best of them, are miserably degraded and enslaved.'

'Then if the man is like the State,' I said, 'must not the same rule prevail? His soul is full of meanness and vulgarity – the best elements in him are enslaved; and there is a small ruling part, which is also the worst and maddest.'

'Inevitably.'

'And would you say that the soul of such a one is the soul of a freeman, or of a slave?'

'He has the soul of a slave, in my opinion.'

'And the State which is enslaved under a tyrant is utterly incapable of acting voluntarily?'

'Utterly incapable.'

'And also the soul which is under a tyrant (I am speaking of the soul taken as a whole) is least capable of doing what she desires; there is a gadfly which goads her, and she is full of trouble and remorse?'

'Certainly.'

'And is the city which is under a tyrant rich or poor?'

'Poor.'

'And the tyrannical soul must be always poor and insatiable?'

'True.'

'And must not such a State and such a man be always full of fear?'

'Yes, indeed.'

'Is there any State in which you will find more of lamentation and sorrow and groaning and pain?'

'Certainly not.'

'And is there any man in whom you will find more of this sort of misery than in the tyrannical man, who is in a fury of passions and desires?'

'Impossible.'

'Reflecting upon these and similar evils, you held the tyrannical State to be the most miserable of States?'

'And I was right,' he said.

'Certainly, 'I said. 'And when you see the same evils in the tyrannical man, what do you say of him?'

'I say that he is by far the most miserable of all men.'

'There', I said, 'I think that you are beginning to go wrong.'

'What do you mean?'

'I do not think that he has as yet reached the utmost extreme of misery.'

'Then who is more miserable?'

'One of whom I am about to speak.'

'Who is that?'

'He who is of a tyrannical nature, and instead of leading a private life has been cursed with the further misfortune of being a public tyrant.'

'From what has been said, I gather that you are right.'

'Yes,' I replied, 'but in this high argument you should be a little more certain, and should not conjecture only; for of all questions, this respecting good and evil is the greatest.'

'Very true,' he said.

'Let me then offer you an illustration, which may, I think, throw a light upon this subject.'

'What is your illustration?'

'The case of rich individuals in cities who possess many slaves: from them you may form an idea of the tyrant's condition, for they both have slaves; the only difference is that he has more slaves.'

'Yes, that is the difference.'

'You know that they live securely and have nothing to apprehend from their servants?'

'What should they fear?'

'Nothing. But do you observe the reason of this?'

'Yes: the reason is that the whole city is leagued together for the protection of each individual.'

'Very true,' I said. 'But imagine one of these owners, the master say of some fifty slaves, together with his family and property and slaves, carried off by a god into the wilderness, where there are no freemen to help him – will he not be in an agony of fear lest he and his wife and children should be put to death by his slaves?'

'Yes,' he said, 'he will be in the utmost fear.'

'The time has arrived when he will be compelled to flatter divers of his slaves, and make many promises to them of freedom and other things, much against his will – he will have to cajole his own servants.'

'Yes,' he said, 'that will be the only way of saving himself.'

'And suppose the same god, who carried him away, to surround him with neighbours who will not suffer one man to be the master of another, and who, if they could catch the offender, would take his life?'

'His case will be still worse, if you suppose him to be everywhere surrounded and watched by enemies.'

'And is not this the sort of prison in which the tyrant will be bound – he who, being by nature such as we have described, is full of all sorts of fears and lusts? His soul is dainty and greedy, and yet alone, of all men in the city, he is never allowed to go on a journey, or to see the things which other freemen desire to see, but he lives in his hole like a woman hidden in the house, and is jealous of any other citizen who goes into foreign parts and sees anything of interest.'

'Very true,' he said.

'And amid evils such as these will not he who is ill-governed in his own person – the tyrannical man, I mean, whom you just now decided to be the most miserable of all – will not he be yet more miserable when, instead of leading a private life, he is constrained by fortune to be a public tyrant? He has to be master of others when he is not master of himself: he is like a diseased or paralytic man who is compelled to pass his life, not in retirement, but fighting and combating with other men.'

'Yes,' he said, 'the similitude is most exact.'

'Is not his case utterly miserable? And does not the actual tyrant lead a worse life than he whose life you determined to be the worst?'

'Certainly.'

'He who is the real tyrant, whatever men may think, is the real slave, and is obliged to practise the greatest adulation and servility, and to be the flatterer of the vilest of mankind. He has desires which he is utterly unable to satisfy, and has more wants than anyone, and is truly poor, if you know how to inspect the whole soul of him: all his life long he is beset with fear and is full of convulsions, and distractions, even as the State which he resembles. And surely the resemblance holds?'

'Very true,' he said.

'Moreover, as we were saying before, he grows worse from having power: he becomes and is of necessity more jealous, more faithless, more unjust, more friendless, more impious, than he was at first; he is the purveyor and cherisher of every sort of vice, and the consequence is that he is supremely miserable, and that he makes everybody else as miserable as himself.'

'No man of any sense will dispute your words.'

'Come then,' I said, 'and as the general umpire in theatrical contests proclaims the result, do you also decide who in your opinion is first in the scale of happiness, and who second, and in what order the others follow: there are five of them in all – they are the royal, timocratical, oligarchical, democratical, tyrannical.'

'The decision will be easily given, he replied: they shall be choruses coming on the stage, and I must judge them in the order in which they enter, by the criterion of virtue and vice, happiness and misery.'

'Need we hire a herald, or shall I announce that the son of Ariston [the best] has decided that the best and justest is also the happiest, and that this is he who is the most royal man and king over himself; and that the worst and most unjust man is also the most miserable, and that this is he who being the greatest tyrant of himself is also the greatest tyrant of his State?'

'Make the proclamation yourself,' he said.

'And shall I add, "whether seen or unseen by gods and men"?'

'Let the words be added.'

'Then this', I said, 'will be our first proof; and there is another, which may also have some weight.'

'What is that?'

'The second proof is derived from the nature of the soul: seeing that the individual soul, like the State, has been divided by us into three principles, the division may, I think, furnish a new demonstration.'

'Of what nature?'

'It seems to me that to these three principles three pleasures correspond; also three desires and governing powers.'

'How do you mean?' he said.

'There is one principle with which, as we were saying, a man learns, another with which he is angry; the third, having many forms, has no special name, but is denoted by the general term appetitive, from the extraordinary strength and vehemence of the desires of eating and drinking and the other sensual appetites which are the main elements of it; also money-loving, because such desires are generally satisfied by the help of money.'

'That is true,' he said.

'If we were to say that the loves and pleasures of this third part were concerned with gain, we should then be able to fall back on a single notion; and might truly and intelligibly describe this part of the soul as loving gain or money.'

'I agree with you.'

'Again, is not the passionate element wholly set on ruling and conquering and getting fame?'

'True.'

'Suppose we call it the contentious or ambitious – would the term be suitable?'

'Extremely suitable.'

'On the other hand, everyone sees that the principle of knowledge is wholly directed to the truth, and cares less than either of the others for gain or fame.'

'Far less.'

'"Lover of wisdom", "lover of knowledge" are titles which we may fitly apply to that part of the soul?'

'Certainly.'

'One principle prevails in the souls of one class of men, another in others, as may happen?'

'Yes.'

'Then we may begin by assuming that there are three classes of men – lovers of wisdom, lovers of honour, lovers of gain?'

'Exactly.'

'And there are three kinds of pleasure, which are their several objects?'

'Very true.'

'Now, if you examine the three classes of men, and ask of them in turn which of their lives is pleasantest, each will be found praising his own and depreciating that of others: the money-maker will contrast the vanity of honour or of learning if they bring no money with the solid advantages of gold and silver?'

'True,' he said.

'And the lover of honour – what will be his opinion? Will he not think that the pleasure of riches is vulgar, while the pleasure of learning, if it brings no distinction, is all smoke and nonsense to him?'

'Very true.'

'And are we to suppose', I said, 'that the philosopher sets any value on other pleasures in comparison with the pleasure of knowing the truth, and in that pursuit abiding, ever learning, not so far indeed from the heaven of pleasure? Does he not call the other pleasures necessary, under the idea that if there were no necessity for them, he would rather not have them?'

'There can be no doubt of that,' he replied.

'Since, then, the pleasures of each class and the life of each are in dispute, and the question is not which life is more or less honourable, or better or worse, but which is the more pleasant or painless – how shall we know who speaks truly?'

'I cannot myself tell,' he said.

'Well, but what ought to be the criterion? Is any better than experience and wisdom and reason?'

'There cannot be a better,' he said.

'Then,' I said, 'reflect. Of the three individuals, which has the greatest experience of all the pleasures which we enumerated? Has the lover of gain, in learning the nature of essential truth, greater experience of the pleasure of knowledge than the philosopher has of the pleasure of gain?'

'The philosopher', he replied 'has greatly the advantage; for he has of necessity always known the taste of the other pleasures from his childhood upwards: but the lover of gain in all his experience has not of necessity tasted – or, I should rather say, even had he desired, could hardly have tasted – the sweetness of learning and knowing truth.'

'Then the lover of wisdom has a great advantage over the lover of gain, for he has a double experience?'

'Yes, very great.'

'Again, has he greater experience of the pleasures of honour, or the lover of honour of the pleasures of wisdom?'

'Nay,' he said, 'all three are honoured in proportion as they attain their object; for the rich man and the brave man and the wise man alike have their crowd of admirers, and as they all receive honour they all have experience of the pleasures of honour; but the delight which is to be found in the knowledge of true being is known to the philosopher only.'

'His experience, then, will enable him to judge better than anyone?'

'Far better.'

'And he is the only one who has wisdom as well as experience?'

'Certainly.'

'Further, the very faculty which is the instrument of judgment is not possessed by the covetous or ambitious man, but only by the philosopher?'

'What faculty?'

'Reason, with whom, as we were saying, the decision ought to rest.'

'Yes.'

'And reasoning is peculiarly his instrument?'

'Certainly.'

'If wealth and gain were the criterion, then the praise or blame of the lover of gain would surely be the most trustworthy?'

'Assuredly.'

'Or if honour or victory or courage, in that case the judgement of the ambitious or pugnacious would be the truest?'

'Clearly.'

'But since experience and wisdom and reason are the judges –'

'The only inference possible', he replied, 'is that pleasures which are approved by the lover of wisdom and reason are the truest.'

'And so we arrive at the result, that the pleasure of the intelligent part of the soul is the pleasantest of the three, and that he of us in whom this is the ruling principle has the pleasantest life.'

'Unquestionably,' he said, 'the wise man speaks with authority when he approves of his own life.'

'And what does the judge affirm to be the life which is next, and the pleasure which is next?'

'Clearly that of the soldier and lover of honour; who is nearer to himself than the money-maker.'

'Last comes the lover of gain?'

'Very true,' he said.

'Twice in succession, then, has the just man overthrown the unjust in this conflict; and now comes the third trial, which is dedicated to Olympian Zeus the saviour: a sage whispers in my ear that no pleasure except that of the wise is quite true and pure – all others are a shadow only; and surely this will prove the greatest and most decisive of falls?'

'Yes, the greatest; but will you explain yourself?'

'I will work out the subject and you shall answer my questions.'

'Proceed.'

'Say, then, is not pleasure opposed to pain?'

'True.'

'And there is a neutral state which is neither pleasure nor pain?'

'There is.'

'A state which is intermediate, and a sort of repose of the soul about either – that is what you mean?'

'Yes.'

'You remember what people say when they are sick?'

'What do they say?'

'That after all nothing is pleasanter than health. But then they never knew this to be the greatest of pleasures until they were ill.'

'Yes, I know,' he said.

'And when persons are suffering from acute pain you must have heard them say that there is nothing pleasanter than to get rid of their pain?'

'I have.'

'And there are many other cases of suffering in which the mere rest and cessation of pain, and not any positive enjoyment, is extolled by them as the greatest pleasure?'

'Yes,' he said; 'at the time they are pleased and well content to be at rest.'

'Again, when pleasure ceases, that sort of rest or cessation will be painful?'

'Doubtless,' he said.

'Then the intermediate state of rest will be pleasure and will also be pain?'

'So it would seem.'

'But can that which is neither become both?'

'I should say not.'

'And both pleasure and pain are motions of the soul, are they not?'

'Yes.'

'But that which is neither was just now shown to be rest and not motion, and in a mean between them?'

'Yes.'

'How, then, can we be right in supposing that the absence of pain is pleasure, or that the absence of pleasure is pain?'

'Impossible.'

'This, then, is an appearance only and not a reality; that is to say, the rest is pleasure at the moment and in comparison to what is painful, and painful in comparison to what is pleasant; but all these representations, when tried by the test of true pleasure, are not real but a sort of imposition?'

'That is the inference.'

'Look at the other class of pleasures which have no antecedent pains and you will no longer suppose, as you perhaps may at present, that pleasure is only the cessation of pain, or pain of pleasure.'

'What are they,' he said, 'and where shall I find them?'

'There are many of them: take as an example the pleasures of smell, which are very great and have no antecedent pains; they come in a moment, and when they depart leave no pain behind them.'

'Most true,' he said.

'Let us not, then, be induced to believe that pure pleasure is the cessation of pain, or pain of pleasure.'

'No.'

'Still, the more numerous and violent pleasures which reach the soul through the body are generally of this sort – they are reliefs of pain.'

'That is true.'

'And the anticipations of future pleasures and pains are of a like nature?'

'Yes.'

'Shall I give you an illustration of them?'

'Let me hear.'

'You would allow', I said, 'that there is in nature an upper and lower and middle region?'

'I should.'

'And if a person were to go from the lower to the middle region, would he not imagine that he is going up; and he who is standing in the middle, and sees whence he has come, would imagine that he is already in the upper region, if he has never seen the true upper world?'

'To be sure,' he said; 'how can he think otherwise?'

'But if he were taken back again he would imagine, and truly imagine, that he was descending?'

'No doubt.'

'All that would arise out of his ignorance of the true upper and middle and lower regions?'

'Yes.'

'Then can you wonder that persons who are inexperienced in the truth, as they have wrong ideas about many other things, should also have wrong ideas about pleasure and pain and the intermediate state; so that when they are only being drawn towards the painful they feel pain and think the pain which they experience to be real, and in like manner, when drawn away from pain to the neutral or intermediate state, they firmly believe that they have reached the goal of satiety and pleasure; they, not knowing pleasure, err in contrasting pain with the absence of pain, which is like contrasting black with grey instead of white – can you wonder, I say, at this?'

'No, indeed; I should be much more disposed to wonder at the opposite.'

'Look at the matter thus: hunger, thirst and the like are inanitions of the bodily state?'

'Yes.'

'And ignorance and folly are inanitions of the soul?'

'True.'

'And food and wisdom are the corresponding satisfactions of either?'

'Certainly.'

'And is the satisfaction derived from that which has less or from that which has more existence the truer?'

'Clearly, from that which has more.'

'What classes of things have a greater share of pure existence in your judgment – those of which food and drink and condiments and all kinds of sustenance are examples, or the class which contains true opinion and knowledge and mind and all the different kinds of virtue? Put the question in this way: which has a more pure being – that which is concerned with the invariable, the immortal and the true, and is of such a nature, and is found in such natures; or that which is concerned with and found in the variable and mortal, and is itself variable and mortal?'

'Far purer', he replied, 'is the being of that which is concerned with the invariable.'

'And does the essence of the invariable partake of knowledge in the same degree as of essence?'

'Yes, of knowledge in the same degree.'

'And of truth in the same degree?'

'Yes.'

'And, conversely, that which has less of truth will also have less of essence?'

'Necessarily.'

'Then, in general, those kinds of things which are in the service of the body have less of truth and essence than those which are in the service of the soul?'

'Far less.'

'And has not the body itself less of truth and essence than the soul?'

'Yes.'

'What is filled with more real existence, and actually has a more real existence, is more really filled than that which is filled with less real existence and is less real?'

'Of course.'

'And if there be a pleasure in being filled with that which is according to nature, that which is more really filled with more real being will more really and truly enjoy true pleasure; whereas that which participates in less real being will be less truly and surely satisfied, and will participate in an illusory and less real pleasure?'

'Unquestionably.'

'Those, then, who know not wisdom and virtue, and are always busy with gluttony and sensuality, go down and up again as far as the mean; and in this region they move at random throughout life, but they never pass into the true upper world; thither they neither look, nor do they ever find their way, neither are they truly filled with true being, nor do they taste of pure and abiding pleasure. Like cattle, with their eyes always looking down and their heads stooping to the earth, that is to the dining-table, they fatten and feed and breed, and, in their excessive love of these delights, they kick and butt at one another with horns and hoofs which are made of iron; and they kill one another by reason of their insatiable lust. For they fill themselves with that which is not substantial, and the part of themselves which they fill is also unsubstantial and incontinent.'

'Verily, Socrates,' said Glaucon, 'you describe the life of the many like an oracle.'

'Their pleasures are mixed with pains – how can they be otherwise? For they are mere shadows and pictures of the true, and are coloured by contrast, which exaggerates both light and shade, and so they implant in the minds of fools insane desires of themselves; and they are fought about as Stesichorus says that the Greeks fought about the shadow of Helen at Troy in ignorance of the truth.'

'Something of that sort must inevitably happen.'

'And must not the like happen with the spirited or passionate element of the soul? Will not the passionate man who carries his passion into action, be in the like case, whether he is envious and ambitious, or violent and contentious, or angry and discontented, if he be seeking to attain honour and victory and the satisfaction of his anger without reason or sense?'

'Yes,' he said, 'the same will happen with the spirited element also.'

'Then may we not confidently assert that the lovers of money and honour, when they seek their pleasures under the guidance and in the company of reason and knowledge, and pursue after and win the pleasures which wisdom shows them, will also have the truest pleasures in the highest degree which is attainable to them, inasmuch as they follow truth; and they will have the pleasures which are natural to them, if that which is best for each one is also most natural to him?'

'Yes, certainly; the best is the most natural.'

'And when the whole soul follows the philosophical principle, and there is no division, the several parts are just, and do each of them their own business, and enjoy severally the best and truest pleasures of which they are capable?'

'Exactly.'

'But when either of the two other principles prevails, it fails in attaining its own pleasure, and compels the rest to pursue after a pleasure which is a shadow only and which is not their own?'

'True.'

'And the greater the interval which separates them from philosophy and reason, the more strange and illusive will be the pleasure?'

'Yes.'

'And is not that farthest from reason which is at the greatest distance from law and order?'

'Clearly.'

'And the lustful and tyrannical desires are, as we saw, at the greatest distance?'

'Yes.'

'And the royal and orderly desires are nearest?'

'Yes.'

'Then the tyrant will live at the greatest distance from true or natural pleasure, and the king at the least?'

'Certainly.'

'But if so, the tyrant will live most unpleasantly, and the king most pleasantly?'

'Inevitably.'

'Would you know the measure of the interval which separates them?'

'Will you tell me?'

'There appear to be three pleasures, one genuine and two spurious: now the transgression of the tyrant reaches a point beyond the spurious; he has run away from the region of law and reason, and taken up his abode with certain slave pleasures which are his satellites, and the measure of his inferiority can only be expressed in a figure.'

'How do you mean?'

'I assume', I said, 'that the tyrant is in the third place from the oligarch; the democrat was in the middle?'

'Yes.'

'And if there is truth in what has preceded, he will be wedded to an image of pleasure which is thrice removed as to truth from the pleasure of the oligarch?'

'He will.'

'And the oligarch is third from the royal; since we count as one royal and aristocratical?'

'Yes, he is third.'

'Then the tyrant is removed from true pleasure by the space of a number which is three times three?'

'Manifestly.'

'The shadow then of tyrannical pleasure determined by the number of length will be a plane figure.'

'Certainly.'

'And if you raise the power and make the plane a solid, there is no difficulty in seeing how vast is the interval by which the tyrant is parted from the king.'

'Yes; the arithmetician will easily do the sum.'

'Or if some person begins at the other end and measures the interval by which the king is parted from the tyrant in truth of pleasure, he will find him, when the multiplication is complete, living 729 times more pleasantly, and the tyrant more painfully by this same interval.'

'What a wonderful calculation! And how enormous is the distance which separates the just from the unjust in regard to pleasure and pain!'

'Yet a true calculation,' I said, 'and a number which nearly concerns human life, if human beings are concerned with days and nights and months and years.'

'Yes,' he said, 'human life is certainly concerned with them.'

'Then if the good and just man be thus superior in pleasure to the evil and unjust, his superiority will be infinitely greater in propriety of life and in beauty and virtue?'

'Immeasurably greater.'

'Well,' I said, 'and now having arrived at this stage of the argument, we may revert to the words which brought us hither: was not someone saying that injustice was a gain to the perfectly unjust who was reputed to be just?'

'Yes, that was said.'

'Now then, having determined the power and quality of justice and injustice, let us have a little conversation with him.'

'What shall we say to him?'

'Let us make an image of the soul, that he may have his own words presented before his eyes.'

'Of what sort?'

'An ideal image of the soul, like the composite creations of ancient mythology, such as the Chimera or Scylla or Cerberus, and there are many others in which two or more different natures are said to grow into one.'

'There are said to have been such unions.'

'Then do you now model the form of a multitudinous, many-headed monster, having a ring of heads of all manner of beasts, tame and wild, which he is able to generate and metamorphose at will.'

'You suppose marvellous powers in the artist; but, as language is more pliable than wax or any similar substance, let there be such a model as you propose.'

'Suppose now that you make a second form as of a lion, and a third of a man, the second smaller than the first, and the third smaller than the second.'

'That', he said, 'is an easier task; and I have made them as you say.'

'And now join them, and let the three grow into one.'

'That has been accomplished.'

'Next fashion the outside of them into a single image, as of a man, so that he who is not able to look within, and sees only the outer hull, may believe the beast to be a single human creature.'

'I have done so,' he said.

'And now, to him who maintains that it is profitable for the human creature to be unjust, and unprofitable to be just, let us reply that, if he be right, it is profitable for this creature to feast the multitudinous monster and strengthen the lion and the lion-like qualities, but to starve and weaken the man, who is consequently liable to be dragged about at the mercy of either of the other two; and he is not to attempt to familiarize or harmonize them with one another – he ought rather to suffer them to fight and bite and devour one another.'

'Certainly,' he said; 'that is what the approver of injustice says.'

'To him the supporter of justice makes answer that he should ever so speak and act as to give the man within him in some way or other the most complete mastery over the entire human creature.'

'He should watch over the many-headed monster like a good husbandman, fostering and cultivating the gentle qualities, and preventing the wild ones from growing; he should be making the lion-heart his ally, and in common care of them all should be uniting the several parts with one another and with himself.'

'Yes,' he said, 'that is quite what the maintainer of justice says.'

'And so from every point of view, whether of pleasure, honour or advantage, the approver of justice is right and speaks the truth, and the disapprover is wrong and false and ignorant.'

'Yes, from every point of view.'

'Come, now, and let us gently reason with the unjust, who is not intentionally in error. "Sweet Sir," we will say to him, "what think you of things esteemed noble and ignoble? Is not the noble that which subjects the beast to the man, or rather to the god in man; and the ignoble that which subjects the man to the beast?" He can hardly avoid saying yes – can he now?'

'Not if he has any regard for my opinion.'

'But, if he agree so far, we may ask him to answer another question: "Then how would a man profit if he received gold and silver on the condition that he was to enslave the noblest part of him to the worst? Who can imagine that a man who sold his son or daughter into slavery for money, especially if he sold them into the hands of fierce and evil men, would be the gainer, however large might be the sum which he received? And will anyone say that he is not a miserable caitiff who remorselessly sells his own divine being to that which is most godless and detestable? Eriphyle took the necklace as the price of her husband's life, but he is taking a bribe in order to compass a worse ruin."'

'Yes,' said Glaucon, 'far worse – I will answer for him.'

'Has not the intemperate been censured of old, because in him the huge multiform monster is allowed to be too much at large?'

'Clearly.'

'And men are blamed for pride and bad temper when the lion and serpent element in them disproportionately grows and gains strength?'

'Yes.'

'And luxury and softness are blamed, because they relax and weaken this same creature, and make a coward of him?'

'Very true.'

'And is not a man reproached for flattery and meanness who subordinates the spirited animal to the unruly monster, and, for the sake of money, of which he can never have enough, habituates him in the days of his youth to be trampled in the mire, and from being a lion to become a monkey?'

'True,' he said.

'And why are mean employments and manual arts a reproach? Only because they imply a natural weakness of the higher principle; the individual is unable to control the creatures within him, but has to court them, and his great study is how to flatter them.'

'Such appears to be the reason.'

'And therefore, being desirous of placing him under a rule like that of the best, we say that he ought to be the servant of the best, in whom the Divine rules; not, as Thrasymachus supposed, to the injury of the servant, but because everyone had better be ruled by divine wisdom dwelling within him; or, if this be impossible, then by an external authority, in order that we may be all, as far as possible, under the same government, friends and equals.'

'True,' he said.

'And this is clearly seen to be the intention of the law, which is the ally of the whole city; and is seen also in the authority which we exercise over children, and the refusal to let them be free until we have established in them a principle analogous to the constitution of a state, and by cultivation of this higher element have set up in their hearts a guardian and ruler like our own, and when this is done they may go their ways.'

'Yes,' he said, 'the purpose of the law is manifest.'

'From what point of view, then, and on what ground can we say that a man is profited by injustice or intemperance or other baseness, which will make him a worse man, even though he acquire money or power by his wickedness?'

'From no point of view at all.'

'What shall he profit, if his injustice be undetected and unpunished? He who is undetected only gets worse, whereas he who is detected and punished has the brutal part of his nature silenced and humanized; the gentler element in him is liberated, and his whole soul is perfected and ennobled by the acquirement of justice and temperance and wisdom, more than the body ever is by receiving gifts of beauty, strength and health, in proportion as the soul is more honourable than the body.'

'Certainly,' he said.

'To this nobler purpose the man of understanding will devote the energies of his life. And in the first place, he will honour studies which impress these qualities on his soul and disregard others?'

'Clearly,' he said.

'In the next place, he will regulate his bodily habit and training, and so far will he be from yielding to brutal and irrational pleasures that he will regard even health as quite a secondary matter; his first object will be not that he may be fair or strong or well, unless he is likely thereby to gain temperance, but he will always desire so to attemper the body as to preserve the harmony of the soul?'

'Certainly he will, if he has true music in him.'

'And in the acquisition of wealth there is a principle of order and harmony which he will also observe; he will not allow himself to be dazzled by the foolish applause of the world, and heap up riches to his own infinite harm?'

'Certainly not,' he said.

'He will look at the city which is within him, and take heed that no disorder occur in it, such as might arise either from superfluity or from want; and upon this principle he will regulate his property and gain or spend according to his means.'

'Very true.'

'And, for the same reason, he will gladly accept and enjoy such honours as he deems likely to make him a better man; but those, whether private or public, which are likely to disorder his life, he will avoid?'

'Then, if that is his motive, he will not be a statesman.'

'By the dog of Egypt, he will! In the city which is his own he certainly will, though in the land of his birth perhaps not, unless he have a divine call.'

'I understand: you mean that he will be a ruler in the city of which we are the founders, and which exists in idea only; for I do not believe that there is such an one anywhere on earth?'

'In heaven,' I replied, 'there is laid up a pattern of it, methinks, which he who desires may behold, and beholding, may set his own house in order. But whether such an one exists, or ever will exist in fact, is no matter; for he will live after the manner of that city, having nothing to do with any other.'

'I think so,' he said.

Book X

'Of the many excellences which I perceive in the order of our State, there is none which upon reflection pleases me better than the rule about poetry.'

'To what do you refer?'

'To the rejection of imitative poetry, which certainly ought not to be received; as I see far more clearly now that the parts of the soul have been distinguished.'

'What do you mean?'

'Speaking in confidence, for I should not like to have my words repeated to the tragedians and the rest of the imitative tribe – but I do not mind saying to you that all poetical imitations are ruinous to the understanding of the hearers, and that the knowledge of their true nature is the only antidote to them.'

'Explain the purport of your remark.'

'Well, I will tell you, although I have always from my earliest youth had an awe and love of Homer, which even now makes the words falter on my lips, for he is the great captain and teacher of the whole of that charming tragic company; but a man is not to be reverenced more than the truth, and therefore I will speak out.'

'Very good,' he said.

'Listen to me then, or rather, answer me.'

'Put your question.'

'Can you tell me what imitation is? For I really do not know.'

'A likely thing, then, that I should know.'

'Why not? For the duller eye may often see a thing sooner than the keener.'

'Very true,' he said. 'But in your presence, even if I had any faint notion, I could not muster courage to utter it. Will you enquire yourself?'

'Well, then, shall we begin the enquiry in our usual manner: whenever a number of individuals have a common name, we assume them to have also a corresponding idea or form. Do you understand me?'

'I do.'

'Let us take any common instance; there are beds and tables in the world – plenty of them, are there not?'

'Yes.'

'But there are only two ideas or forms of them – one the idea of a bed, the other of a table.'

'True.

'And the maker of either of them makes a bed or he makes a table for our use, in accordance with the idea – that is our way of speaking in this and similar instances – but no artificer makes the ideas themselves; how could he?'

'Impossible.'

'And there is another artist – I should like to know what you would say of him.'

'Who is he?'

'One who is the maker of all the works of all other workmen.'

'What an extraordinary man!'

'Wait a little, and there will be more reason for your saying so. For this is he who is able to make not only vessels of every kind, but plants and animals, himself and all other things – the earth and heaven, and the things which are in heaven or under the earth; he makes the gods also.'

'He must be a wizard and no mistake.'

'Oh! You are incredulous, are you? Do you mean that there is no such maker or creator, or that in one sense there might be a maker of all these things but in another not? Do you see that there is a way in which you could make them all yourself?'

'What way?'

'An easy way enough; or rather, there are many ways in which the feat might be quickly and easily accomplished, none quicker than that of turning a mirror round and round – you would soon enough make the sun and the heavens, and the earth and yourself, and other animals and plants, and all the other things of which we were just now speaking, in the mirror.'

'Yes,' he said; 'but they would be appearances only.'

'Very good,' I said, 'you are coming to the point now. And the painter too is, as I conceive, just such another – a creator of appearances, is he not?'

'Of course.'

'But then I suppose you will say that what he creates is untrue. And yet there is a sense in which the painter also creates a bed?'

'Yes,' he said, 'but not a real bed.'

'And what of the maker of the bed? Were you not saying that he too makes not the idea which, according to our view, is the essence of the bed, but only a particular bed?'

'Yes, I did.'

'Then if he does not make that which exists he cannot make true existence, but only some semblance of existence; and if anyone were to say that the work of the maker of the bed, or of any other workman, has real existence, he could hardly be supposed to be speaking the truth.'

'At any rate,' he replied, 'philosophers would say that he was not speaking the truth.'

'No wonder, then, that his work too is an indistinct expression of truth.'

'No wonder.'

'Suppose now that by the light of the examples just offered we enquire who this imitator is?'

'If you please.'

'Well, then, here are three beds: one existing in nature, which is made by God, as I think that we may say – for no one else can be the maker?'

'No.'

'There is another which is the work of the carpenter?'

'Yes.'

'And the work of the painter is a third?'

'Yes.'

'Beds, then, are of three kinds, and there are three artists who superintend them: God, the maker of the bed, and the painter?'

'Yes, there are three of them.'

'God, whether from choice or from necessity, made one bed in nature and one only; two or more such ideal beds neither ever have been nor ever will be made by God.'

'Why is that?'

'Because even if He had made but two, a third would still appear behind them which both of them would have for their idea, and that would be the ideal bed and the two others.'

'Very true,' he said.

'God knew this, and He desired to be the real maker of a real bed, not a particular maker of a particular bed, and therefore He created a bed which is essentially and by nature one only.'

'So we believe.'

'Shall we, then, speak of Him as the natural author or maker of the bed?'

'Yes,' he replied; 'inasmuch as by the natural process of creation He is the author of this and of all other things.'

'And what shall we say of the carpenter – is not he also the maker of the bed?'

'Yes.'

'But would you call the painter a creator and maker?'

'Certainly not.'

'Yet if he is not the maker, what is he in relation to the bed?'

'I think', he said, 'that we may fairly designate him as the imitator of that which the others make.'

'Good,' I said. 'Then you call him who is third in the descent from nature an imitator?'

'Certainly,' he said.

'And the tragic poet is an imitator, and therefore, like all other imitators, he is thrice removed from the king and from the truth?'

'That appears to be so. '

'Then about the imitator we are agreed. And what about the painter? I would like to know whether he may be thought to imitate that which originally exists in nature, or only the creations of artists?'

'The latter.'

'As they are or as they appear? You have still to determine this.'

'What do you mean?'

'I mean that you may look at a bed from different points of view, obliquely or directly or from any other point of view, and the bed will appear different, but there is no difference in reality. And the same of all things.'

'Yes,' he said, 'the difference is only apparent.'

'Now let me ask you another question: which is the art of painting designed to be – an imitation of things as they are, or as they appear – of appearance or of reality?'

'Of appearance.'

'Then the imitator', I said, 'is a long way off the truth, and can do all things because he lightly touches on a small part of them, and that part an image. For example: a painter will paint a cobbler, carpenter or any other artist, though he knows nothing of their arts; and, if he is a good artist, he may deceive children or simple persons, when he shows them his picture of a carpenter from a distance, and they will fancy that they are looking at a real carpenter.'

'Certainly.'

'And whenever anyone informs us that he has found a man knows all the arts, and all things else that anybody knows, and every single thing with a higher degree of accuracy than any other man – whoever tells us this, I think that we can only imagine to be a simple creature who is likely to have been deceived by some wizard or actor whom he met, and whom he thought all-knowing, because he himself was unable to analyse the nature of knowledge and ignorance and imitation.'

'Most true.'

'And so, when we hear persons saying that the tragedians, and Homer, who is at their head, know all the arts and all things human, virtue as well as vice, and divine things too, for that the good poet cannot compose well unless he knows his subject, and that he who has not this knowledge can never be a poet, we ought to consider whether here also there may not be a similar illusion. Perhaps they may have come across imitators and been deceived by them; they may not have remembered when they saw their works that these were but imitations thrice removed from the truth, and could easily be made without any knowledge of the truth, because they are appearances only and not realities? Or, after all, they may be in the right, and poets do really know the things about which they seem to the many to speak so well?'

'The question', he said, 'should by all means be considered.'

'Now do you suppose that if a person were able to make the original as well as the image, he would seriously devote himself to the image-making branch? Would he allow imitation to be the ruling principle of his life, as if he had nothing higher in him?'

'I should say not.'

'The real artist, who knew what he was imitating, would be interested in realities and not in imitations; and would desire to leave as memorials of himself works many and fair; and, instead of being the author of encomiums, he would prefer to be the theme of them.'

'Yes,' he said, 'that would be to him a source of much greater honour and profit.'

'Then', I said, 'we must put a question to Homer; not about medicine, or any of the arts to which his poems only incidentally refer: we are not going to ask him, or any other poet, whether he has cured patients like Asclepius, or left behind him a school of medicine such as the Asclepiads were, or whether he only talks about medicine and other arts at second hand; but we have a right to know respecting military tactics, politics, education, which are the chiefest and noblest subjects of his poems, and we may fairly ask him about them. "Friend Homer," then we say to him, "if you are only in the second remove from truth in what you say of virtue, and not in the third – not an image maker or imitator – and if you are able to discern what pursuits make men better or worse in private or public life, tell us what State was ever better governed by your help? The good order of Lacedaemon is due to Lycurgus, and many other cities great and small have been similarly benefited by others; but who says that you have been a good legislator to them and have done them any good? Italy and Sicily boast of Charondas, and there is Solon who is renowned among us; but what city has anything to say about you?" Is there any city which he might name?'

'I think not,' said Glaucon. 'Not even the Homerids themselves pretend that he was a legislator.'

'Well, but is there any war on record which was carried on successfully by him, or aided by his counsels, when he was alive?'

'There is not.'

'Or is there any invention of his, applicable to the arts or to human life, such as Thales the Milesian or Anacharsis the Scythian, and other ingenious men have conceived, which is attributed to him?'

'There is absolutely nothing of the kind.'

'But, if Homer never did any public service, was he privately a guide or teacher of any? Had he in his lifetime friends who loved to associate with him, and who handed down to posterity an Homeric way of life, such as was established by Pythagoras who was so greatly beloved for his wisdom, and whose followers are to this day quite celebrated for the order which was named after him?'

'Nothing of the kind is recorded of him. For surely, Socrates, Creophylus, the companion of Homer, that child of flesh, whose name always makes us laugh, might be more justly ridiculed for his stupidity, if, as is said, Homer was greatly neglected by him and others in his own day when he was alive?'

'Yes,' I replied, 'that is the tradition. But can you imagine, Glaucon, that if Homer had really been able to educate and improve mankind – if he had possessed knowledge and not been a mere imitator – can you imagine, I say, that he would not have had many followers, and been honoured and loved by them? Protagoras of Abdera, and Prodicus of Ceos, and a host of others, have only to whisper to their contemporaries: "You will never be able to manage either your own house or your own State until you appoint us to be your ministers of education" – and this ingenious device of theirs has such an effect in making them love them that their companions all but carry them about on their shoulders. And is it conceivable that the contemporaries of Homer, or again of Hesiod, would have allowed either of them to go about as rhapsodists, if they had really been able to make mankind virtuous? Would they not have been as unwilling to part with them as with gold, and have compelled them to stay at home with them? Or, if the master would not stay, then the disciples would have followed him about everywhere, until they had got education enough?'

'Yes, Socrates, that, I think, is quite true.'

'Then must we not infer that all these poetical individuals, beginning with Homer, are only imitators: they copy images of virtue and the like, but the truth they never reach? The poet is like a painter who, as we have already observed, will make a likeness of a cobbler though he understands nothing of cobbling; and his picture is good enough for those who know no more than he does, and judge only by colours and figures.'

'Quite so.'

'In like manner the poet with his words and phrases may be said to lay on the colours of the several arts, himself understanding their nature only enough to imitate them; and other people, who are as ignorant as he is, and judge only from his words, imagine that if he speaks of cobbling, or of military tactics, or of anything else, in metre and harmony and rhythm, he speaks very well – such is the sweet influence which melody and rhythm by nature have. And I think that you must have observed again and again what a poor appearance the tales of poets make when stripped of the colours which music puts upon them, and recited in simple prose.'

'Yes,' he said.

'They are like faces which were never really beautiful, but only blooming; and now the bloom of youth has passed away from them?'

'Exactly.'

'Here is another point: the imitator or maker of the image knows nothing of true existence; he knows appearances only. Am I not right?'

'Yes.'

'Then let us have a clear understanding, and not be satisfied with half an explanation.'

'Proceed.'

'Of the painter we say that he will paint reins, and he will paint a bit?'

'Yes.'

'And the worker in leather and brass will make them?'

'Certainly.

'But does the painter know the right form of the bit and reins? Nay, hardly even the workers in brass and leather who make them; only the horseman who knows how to use them – he knows their right form.'

'Most true.'

'And may we not say the same of all things?'

'What?'

'That there are three arts which are concerned with all things: one which uses, another which makes, a third which imitates them?'

'Yes.'

'And the excellence or beauty or truth of every structure, animate or inanimate, and of every action of man, is relative to the use for which nature or the artist has intended them.'

'True.'

'Then the user of them must have the greatest experience of them, and he must indicate to the maker the good or bad qualities which develop themselves in use; for example, the flute-player will tell the flute-maker which of his flutes is satisfactory to the performer; he will tell him how he ought to make them, and the other will attend to his instructions?'

'Of course.'

'The one knows and therefore speaks with authority about the goodness and badness of flutes, while the other, confiding in him, will do what he is told by him?'

'True.'

'The instrument is the same, but about the excellence or badness of it the maker will only attain to a correct belief; and this he will gain from him who knows, by talking to him and being compelled to hear what he has to say, whereas the user will have knowledge?'

'True.'

'But will the imitator have either? Will he know from use whether or no his drawing is correct or beautiful? Or will he have right opinion from being compelled to associate with another who knows and gives him instructions about what he should draw?'

'Neither.'

'Then he will no more have true opinion than he will have knowledge about the goodness or badness of his imitations?'

'I suppose not.'

'The imitative artist will be in a brilliant state of intelligence about his own creations?'

'Nay, very much the reverse.'

'And still he will go on imitating without knowing what makes a thing good or bad, and may be expected therefore to imitate only that which appears to be good to the ignorant multitude?'

'Just so.'

'Thus far, then, we are pretty well agreed that the imitator has no knowledge worth mentioning of what he imitates. Imitation is only a kind of play or sport, and the tragic poets, whether they write in iambic or in Heroic verse, are imitators in the highest degree?'

'Very true.'

'And now tell me, I conjure you, has not imitation been shown by us to be concerned with that which is thrice removed from the truth?'

'Certainly.'

'And what is the faculty in man to which imitation is addressed?'

'What do you mean?'

'I will explain: the body which is large when seen near, appears small when seen at a distance?'

'True.'

'And the same object appears straight when looked at out of the water, and crooked when in the water; and the concave becomes convex, owing to the illusion about colours to which the sight is liable. Thus every sort of confusion is revealed within us; and this is that weakness of the human mind on which the art of conjuring and of deceiving by light and shadow and other ingenious devices imposes, having an effect upon us like magic.'

'True.'

'And the arts of measuring and numbering and weighing come to the rescue of the human understanding – there is the beauty of them – and the apparent greater or less, or more or heavier, no longer have the mastery over us, but give way before calculation and measure and weight?'

'Most true.'

'And this, surely, must be the work of the calculating and rational principle in the soul'

'To be sure.'

'And when this principle measures and certifies that some things are equal, or that some are greater or less than others, there occurs an apparent contradiction?'

'True.'

'But were we not saying that such a contradiction is impossible; that the same faculty cannot have contrary opinions at the same time about the same thing?'

'Very true.'

'Then that part of the soul which has an opinion contrary to measure is not the same with that which has an opinion in accordance with measure?'

'True.'

'And the better part of the soul is likely to be that which trusts to measure and calculation?'

'Certainly.'

'And that which is opposed to them is one of the inferior principles of the soul?'

'No doubt.'

'This was the conclusion at which I was seeking to arrive when I said that painting or drawing, and imitation in general, when doing their own proper work, are far removed from truth, and the companions and friends and associates of a principle within us which is equally removed from reason, and that they have no true or healthy aim.'

'Exactly. '

'The imitative art is an inferior who marries an inferior, and has inferior offspring.'

'Very true.'

'And is this confined to the sight only, or does it extend to the hearing also, relating in fact to what we term poetry?'

'Probably the same would be true of poetry.'

'Do not rely', I said, 'on a probability derived from the analogy of painting; but let us examine further and see whether the faculty with which poetical imitation is concerned is good or bad.'

'By all means.'

'We may state the question thus: imitation imitates the actions of men, whether voluntary or involuntary, on which, as they imagine, a good or bad result has ensued, and they rejoice or sorrow accordingly. Is there anything more?'

'No, there is nothing else.'

'But in all this variety of circumstances is the man at unity with himself – or rather, as in the instance of sight there was confusion and opposition in his opinions about the same things, so here also is there not strife and inconsistency in his life? Though I need hardly raise the question again, for I remember that all this has been already admitted; and the soul has been acknowledged by us to be full of these and ten thousand similar oppositions occurring at the same moment?'

'And we were right,' he said.

'Yes,' I said, 'thus far we were right; but there was an omission which must now be supplied.'

'What was the omission?'

'Were we not saying that a good man, who has the misfortune to lose his son or anything else which is most dear to him, will bear the loss with more equanimity than another?'

'Yes.'

'But will he have no sorrow, or shall we say that although he cannot help sorrowing, he will moderate his sorrow?'

'The latter', he said, 'is the truer statement.'

'Tell me: will he be more likely to struggle and hold out against his sorrow when he is seen by his equals, or when he is alone?'

'It will make a great difference whether he is seen or not.'

'When he is by himself he will not mind saying or doing many things which he would be ashamed of anyone hearing or seeing him do?'

'True.'

'There is a principle of law and reason in him which bids him resist, as well as a feeling of his misfortune which is forcing him to indulge his sorrow?'

'True.'

'But when a man is drawn in two opposite directions, to and from the same object, this, as we affirm, necessarily implies two distinct principles in him?'

'Certainly.'

'One of them is ready to follow the guidance of the law?'

'How do you mean?'

'The law would say that to be patient under suffering is best, and that we should not give way to impatience, as there is no knowing whether such things are good or evil; and nothing is gained by impatience; also, because no human thing is of serious importance, and grief stands in the way of that which at the moment is most required.'

'What is most required?' he asked.

'That we should take counsel about what has happened, and when the dice have been thrown order our affairs in the way which reason deems best; not, like children who have had a fall, keeping hold of the part struck and wasting time in setting up a howl, but always accustoming the soul forthwith to apply a remedy, raising up that which is sickly and fallen, banishing the cry of sorrow by the healing art.'

'Yes,' he said, 'that is the true way of meeting the attacks of fortune.'

'Yes,' I said; 'and the higher principle is ready to follow this suggestion of reason?'

'Clearly.'

'And the other principle, which inclines us to recollection of our troubles and to lamentation, and can never have enough of them, we may call irrational, useless, and cowardly?'

'Indeed, we may.'

'And does not the latter – I mean the rebellious principle – furnish a great variety of materials for imitation? Whereas the wise and calm temperament, being always nearly equable, is not easy to imitate or to appreciate when imitated, especially at a public festival when a promiscuous crowd is assembled in a theatre. For the feeling represented is one to which they are strangers.'

'Certainly.'

'Then the imitative poet who aims at being popular is not by nature made, nor is his art intended, to please or to affect the principle in the soul; but he will prefer the passionate and fitful temper, which is easily imitated?'

'Clearly.'

'And now we may fairly take him and place him by the side of the painter, for he is like him in two ways: first, inasmuch as his creations have an inferior degree of truth – in this, I say, he is like him; and he is also like him in being concerned with an inferior part of the soul; and therefore we shall be right in refusing to admit him into a well-ordered State, because he awakens and nourishes and strengthens the feelings and impairs the reason. As in a city when the evil are permitted to have authority and the good are put out of the way, so in the soul of man, as we maintain, the imitative poet implants an evil constitution, for he indulges the irrational nature which has no discernment of greater and less, but thinks the same thing at one time great and at another small – he is a manufacturer of images and is very far removed from the truth.'

'Exactly.'

'But we have not yet brought forward the heaviest count in our accusation: the power which poetry has of harming even the good (and there are very few who are not harmed), is surely an awful thing?'

'Yes, certainly, if the effect is what you say.'

'Hear and judge: the best of us, as I conceive, when we listen to a passage of Homer, or one of the tragedians, in which he represents some pitiful hero who is drawling out his sorrows in a long oration, or weeping, and smiting his breast – the best of us, you know, delight in giving way to sympathy, and are in raptures at the excellence of the poet who stirs our feelings most.'

'Yes, of course I know.'

'But when any sorrow of our own happens to us, then you may observe that we pride ourselves on the opposite quality – we would fain be quiet and patient; this is the manly part, and the other which delighted us in the recitation is now deemed to be the part of a woman.'

'Very true,' he said.

'Now can we be right in praising and admiring another who is doing that which anyone of us would abominate and be ashamed of in his own person?'

'No,' he said, 'that is certainly not reasonable.'

'Nay,' I said, 'quite reasonable from one point of view.'

'What point of view?'

'If you consider', I said, 'that when in misfortune we feel a natural hunger and desire to relieve our sorrow by weeping and lamentation, and that this feeling which is kept under control in our own calamities is satisfied and delighted by the poets; the better nature in each of us, not having been sufficiently trained by reason or habit, allows the sympathetic element to break loose because the sorrow is another's; and the spectator fancies that there can be no disgrace to himself in praising and pitying anyone who comes telling him what a good man he is, and making a fuss about his troubles; he thinks that the pleasure is a gain, and why should he be supercilious and lose this and the poem too? Few persons ever reflect, as I should imagine, that from the evil of other men something of evil is communicated to themselves. And so the feeling of sorrow which has gathered strength at the sight of the misfortunes of others is with difficulty repressed in our own.'

'How very true!'

'And does not the same hold also of the ridiculous? There are jests which you would be ashamed to make yourself, and yet on the comic stage, or indeed in private, when you hear them, you are greatly amused by them, and are not at all disgusted at their unseemliness; the case of pity is repeated – there is a principle in human nature which is disposed to raise a laugh, and this which you once restrained by reason, because you were afraid of being thought a buffoon, is now let out again; and having stimulated the risible faculty at the theatre, you are betrayed unconsciously to yourself into playing the comic poet at home.'

'Quite true,' he said.

'And the same may be said of lust and anger and all the other affections, of desire and pain and pleasure, which are held to be inseparable from every action – in all of them poetry feeds and waters the passions instead of drying them up; she lets them rule, although they ought to be controlled, if mankind are ever to increase in happiness and virtue.'

'I cannot deny it.'

'Therefore, Glaucon,' I said, 'whenever you meet with any of the eulogists of Homer declaring that he has been the educator of Hellas, and that he is profitable for education and for the ordering of human things, and that you should take him up again and again and get to know him and regulate your whole life according to him, we may love and honour those who say these things – they are excellent people, as far as their lights extend; and we are ready to acknowledge that Homer is the greatest of poets and first of tragedy writers; but we must remain firm in our conviction that hymns to the gods and praises of famous men are the only poetry which ought to be admitted into our State. For if you go beyond this and allow the honeyed muse to enter, either in epic or lyric verse, not law and the reason of mankind, which by common consent have ever been deemed best, but pleasure and pain will be the rulers in our State.'

'That is most true,' he said.

'And now since we have reverted to the subject of poetry, let this our defence serve to show the reasonableness of our former judgment in sending away out of our State an art having the tendencies which we have described; for reason constrained us. But that she may impute to us any harshness or want of politeness, let us tell her that there is an ancient quarrel between philosophy and poetry; of which there are many proofs, such as the saying of "the yelping hound howling at her lord", or of one "mighty in the vain talk of fools", and "the mob of sages circumventing Zeus", and the "subtle thinkers who are beggars after all"; and there are innumerable other signs of ancient enmity between them. Notwithstanding this, let us assure our sweet friend and the sister arts of imitation that if she will only prove her title to exist in a well-ordered State we shall be delighted to receive her – we are very conscious of her charms; but we may not on that account betray the truth. I dare say, Glaucon, that you are as much charmed by her as I am, especially when she appears in Homer?'

'Yes, indeed, I am greatly charmed.'

'Shall I propose, then, that she be allowed to return from exile, but upon this condition only – that she make a defence of herself in lyrical or some other metre?'

'Certainly.'

'And we may further grant to those of her defenders who are lovers of poetry and yet not poets the permission to speak in prose on her behalf: let them show not only that she is pleasant but also useful to States and to human life, and we will listen in a kindly spirit; for if this can be proved we shall surely be the gainers – I mean, if there is a use in poetry as well as a delight?'

'Certainly,' he said, 'we shall be the gainers.'

'If her defence fails, then, my dear friend, like other persons who are enamoured of something, but put a restraint upon themselves when they think their desires are opposed to their interests, so too must we after the manner of lovers give her up, though not without a struggle. We too are inspired by that love of poetry which the education of noble States has implanted in us, and therefore we would have her appear at her best and truest; but so long as she is unable to make good her defence, this argument of ours shall be a charm to us, which we will repeat to ourselves while we listen to her strains; that we may not fall away into the childish love of her which captivates the many. At all events we are well aware that poetry being such as we have described is not to be regarded seriously as attaining to the truth; and he who listens to her, fearing for the safety of the city which is within him, should be on his guard against her seductions and make our words his law.'

'Yes,' he said, 'I quite agree with you.'

'Yes,' I said, 'my dear Glaucon, for great is the issue at stake, greater than appears, whether a man is to be good or bad. And what will anyone be profited if under the influence of honour or money or power, aye, or under the excitement of poetry, he neglect justice and virtue?'

'Yes,' he said; 'I have been convinced by the argument, as I believe that anyone else would have been.'

'And yet no mention has been made of the greatest prizes and rewards which await virtue.'

'What, are there any greater still? If there are, they must be of an inconceivable greatness.'

'Why,' I said, 'what was ever great in a short time? The whole period of three score years and ten is surely but a little thing in comparison with eternity?'

'Say rather "nothing",' he replied.

'And should an immortal being seriously think of this little space rather than of the whole?'

'Of the whole, certainly. But why do you ask?'

'Are you not aware', I said, 'that the soul of man is immortal and imperishable?'

He looked at me in astonishment, and said: 'No, by heaven. And are you really prepared to maintain this?'

'Yes,' I said, 'I ought to be, and you too – there is no difficulty in proving it.'

'I see a great difficulty; but I should like to hear you state this argument of which you make so light.'

'Listen, then.'

'I am attending.'

'There is a thing which you call good and another which you call evil?'

'Yes,' he replied.

'Would you agree with me in thinking that the corrupting and destroying element is the evil, and the saving and improving element the good?'

'Yes.'

'And you admit that every thing has a good and also an evil; as ophthalmia is the evil of the eyes and disease of the whole body; as mildew is of corn, and rot of timber, or rust of copper and iron: in everything, or in almost everything, there is an inherent evil and disease?'

'Yes,' he said.

'And anything which is infected by any of these evils is made evil, and at last wholly dissolves and dies?'

'True.'

'The vice and evil which is inherent in each is the destruction of each; and if this does not destroy them there is nothing else that will; for good certainly will not destroy them, nor again that which is neither good nor evil.'

'Certainly not.'

'If, then, we find any nature which, having this inherent corruption, cannot be dissolved or destroyed, we may be certain that of such a nature there is no destruction?'

'That may be assumed.'

'Well,' I said, 'and is there no evil which corrupts the soul?'

'Yes,' he said, 'there are all the evils which we were just now passing in review: unrighteousness, intemperance, cowardice, ignorance.'

'But does any of these dissolve or destroy her? – And here do not let us fall into the error of supposing that the unjust and foolish man, when he is detected, perishes through his own injustice, which is an evil of the soul. Take the analogy of the body: the evil of the body is a disease which wastes and reduces and annihilates the body; and all the things of which we were just now speaking come to annihilation through their own corruption attaching to them and inhering in them and so destroying them. Is not this true?'

'Yes.'

'Consider the soul in like manner. Does the injustice or other evil which exists in the soul waste and consume her? Do they by attaching to the soul and inhering in her at last bring her to death, and so separate her from the body?'

'Certainly not.'

'And yet,' I said, 'it is unreasonable to suppose that anything can perish from without through affection of external evil which could not be destroyed from within by a corruption of its own?'

'It is,' he replied.

'Consider,' I said, 'Glaucon, that even the badness of food, whether staleness, decomposition or any other bad quality, when confined to the actual food, is not supposed to destroy the body; although, if the badness of food communicates corruption to the body, then we should say that the body has been destroyed by a corruption of itself, which is disease, brought on by this; but that the body, being one thing, can be destroyed by the badness of food, which is another, and which does not engender any natural infection – this we shall absolutely deny?'

'Very true.'

'And, on the same principle, unless some bodily evil can produce an evil of the soul, we must not suppose that the soul, which is one thing, can be dissolved by any merely external evil which belongs to another?'

'Yes,' he said, 'there is reason in that.'

'Either, then, let us refute this conclusion or, while it remains unrefuted, let us never say that fever, or any other disease, or the knife put to the throat, or even the cutting up of the whole body into the minutest pieces, can destroy the soul, until she herself is proved to become more unholy or unrighteous in consequence of these things being done to the body; but that the soul, or anything else if not destroyed by an internal evil, can be destroyed by an external one, is not to be affirmed by any man.'

'And surely,' he replied, 'no one will ever prove that the souls of men become more unjust in consequence of death.'

'But if someone who would rather not admit the immortality of the soul boldly denies this, and says that the dying do really become more evil and unrighteous, then, if the speaker is right, I suppose that injustice, like disease, must be assumed to be fatal to the unjust, and that those who take this disorder die by the natural inherent power of destruction which evil has, and which kills them sooner or later, but in quite another way from that in which, at present, the wicked receive death at the hands of others as the penalty of their deeds?'

'Nay,' he said, 'in that case injustice, if fatal to the unjust, will not be so very terrible to him, for he will be delivered from evil. But I rather suspect the opposite to be the truth, and that injustice which, if it have the power, will murder others, keeps the murderer alive – aye, and well awake too; so far removed is her dwelling-place from being a house of death.'

'True,' I said; 'if the inherent natural vice or evil of the soul is unable to kill or destroy her, hardly will that which is appointed to be the destruction of some other body, destroy a soul or anything else except that of which it was appointed to be the destruction.'

'Yes, that can hardly be.'

'But the soul which cannot be destroyed by an evil, whether inherent or external, must exist for ever, and if existing for ever, must be immortal?'

'Certainly.'

'That is the conclusion,' I said. 'And, if a true conclusion, then the souls must always be the same, for if none be destroyed they will not diminish in number. Neither will they increase, for the increase of the immortal natures must come from something mortal, and all things would thus end in immortality.'

'Very true.'

'But this we cannot believe – reason will not allow us – any more than we can believe the soul, in her truest nature, to be full of variety and difference and dissimilarity.'

'What do you mean?' he said.

'The soul', I said, 'being, as is now proven, immortal, must be the fairest of compositions and cannot be compounded of many elements?'

'Certainly not.'

'Her immortality is demonstrated by the previous argument, and there are many other proofs; but to see her as she really is, not as we now behold her, marred by communion with the body and other miseries, you must contemplate her with the eye of reason, in her original purity; and then her beauty will be revealed, and justice and injustice and all the things which we have described will be manifested more clearly. Thus far, we have spoken the truth concerning her as she appears at present, but we must remember also that we have seen her only in a condition which may be compared to that of the sea-god Glaucus, whose original image can hardly be discerned because his natural members are broken off and crushed and damaged by the waves in all sorts of ways, and incrustations have grown over them of seaweed and shells and stones, so that he is more like some monster than he is to his own natural form. And the soul which we behold is in a similar condition, disfigured by ten thousand ills. But not there, Glaucon, not there must we look.'

'Where then?'

'At her love of wisdom. Let us see whom she affects, and what society and converse she seeks in virtue of her near kindred with the immortal and eternal and divine; also how different she would become if wholly following this superior principle, and borne by a divine impulse out of the ocean in which she now is, and disengaged from the stones and shells and things of earth and rock which in wild variety spring up around her because she feeds upon earth, and is overgrown by the good things of this life as they are termed: then you would see her as she is, and know whether she has one shape only or many, or what her nature is. Of her affections and of the forms which she takes in this present life I think that we have now said enough.'

'True,' he replied.

'And thus', I said, 'we have fulfilled the conditions of the argument; we have not introduced the rewards and glories of justice, which, as you were saying, are to be found in Homer and Hesiod; but justice in her own nature has been shown to be best for the soul in her own nature. Let a man do what is just, whether he have the ring of Gyges or not, and even if in addition to the ring of Gyges he put on the helmet of Hades.'

'Very true.'

'And now, Glaucon, there will be no harm in further enumerating how many and how great are the rewards which justice and the other virtues procure to the soul from gods and men, both in life and after death.'

'Certainly not,' he said.

'Will you repay me, then, what you borrowed in the argument?'

'What did I borrow?'

'The assumption that the just man should appear unjust and the unjust just; for you were of opinion that even if the true state of the case could not possibly escape the eyes of gods and men, still this admission ought to be made for the sake of the argument, in order that pure justice might be weighed against pure injustice. Do you remember?'

'I should be much to blame if I had forgotten.'

'Then, as the cause is decided, I demand on behalf of justice that the estimation in which she is held by gods and men and which we acknowledge to be her due should now be restored to her by us; since she has been shown to confer reality, and not to deceive those who truly possess her, let what has been taken from her be given back, that so she may win that palm of appearance which is hers also, and which she gives to her own.'

'The demand', he said, 'is just.'

'In the first place,' I said, '– and this is the first thing which you will have to give back – the nature both of the just and unjust is truly known to the gods.'

'Granted.'

'And if they are both known to them, one must be the friend and the other the enemy of the gods, as we admitted from the beginning?'

'True.'

'And the friend of the gods may be supposed to receive from them all things at their best, excepting only such evil as is the necessary consequence of former sins?'

'Certainly.'

'Then this must be our notion of the just man, that even when he is in poverty or sickness, or any other seeming misfortune, all things will in the end work together for good to him in life and death: for the gods have a care of anyone whose desire is to become just and to be like God, as far as man can attain the divine likeness, by the pursuit of virtue?'

'Yes,' he said, 'if he is like God he will surely not be neglected by him.'

'And of the unjust may not the opposite be supposed?'

'Certainly.'

'Such, then, are the palms of victory which the gods give the just?'

'That is my conviction.'

'And what do they receive of men? Look at things as they really are, and you will see that the clever unjust are in the case of runners, who run well from the starting-place to the goal but not back again from the goal: they go off at a great pace, but in the end only look foolish, slinking away with their ears draggling on their shoulders, and without a crown; but the true runner comes to the finish and receives the prize and is crowned. And this is the way with the just: he who endures to the end of every action and occasion of his entire life has a good report and carries off the prize which men have to bestow.'

'True.'

'And now you must allow me to repeat of the just the blessings which you were attributing to the fortunate unjust. I shall say of them, what you were saying of the others, that as they grow older, they become rulers in their own city if they care to be; they marry whom they like and give in marriage to whom they will; all that you said of the others I now say of these. And, on the other hand, of the unjust I say that the greater number, even though they escape in their youth, are found out at last and look foolish at the end of their course, and when they come to be old and miserable are flouted alike by stranger and citizen; they are beaten and then come those things unfit for ears polite, as you truly term them; they will be racked and have their eyes burned out, as you were saying. And you may suppose that I have repeated the remainder of your tale of horrors. But will you let me assume, without reciting them, that these things are true?'

'Certainly,' he said, 'what you say is true.'

'These, then, are the prizes and rewards and gifts which are bestowed upon the just by gods and men in this present life, in addition to the other good things which justice of herself provides.'

'Yes,' he said, 'and they are fair and lasting.'

'And yet', I said, 'all these are as nothing, either in number or greatness, in comparison with those other recompenses which await both just and unjust after death. And you ought to hear them, and then both just and unjust will have received from us a full payment of the debt which the argument owes to them.'

'Speak,' he said. 'There are few things which I would more gladly hear.'

'Well,' I said, 'I will tell you a tale; not one of the tales which Odysseus tells to the hero Alcinous, yet this too is a tale of a hero, Er, the son of Armenius, a Pamphylian by birth. He was slain in battle, and ten days afterwards, when the bodies of the dead were taken up already in a state of corruption, his body was found unaffected by decay, and carried away home to be buried. And on the twelfth day, as he was lying on the funeral pile, he returned to life and told them what he had seen in the other world. He said that when his soul left the body he went on a journey with a great company, and that they came to a mysterious place at which there were two openings in the earth; they were near together, and over against them were two other openings in the heaven above. In the intermediate space there were judges seated, who commanded the just, after they had given judgment on them and had bound their sentences in front of them, to ascend by the heavenly way on the right hand; and in like manner the unjust were bidden by them to descend by the lower way on the left hand; these also bore the symbols of their deeds, but fastened on their backs. He drew near, and they told him that he was to be the messenger who would carry the report of the other world to men, and they bade him hear and see all that was to be heard and seen in that place. Then he beheld and saw on one side the souls departing at either opening of heaven and earth when sentence had been given on them; and at the two other openings other souls, some ascending out of the earth dusty and worn with travel, some descending out of heaven clean and bright. And arriving ever and anon they seemed to have come from a long journey, and they went forth with gladness into the meadow, where they encamped as at a festival; and those who knew one another embraced and conversed, the souls which came from earth curiously enquiring about the things above, and the souls which came from heaven about the things beneath. And they told one another of what had happened by the way, those from below weeping and sorrowing at the remembrance of the things which they had endured and seen in their journey beneath the earth (now the journey lasted a thousand years), while those from above were describing heavenly delights and visions of inconceivable beauty. The Story, Glaucon, would take too long to tell, but the sum was this: he said that for every wrong which they had done to anyone they suffered tenfold; or once in a hundred years – such being reckoned to be the length of man's life, and the penalty being thus paid ten times in a thousand years. If, for example, there were any who had been the cause of many deaths, or had betrayed or enslaved cities or armies, or been guilty of any other evil behaviour, for each and all of their offences they received punishment ten times over, and the rewards of beneficence and justice and holiness were in the same proportion. I need hardly repeat what he said concerning young children dying almost as soon as they were born. Of piety and impiety to gods and parents, and of murderers, there were retributions other and greater far which he described. He mentioned that he was present when one of the spirits asked another, "Where is Ardiaeus the Great?" (Now this Ardiaeus lived a thousand years before the time of Er: he had been the tyrant of some city of Pamphylia, and had murdered his aged father and his elder brother, and was said to have committed many other abominable crimes.) The answer of the other spirit was: "He comes not hither and will never come. And this", said he, "was one of the dreadful sights which we ourselves witnessed. We were at the mouth of the cavern, and, having completed all our experiences, were about to reascend, when of a sudden Ardiaeus appeared and several others, most of whom were tyrants; and there were also besides the tyrants private individuals who had been great criminals: they were just, as they fancied, about to return into the upper world, but the mouth, instead of admitting them, gave a roar, whenever any of these incurable sinners or someone who had not been sufficiently punished tried to ascend; and then wild men of fiery aspect, who were standing by and heard the sound, seized and carried them off; and Ardiaeus and others they bound head and foot and hand, and threw them down and flayed them with scourges, and dragged them along the road at the side, carding them on thorns like wool, and declaring to the passers-by what were their crimes, and that they were being taken away to be cast into hell." And of all the many terrors which they had endured, he said that there was none like the terror which each of them felt at that moment, lest they should hear the voice; and when there was silence, one by one they ascended with exceeding joy. These, said Er, were the penalties and retributions, and there were blessings as great.

'Now, when the spirits which were in the meadow had tarried seven days, on the eighth they were obliged to proceed on their journey, and, on the fourth day after, he said that they came to a place where they could see from above a line of light, straight as a column, extending right through the whole heaven and through the earth, in colour resembling the rainbow, only brighter and purer; another day's journey brought them to the place, and there, in the midst of the light, they saw the ends of the chains of heaven let down from above: for this light is the belt of heaven, and holds together the circle of the universe, like the under-girders of a trireme. From these ends is extended the spindle of Necessity, on which all the revolutions turn. The shaft and hook of this spindle are made of steel, and the whorl is made partly of steel and also partly of other materials. Now the whorl is in form like the whorl used on earth; and the description of it implied that there is one large hollow whorl which is quite scooped out, and into this is fitted another lesser one, and another, and another, and four others, making eight in all, like vessels which fit into one another; the whorls show their edges on the upper side, and on their lower side all together form one continuous whorl. This is pierced by the spindle, which is driven home through the centre of the eighth. The first and outermost whorl has the rim broadest, and the seven inner whorls are narrower, in the following proportions – the sixth is next to the first in size, the fourth next to the sixth; then comes the eighth; the seventh is fifth, the fifth is sixth, the third is seventh, last and eighth comes the second. The largest (of fixed stars) is spangled, and the seventh (or sun) is brightest; the eighth (or moon) coloured by the reflected light of the seventh; the second and fifth (Saturn and Mercury) are in colour like one another, and yellower than the preceding; the third (Venus) has the whitest light; the fourth (Mars) is reddish; the sixth (Jupiter) is in whiteness second. Now the whole spindle has the same motion; but, as the whole revolves in one direction, the seven inner circles move slowly in the other, and of these the swiftest is the eighth; next in swiftness are the seventh, sixth, and fifth, which move together; third in swiftness appeared to move according to the law of this reversed motion the fourth; the third appeared fourth and the second fifth. The spindle turns on the knees of Necessity; and on the upper surface of each circle is a siren, who goes round with them, hymning a single tone or note. The eight together form one harmony; and round about, at equal intervals, there is another band, three in number, each sitting upon her throne: these are the Fates, daughters of Necessity, who are clothed in white robes and have chaplets upon their heads, Lachesis and Clotho and Atropos, who accompany with their voices the harmony of the sirens – Lachesis singing of the past, Clotho of the present, Atropos of the future; Clotho from time to time assisting with a touch of her right hand the revolution of the outer circle of the whorl or spindle, and Atropos with her left hand touching and guiding the inner ones, and Lachesis laying hold of either in turn, first with one hand and then with the other.

'When Er and the spirits arrived, their duty was to go at once to Lachesis; but first of all there came a prophet who arranged them in order; then he took from the knees of Lachesis lots and samples of lives, and having mounted a high pulpit, spoke as follows: "Hear the word of Lachesis, the daughter of Necessity. Mortal souls, behold a new cycle of life and mortality. Your genius will not be allotted to you, but you choose your genius; and let him who draws the first lot have the first choice, and the life which he chooses shall be his destiny. Virtue is free, and as a man honours or dishonours her he will have more or less of her; the responsibility is with the chooser – God is justified." When the Interpreter had thus spoken he scattered lots indifferently among them all, and each of them took up the lot which fell near him, all but Er himself (he was not allowed), and each as he took his lot perceived the number which he had obtained. Then the Interpreter placed on the ground before them the samples of lives; and there were many more lives than the souls present, and they were of all sorts. There were lives of every animal and of man in every condition. And there were tyrannies among them, some lasting out the tyrant's life, others which broke off in the middle and came to an end in poverty and exile and beggary; and there were lives of famous men, some who were famous for their form and beauty as well as for their strength and success in games, or, again, for their birth and the qualities of their ancestors; and some who were the reverse of famous for the opposite qualities. And of women likewise; there was not, however, any definite character to them, because the soul, when choosing a new life, must of necessity become different. But there was every other quality, and they all mingled with one another, and also with elements of wealth and poverty, and disease and health; and there were mean states also. And here, my dear Glaucon, is the supreme peril of our human state; and therefore the utmost care should be taken. Let each one of us leave every other kind of knowledge and seek and follow one thing only, if peradventure he may be able to learn and may find someone who will make him able to learn and discern between good and evil, and so to choose always and everywhere the better life as he has opportunity. He should consider the bearing of all these things which have been mentioned severally and collectively upon virtue; he should know what the effect of beauty is when combined with poverty or wealth in a particular soul, and what are the good and evil consequences of noble and humble birth, of private and public station, of strength and weakness, of cleverness and dullness, and of all the soul, and the operation of them when conjoined; he will then look at the nature of the soul, and from the consideration of all these qualities he will be able to determine which is the better and which is the worse; and so he will choose, giving the name of evil to the life which will make his soul more unjust, and good to the life which will make his soul more just; all else he will disregard. For we have seen and know that this is the best choice both in life and after death. A man must take with him into the world below an adamantine faith in truth and right, that there too he may be undazzled by the desire of wealth or the other allurements of evil, lest, coming upon tyrannies and similar villainies, he do irremediable wrongs to others and suffer yet worse himself; but let him know how to choose the mean and avoid the extremes on either side, as far as possible, not only in this life but in all that which is to come. For this is the way of happiness.

'And according to the report of the messenger from the other world this was what the prophet said at the time: "Even for the last comer, if he chooses wisely and will live diligently, there is appointed a happy and not undesirable existence. Let not him who chooses first be careless, and let not the last despair." And when he had spoken, he who had the first choice came forward and in a moment chose the greatest tyranny; his mind having been darkened by folly and sensuality, he had not thought out the whole matter before he chose, and did not at first sight perceive that he was fated, among other evils, to devour his own children. But when he had time to reflect, and saw what was in the lot, he began to beat his breast and lament over his choice, forgetting the proclamation of the prophet; for, instead of throwing the blame of his misfortune on himself, he accused chance and the gods, and everything rather than himself. Now he was one of those who came from heaven, and in a former life had dwelt in a well-ordered State, but his virtue was a matter of habit only, and he had no philosophy. And it was true of others who were similarly overtaken, that the greater number of them came from heaven and therefore they had never been schooled by trial, whereas the pilgrims who came from earth, having themselves suffered and seen others suffer, were not in a hurry to choose. And owing to this inexperience of theirs, and also because the lot was a chance, many of the souls exchanged a good destiny for an evil or an evil for a good. For if a man had always on his arrival in this world dedicated himself from the first to sound philosophy, and had been moderately fortunate in the number of the lot, he might, as the messenger reported, be happy here, and also his journey to another life and return to this, instead of being rough and underground, would be smooth and heavenly. Most curious, he said, was the spectacle – sad and laughable and strange; for the choice of the souls was in most cases based on their experience of a previous life. There he saw the soul which had once been Orpheus choosing the life of a swan out of enmity to the race of women, hating to be born of a woman because they had been his murderers; he beheld also the soul of Thamyras choosing the life of a nightingale; birds, on the other hand, like the swan and other musicians, wanting to be men. The soul which obtained the twentieth lot chose the life of a lion, and this was the soul of Ajax the son of Telamon, who would not be a man, remembering the injustice which was done him the judgment about the arms. The next was Agamemnon, who took the life of an eagle, because, like Ajax, he hated human nature by reason of his sufferings. About the middle came the lot of Atalanta; she, seeing the great fame of an athlete, was unable to resist the temptation: and after her there followed the soul of Epeus, the son of Panopeus, passing into the nature of a woman cunning in the arts; and far away among the last who chose, the soul of the jester Thersites was putting on the form of a monkey. There came also the soul of Odysseus having yet to make a choice, and his lot happened to be the last of them all. Now the recollection of former tolls had disenchanted him of ambition, and he went about for a considerable time in search of the life of a private man who had no cares; he had some difficulty in finding this, which was lying about and had been neglected by everybody else; and when he saw it, he said that he would have done the same had his lot been first instead of last, and that he was delighted to have it. And not only did men pass into animals, but I must also mention that there were animals tame and wild who changed into one another and into corresponding human natures – the good into the gentle and the evil into the savage, in all sorts of combinations.

'All the souls had now chosen their lives, and they went in the order of their choice to Lachesis, who sent with them the genius whom they had severally chosen, to be the guardian of their lives and the fulfiller of the choice: this genius led the souls first to Clotho, and drew them within the revolution of the spindle impelled by her hand, thus ratifying the destiny of each; and then, when they were fastened to this, carried them to Atropos, who spun the threads and made them irreversible, whence without turning round they passed beneath the throne of Necessity; and when they had all passed, they marched on in a scorching heat to the plain of Forgetfulness, which was a barren waste destitute of trees and verdure; and then towards evening they encamped by the river of Unmindfulness, whose water no vessel can hold; of this they were all obliged to drink a certain quantity, and those who were not saved by wisdom drank more than was necessary; and each one as he drank forgot all things. Now after they had gone to rest, about the middle of the night there was a thunderstorm and earthquake, and then in an instant they were driven upwards in all manner of ways to their birth, like stars shooting. He himself was hindered from drinking the water. But in what manner or by what means he returned to the body he could not say; only, in the morning, awaking suddenly, he found himself lying on the pyre.

'And thus, Glaucon, the tale has been saved and has not perished, and will save us if we are obedient to the word spoken; and we shall pass safely over the river of Forgetfulness and our soul will not be defiled. Wherefore my counsel is that we hold fast ever to the heavenly way and follow after justice and virtue always, considering that the soul is immortal and able to endure every sort of good and every sort of evil. Thus shall we live dear to one another and to the gods, both while remaining here and when, like conquerors in the games who go round to gather gifts, we receive our reward. And it shall be well with us both in this life and in the pilgrimage of a thousand years which we have been describing.'